# Latino Metropolis

## Globalization and Community

*Dennis R. Judd, Series Editor*

# Latino Metropolis

*Victor M. Valle and Rodolfo D. Torres*

*Globalization and Community / Volume 7*
*University of Minnesota Press*
*Minneapolis • London*

An earlier and significantly different version of chapter 1 originally appeared in *Socialist Review* 23, no. 4 (1994); reprinted by permission of the author. The article reprinted in chapter 4 originally appeared as "Bank Job: Stafford Called on Roski in Bid to Control Local Lender," by Victor M. Valle and Rodolfo D. Torres, *L.A. Weekly* 20, no. 51 (November 13–19, 1998); reprinted by permission of the authors and courtesy of L.A. Weekly Media, Inc.

Published by the University of Minnesota Press
111 Third Avenue South, Suite 290
Minneapolis, MN 55401-2520
http://www.upress.umn.edu

Printed in the United States of America on acid-free paper

Library of Congress Cataloging-in-Publication Data

Valle, Victor M.
    Latino metropolis / Victor M. Valle and Rodolfo D. Torres.
        p.    cm. — (Globalization and community ; v. 7)
    Includes bibliographical references and index.
    ISBN 0-8166-3029-1 (alk. paper) — ISBN 0-8166-3030-5 (pbk : alk. paper)
    1. Hispanic Americans—California—Los Angeles—Politics and government.
2. Hispanic Americans—California—Los Angeles—Economic conditions.    3. Hispanic Americans—California—Los Angeles—Race identity.    4. Los Angeles
(Calif.)—Race relations.    5. Los Angeles (Calif.)—Politics and government.
6. Los Angeles (Calif.)—Economic conditions.    I. Torres, Rodolfo D., 1949–
II. Title.    III. Series.
    F869.L89 S757 2000
    320.9794'94'08968—dc21

                                                                00-008646

The University of Minnesota is an equal-opportunity educator and employer.


11  10  09  08  07  06  05  04  03  02  01  00              10 9 8 7 6 5 4 3 2 1

To my marvelous son, Jacob David Torres, with love,
I dedicate this book.
—RDT

## NUESTRA REINA

Llegarán más Africanos,
Chinos, Filipinos,
Más Mexicanos, Hondureños,
Nicas, Panameños,
Chilenos, Árabes, Persas,
Más de todos hasta quedarnos
Inundando de familias,
De gatos y abuelas,
Muchachas, tataranietas,
Y los que vienen solos,
Los que todavía se vienen acercando,
Saliendo de los días
A la hora de vernos cara a cara,
En su colmena

Lo estamos propagando
Con los días de trabajo,
Con el sol que sube
La avenida con los camiones

**— Victor Valle**

# Contents

# Foreword

*Saskia Sassen*

This extraordinary account of the Latino population in the Greater Los Angeles area is an important contribution to the political economy of place. In dissecting a particular place, the Greater Eastside of Los Angeles, the authors help us see the possibility of a new kind of Latino politics. Further, by focusing on Latinos in this place they help us understand the shortcomings of existing categories about race relations and such entities as ghettos and barrios. These terms do not capture the distinctive situation and potential of the Latino population in Los Angeles. As a place, Los Angeles and its metropolitan region is a site that captures larger dynamics: globalization, post-Fordism, immigration, politics.

Recovering place is a powerful research strategy, especially when dealing with that which is marked by disadvantage in the current era dominated by images of globalization and high technology. Place is central to the multiple circuits through which the economy is constituted. This holds even in the case of advanced sectors producing highly mobile dematerialized outputs and operating in mostly digitalized networks; as I have long argued, hypermobility needs to be produced, serviced, and maintained, and this requires places and workers. A focus on place allows us to recover the broad variety of types of workers and types of firms that are part of the economy—specifically, in this case, the Los Angeles economy. Thereby we can bring to visibility what is often left out of macro-level analyses. This book does precisely that—it resituates what has been constructed as marginal or evicted from prevailing accounts.

Valle and Torres show us how the residential districts in the Greater Eastside populated by low-income Latinos have been reduced to powerless jurisdictions that function as bedroom communities for the various neighboring cities. These cities have been constituted so as to capture a maximum of public resources for maximum private development. These cities function as private wealth-producing machines, without any of the corresponding responsibilities for distributing public revenue to the residential communities to support schools, water, transportation, and other essentials. Although bound to each other by the economic dynamics of the larger area, these places have been constructed as separate political jurisdictions so that the electorate represented by the workers of these cities cannot influence processes taking place in the cities where they work, no matter how close they are to the residential areas.

Thus the Latino communities that provide the low-wage workers for those cities have been stripped of their political power to influence at least to some extent the politics of those cities through participation in the democratic process. And, the authors suggest, Latino politicians are also disempowered when their constituencies are segregated into low-income, low-resource jurisdictions where their votes cannot affect those with power and wealth.

One of the important implications of this dissecting of place has to do with the possibility of a new kind of politics. The efforts of Latino politicians have been focused on distribution of revitalization funds and redistricting. But Valle and Torres show us that these older political strategies no longer work. And they have kept Latino politicians from being able to mobilize the enormous political resource that is the Latino population and the pursuit of broader agendas that empower both Latinos and their political representatives. Those older categories fuel competition between African Americans and Latinos for resources and recognition. According to the authors, this is not what is needed now. The need is rather for a flexible post-Fordist politics of networked communities. Latinos can participate in such a politics because they inhabit so many of the communities that make up the Greater Eastside and are the workers for the privatized cities that dominate the region. And they can do so because so many politicians in local government in Los Angeles are Latinos. Rather than redistricting or getting more of a share for their particular communities, they should invest their efforts in the shaping of a new politics that cuts across these districts—a politics of the larger place that is the Greater Eastside.

This resonates with some of the findings in my own research focused on cities and the formation of new cross-border networks that connect global cities to each other.[1] I see here the formation of a new kind of geography of centrality that is conceivably also the space for a new type of politics: a politics of the global that goes through the specifics of locality. We can begin to think about a new politics that engages the global scale without having to depend on a world state—a type of state I do not believe is feasible or effective. Similarly, in the case of the Greater Eastside, what Valle and Torres describe is a politics of localities, but with a difference: the residents' recognition that they are part of a larger network of localities in the area. Further, insofar as these are immigrant communities, one might think of networks that connect the Greater Eastside of Los Angeles with communities in Mexico.[2]

Crucial in the analysis in my work on such a networked politics of place is the fact that the places in the network—in this case, global cities—concentrate key resources that are strategic for running the global economic system, such as material infrastructures and structures, and a variety of other resources, including professional talent and multiple specialized service firms. In the case of the Greater Eastside, one could argue that the interdependencies between the economic base of the region and the Latino workforce constitute a parallel instance. I will return to this below, as I think it is crucial for the possibility of this new politics that Valle and Torres call for.

A second important implication that comes out of the analysis in this book is the inadequacy of the prevailing categories in studies of race, race relations, the poor and unemployed, the ghetto and the barrio. Valle and Torres find problematic the construction of the Latino as a racialized subject and as one caught in the same politics of black and white as African Americans. They find the categories of race and race relations do not help Latinos understand their specific situation. Latinos are at the intersection of several racializing dynamics and are, in that regard, an instance of *mestizaje*.

Not unrelated to this subject is the question of the politics of identity and the authors' assertion that it is limiting and that we need to reintroduce class in political analysis. I would like to argue that the crucial issue is empowerment and that a focus on empowerment allows us to recognize sites for political action where labor struggles and identity politics can intersect. The debate about scales, locations, types of leadership, and purposes of various struggles is fruitful, and necessary. Each one of us has multiple identities and multiple sites for action; worker and workplace are but one type. The authors would agree that old-style union organizing still works for certain types of conditions, but that it is not enough and, in many cases, it distorts the struggle for empowerment. Community, household, cultural practices, our bodies—these are all sites for identity and for action. In certain sites labor struggles and identity politics coincide, too; these are the strategic intersections that need to be strengthened rather than rejected. And the fact that labor struggles and identity politics do not coincide in many other sites does *not* mean that they are incompatible, or that such sites cannot be locations for empowerment struggles.

A third issue that emerges strongly from this book is the question of employment and its significance for understanding the distinctiveness of Latinos. Valle and Torres argue that insofar as Latinos in the Greater Eastside are mostly employed, even though at very low wages, the image of the ghetto and the hyperghetto as a place of extreme unemployment does not hold for Latinos. Hence the meaning of ghetto is different for each community, Latino and African American. The issue of immigrant employment is important for the authors' analysis and for the effort to develop a political economy of place and the reinsertion of class in the analysis of Latinos. It warrants elaboration, and I draw again on my own work to expand on this subject.

Immigrant communities and households can be characterized by the weight of social ties that bind people into relations of trust and mutual obligation, the fact of "enforceable trust," and the weight of collective rather than individual economic attainment strategies.[3] The fact that the immigrant household or community can allocate members to a labor market also works to the advantage of employers. Several studies have found that employers generally, not just employers of immigrants, say they prefer hiring production workers through word of mouth. The figures in these same studies suggest that employers do not always get their way: a good proportion of all jobs are *not* filled through word of mouth. Thus we can infer that immigrant communities offer an advantage, given the intensity of their networks and the channeling of newly arrived and long-resident immigrants into immigrant-dominated labor markets. It is probable that a greater share of jobs can be filled through word of mouth when immigrants and their communities are involved. Further, in immigrant communities matters of control and enforceable trust give additional strength to these screening and coaching mechanisms.

Dependencies between employing establishments and communities or households are likely to emerge when the networks used by workers to obtain information about jobs also become recruitment conduits for employers. Networks contain not only information circuits but also screening mechanisms. Employees are likely to know their employers' preferences and channel to them individuals they consider appropriate members of their networks when job openings arise at their workplaces. In the case of immigrant communities, this "knowledge" about employers' preferences and expectations may be crucial when it comes to language proficiency, legal status, and "cultural adjustment." These characteristics of immigrant employment should strengthen the type of political project sketched out by Valle and Torres as it signals interdependencies among Latino communities in the Greater Eastside and between these Latino communities and the privatized cities where they are employed.

Valle and Torres present us with the ingredients of what could become a new, strategic microhistory of the politics of place. To do so, they decode and resituate many familiar elements of the lives of Latinos and their communities in Los Angeles, elements that range from the world of work to the world of cuisine. But they go beyond this in that one of their key concerns is to understand the political options for Latinos in Los Angeles and possibly throughout other large urban areas in the United States.

# Acknowledgments

Our thanks to Carrie Mullen, acquisitions editor, and to Dennis Judd, series editor, for their support, patience, and intelligent judgment in helping shape this collaborative book. Judy Selhorst copyedited the text with extraordinary diligence and skills that added considerably to the final product. We also wish to express our appreciation to Laura Westlund, managing editor, for guiding this manuscript through production and into print.

We wish to express our deep appreciation to Luis F. Mirón, chair of the Department of Education at the University of California, Irvine, and Robert Gish, chair of the Department of Ethnic Studies, California Polytechnic State University, San Luis Obispo, for their support and friendship. It would have been impossible to complete this work without the institutional environment Lou and Robert both provided, for which we will be ever grateful. Rudy also wishes to express thanks to his colleagues at UC Irvine, Joan Bissell, Tim Tift, Gilbert G. Gonzalez, Jeff Garcilazo, and Raul Fernandez, for their encouragement.

We have been assisted over the years by a host of colleagues and friends. They include Itabari Njeri, Mike Davis, Roy Ulrich, Allen Maltun, Antonia Darder, Robert Miles, Peter McLaren, David Theo Goldberg, Steve Small, Charles Kerchner, Mario Barrera, Francisco Vazquez, Goetz Wolff, Noel Samaroo, Dan Moreno, Frederick S. Weaver, Adela de la Torre, George Katsiaficas, Dan Solorzano, Zaragosa Vargas, Peter Bohmer, Ed Escobar, and Darrell Y. Hamamoto. Any omissions from this list are quite inadvertent.

Thanks to colleagues at California State University, Long Beach: Ron Schmidt, Luis Arroyo, Federico Sanchez, Norma Chinchilla, Maulana Karenga, Craig Stone, Anna M. Sandoval, Gerry Riposa, John Attinasi, and Michelle Saint-Germain. A number of librarians have been very helpful.

We want especially to thank Sara Cooper and Mary Tyler of the Southern California Library for Social Studies and Research, and Carolyn Cole of the Los Angeles Public Library. In preparing the manuscript, we were fortunate enough to have two first-rate research and technical assistants, Cliff Akiyama and Dylan Le. During the last phase of the project, Mary Walker provided important technical, editorial, and research assistance. Her skill and attention to detail have enhanced this volume. A special thank-you to Ricardo Duffy for his contribution to the cover art. All chapters were authored collaboratively.

Finally, we cannot say enough in expressing our appreciation to our families. Rudy's wife, Patricia Speier Torres, and Victor's wife, Maria Lau Valle, must be credited as our wise, generous, and ever-patient coauthors. Their love and support allowed us to birth this book. It is time this child of modest gifts stood up and walked in the world.

# Latino Metropolis

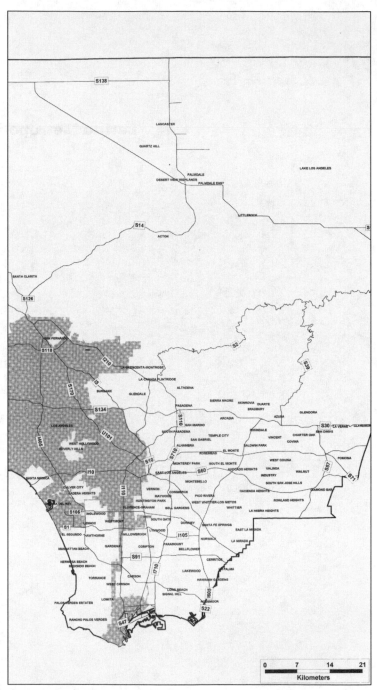

Los Angeles County. Map courtesy of Ali Modarres; reprinted with permission.

# Introduction

> Over the past several decades, Latinos in the United States have emerged as strategic actors in major processes of social transformation. This new reality—the Latinization of the United States—is driven by forces that extend well beyond U.S. borders and asserts itself demographically and politically, in the workplace and in daily life.
>
> **Frank Bonilla, "Changing the Americas from within the United States," 1998**

> The Latino metropolis is, in the first place, the crucible of far-reaching transformations in urban culture and ethnic identity.
>
> **Mike Davis, "Magical Urbanism: Latinos Reinvent the U.S. Big City," 1999**

The beginning of the twenty-first century signifies an epochal transformation in the nature of U.S. society. Nowhere is this more obvious than in the precipitous growth of the immigrant and refugee population in urban centers of the United States. Unlike the peak years of immigration early in the twentieth century, when European peoples predominated, the vast majority of contemporary immigrant and refugee groups have their origins in either Asia or Latin America. Earlier waves of immigration from Asia and Latin America (then primarily Mexico) notwithstanding, the "new immigrants" are entering a society that is vastly different from that entered by their predecessors.[1]

For one, the high-wage manufacturing jobs that were once the basis of a largely middle-class society have been exported overseas, having been supplanted by skilled professions in the information economy that require

3

specialized training through years of increasingly costly education at the postsecondary level.[2] At the lower end of the service and information economy are the legions of Asian and Latino laborers who hold ethnically typed low-wage jobs cleaning, clothing, feeding, and housing those on the other side of the widening class divide. It is the janitorial, clothing, agriculture, and construction industries that are the principal employers of immigrant workers. In extreme instances, immigrants have been found to be working under conditions comparable to slavery.[3]

In the past thirty years, Latinos have become an increasingly important segment of the immigrant population, one whose growing presence and conditions are closely intertwined with the very forces that are causing the ongoing economic restructuring and reshaping of once-familiar international, national, regional, and local landscapes. For nearly four decades, these global political economic changes have greatly stimulated Latino immigration to the United States.

On July 1, 1998, there were an estimated 30.4 million Latinos in the United States, constituting 11.3 percent of the total population. By 2005, the Census Bureau projects that Latinos will overtake African Americans as the largest minority group in the United States. By 2050, there should be more Latinos than all other minorities combined. As of 1998, the Latino population in California stood at 7,687,938, or 26 percent of the state's total population; California could have a Latino majority by the year 2040, according to recent Census Bureau projections. The Latino population of Los Angeles County in 1998 was 4,226,000, or 44 percent; in the city of Los Angeles, where the Latino population was nearly 1,651,000, Latinos made up 45 percent of the total population. It is estimated that by 2002, there will be nearly 4,827,000 Latinos in Los Angeles County and 1,827,460 in the city.[4]

Perhaps more important than sheer numbers, Latinos are the most significant and fastest-growing sector of the working class in the United States. Within a few years, Latinos will make up more than a quarter of the nation's total workforce, a proportion that is, of course, more than three times larger than this group's proportion of the total population. Equally important, Latino men and women are increasingly concentrated in the very industries that have been most influenced by the economic restructuring of the United States. J. Scott and A. S. Paul have described Southern California as the most advanced case of post-Fordist industrialization in the United States, if not the world.[5] Los Angeles County, for example, is the "postindustrial" heartland of the United States, with its industries based on nonunionized low-wage workers who are drawn increasingly from the ranks of immigrants, legal and undocumented. The county is the nation's largest manufacturing center, with 667,800 workers employed in manufacturing as of 1998.[6] It has been estimated that half of these workers are Latinos.

In the city of Los Angeles, the economy has increasingly come to rest on this cheap, nonunionized labor. The deindustrialization of Central Los Angeles in the recent past is linked directly to the reindustrialization of the Eastside based upon low-wage manufacturing. Here Los Angeles seems unique among global cities. In New York, Chicago, even London, downtown central business districts have been regenerated by way of their mediation of global financial markets supplemented by high-end retail stores and low-end service sector jobs.[7] In Los Angeles, by contrast, high-end retail consumption is dispersed across the western portion of the city. Low-wage manufacturing is to the Latinized workforce of Los Angeles what service sector jobs offer other cities in the postindustrial order. At the same time, the political economy of prisons has come to replace the political economy of military bases in the life of "postindustrial" Los Angeles. Commodified material culture reifies this differential experience across the city. Storefronts in Central and East Los Angeles are boarded up, insulated from the perceived dangers of "the street," the goods on offer cluttered and contained behind the restricting and restrictive presence of close surveillance, suggesting always the possibility of a future looking through bars. On the Westside, high-end retail stores offer the promise of pleasure for those who can apparently afford to shop there, signifying a future of limitless growth and prosperity. Billboards compete with graffiti in shaping, articulating, and reflecting these differing sensibilities and expectations, desires and anxieties.

## Political Economy of Latino Los Angeles

The Latinization of Los Angeles comes at a time of massive cuts in aid to housing, schools, and social services. The passage of Proposition 187 in 1994 denied undocumented immigrants public services. Proposition 209, the anti-affirmative action initiative, was approved by the voters in 1996, and most recently in 1998, Proposition 227 ended bilingual education. The rich are getting richer, and the middle class is besieged by the threat of unemployment and rising debt levels. [8]

A report released in 1998 by the California Assembly Select Committee on the California Middle Class, chaired by Assemblyman Wally Knox, indicated that income inequality in Los Angeles has increased significantly. The study on which the report was based found that as of 1996, 41 percent of the residents of L.A. County lived in households with annual income below $20,000, and fully two-thirds lived in households with annual incomes below $40,000. Only 26 percent were in middle-income households making between $40,000 and $100,000, with 8 percent in households making more than $100,000.[9]

California's recovery from the recession of the early 1990s has not mitigated this trend, but rather has magnified the effect of structural inequalities in L.A.'s economy. According to an analysis undertaken by the *Los Angeles Times* in 1999, nearly all the job growth in Los Angeles County, since the low point of the recession in winter 1993, has been in low-income jobs. Although the number of new jobs created is impressive, almost three hundred thousand since 1993, very few of these jobs fall in the middle-class income range of $40,000 to $60,000. L.A.'s economic recovery has produced far more parking lot attendants, waiters, and video store clerks than highly paid workers in information technology, entertainment, or international trade. The majority of new jobs pay less than $25,000 per year, and barely one new job in ten averages $60,000 per year.[10]

The impact of these low salary figures is even more dramatic in light of the high cost of living in Los Angeles County. The high cost of real estate in Los Angeles makes it difficult for low-income workers to buy homes even if several wage earners share the same household. Whereas neighboring Orange County has seen a 10 percent increase in its home ownership rate in the past ten years, the rate for Los Angeles County has scarcely moved in the same period. Many of these new jobs also lack long-term security or health care benefits. According to Mark Drayse, research director of the nonprofit Economic Roundtable, the net effect is that the population is "becoming more polarized."[11]

The current socioeconomic condition of Latinos in Los Angeles can be traced directly to the relentless emergence of the global economy and recent economic policies of expansion, such as the North American Free Trade Agreement (NAFTA), that have weakened the labor participation of Latinos through the transfer of historically well-paying manufacturing jobs to Mexico and other "cheap-labor" manufacturing centers around the world. Such consequences highlight the need for scholars to link the condition of U.S. Latinos in cities to the globalization of the economy. Few scholars have contributed more to our understanding of globalization and economic restructuring than Saskia Sassen, who posits:

> Trends in major cities cannot be understood in isolation of fundamental changes in the broader organization of advanced economies. The combination of economic, political, and technical forces

that has contributed to the decline of mass production as the central element in the economy brought about a decline in a wider institutional framework that shaped the employment relations.[12]

In light of this view, Latino Los Angeles can be fully understood only within the context of the U.S. political economy and the new international division of labor. Without question, the United States is the wealthiest country in the world, yet it is the nation-state with the greatest economic inequality between the rich and the poor and with the most disproportionate wealth distribution of all the "developed" nations of the world. To overlook this economic reality in the analysis of Latino populations is to ignore the most compelling social phenomenon in U.S. society today—the growing gap between rich and poor.[13]

Further, we must address the impact of U.S. economic globalization on cultural production, particularly that of popular culture, in the United States and worldwide. Stuart Hall's writings on culture, globalization, and the world-system clearly address the relationship between global mass culture (which Hall identifies as American) and the economy.

> Global mass culture is dominated by the modern means of cultural production, dominated by the image which crosses and re-crosses linguistic frontiers much more rapidly and more easily, and which speaks across languages in a much more immediate way. It is dominated by all the ways in which visual and graphic arts have entered directly into the reconstitution of popular life, of entertainment and of leisure. It is dominated by television and by film, and by image, imagery, and styles of mass advertising. Its epitome is in all those forms of mass communication of which one might think of satellite television as the prime example. Not because it is the only example but because you could not understand satellite television without understanding its grounding in a particular advanced national economy and culture and yet its whole purpose is precisely that it cannot be limited any longer by national boundaries.[14]

Hall's analysis of the globalized economy and its impact on transnational cultural formations has theoretical and political significance for an understanding of the concept of *mestizaje* as a transcultural style of Latino border crossing. We argue in this volume that, although the notion of *mestizaje* has links to Mexican and Latin American history, its lived experience is radically transformed amid the realities of the U.S. political economy.

If globalization has meant anything, it entails that the shifts Frantz

Fanon suggests in social formation, structure, and culture facing the (former) colonies in the wake of their independence have had deep structural implications also for colonizing and dominant geopolitical powers. Thus Los Angeles, like other cities in the United States, has experienced dramatic structural shifts in its mode of structural formation in the postcolonial period since World War II, and especially in the past twenty-five years. Indeed, these shifts are linked to postcolonial transformations globally. Nor were the decline and shift in L.A.'s manufacturing base unique to that city; rather, these changes represented shifts in the mode of capital accumulation worldwide from Fordist to flexible.[15] Tied to these were a number of related transformations: from manufacturing to service jobs (global financial at the high end, social services in both senses at the low), from global power to global partner, from presumptive (indeed presumptuous) homogeneous military-industrial complex to complex multicultural hybrid, and from a society where work was supposedly work and the rest was leisurely play to one where we are increasingly troubled about finding work that pays a living wage and recreation is big business. Even as it may have responded somewhat differentially to these changes, Los Angeles has witnessed these transformations as visibly as any city in the United States, and in its culture (and cultural industry) it has reflected (as it reflects upon) these changes for the rest of the country (and, more imperialistically, for the rest of the world).

There are further changes attendant to these broader transformations and so more obviously at play in Los Angeles than elsewhere. For one, across roughly the same period the city became identified with new waves of influx, migration, and immigration—and not just from across borders or seas but across the landscape of America (the lure of opportunity, leisure, and play, long associated with the image of that city), thus magnifying its always already diverse character. The shrinking of traditional and "legitimate" opportunities gave way to the emergence of alternative economies (the creation of new opportunities in the face of their absence)—drugs and guns have manifested more visibly, but also new cultural forms have opened up in turn other economic opportunities, as in the case of gangsta rap and hip-hop.

At the same time, as Mike Davis, Edward W. Soja, Roger Keil, and others have documented in relation to Los Angeles, and in what Louis F. Miron suggests is a more general phenomenon (although perhaps especially pressing and visible in Los Angeles), there was a distinct and increasingly self-conscious shift to privatization of the public mandate and public services: you get what you can pay for.[16] In this sense, California's Proposition

187 is only the latest development in this logic of privatizing the health and educational costs for unskilled labor. The law approved by electoral endorsement of Proposition 187 has no design on ending immigration or the employment of immigrants, only on ensuring that continued source of "waged slavery" by refusing education to immigrants and cheapening the labor supply by privatizing its associated costs.

The effect of all this is to render the population that "occupies" Central Los Angeles *invisible* politically and economically, to be policed but not seen or heard (from), a population beyond the boundaries of the political imagination save as that unspoken reserve army of labor keeping unskilled wages, and so the minimum wage, in check. Inflation is kept in hand as well on the backs of the unemployed, for the unemployed tend not to vote, whereas consumers stop by at the polls on the way to the mall (or these days at the mall). In this sense, the Los Angeles implosion in 1992 was not a riot or an uprising or an *intifada,* not an uprising or quite a revolt, but the overflowing of anger no longer containable, at once self-defeating as it was other-directed. This implosion can be understood thus as the bitter and pained insistence on visibility—"We are here, deal with us, in every sense of the term"—in the face of the logic and policies of invisibility.

The revolution, as Gil Scott-Heron once suggested, may not be televised, but Fanon hinted at the fact that it would be deeply linked to technological innovation, although he could not have predicted in the 1950s that the deeper, unseen revolution would turn out to be electronic rather than political. Television and computers are its media, surveillance and supervision its mode, discipline its message, containment its effect. In this context, L.A.'s implosion—and where more fitting in this sense than Los Angeles?—was about making public the privatization of marginalization. Related to these deep structural shifts, as should be apparent and has been commented upon by many others, is the transformation in urban space that accompanied them: peripheral sub-urban spaces decentering the "inner" city and rendering the center marginal. This marginalization is effected by the use of landscape, natural (for example, rivers as dividing lines) and created (as in the placing of highways both to traverse threatening space without having to engage it and to cut off the threat from its expansion—not altogether successful in 1992). Highways, those quintessentially L.A. modes of transportation, thus represent not only communication and speed but containment and territorialization—something the apartheid state in South Africa employed quite self-consciously for a while with devastating effect. Actually, the analogy with South Africa runs deeper. Los Angeles is not unlike Johannesburg by the sea, with lines of "racial" demarcation only more formally drawn under apartheid. And white South Africa has been trying now since the beginning of the 1990s to transform its (sub)urban spaces into a mirror image of Los Angeles, emulating the American legacy of privatized apartheid.

The globalization of capital and its changes in class relations form the very backdrop of contemporary Latino politics and racialized relations, but is conspicuously absent in most contemporary accounts of Latino life in the United States—accounts that ignore the increasing significance of class and the specificity of capitalism as a system of social and political relations of power.

One issue is clear to us. Despite claims by some on the Left (whose theoretical orientations could be described as "postmodernist" or "post-Marxist") that class politics is an anachronism, we maintain that the concept of class has increasing analytic value as we enter the twenty-first century. We are guided here by David Harvey's definition of class:

> I insist that class is not a thing, an entity, or a "permanence"
> (though under given conditions it can indeed assume such a form)
> but fundamentally a process. But what kind of process? Marx ap-
> pears to define class relationally as command (or noncommand)
> over the means of production. I prefer to define class as *situated-
> ness or positionality* in relation to process of capital accumulation.[17]

We also recognize that there is a theoretical tension between our insistence on the need for a renewed class approach at a time when it has become fashionable for some on the academic Left to question its analytic utility and our often implicit constructivist and discursive mapping of racialized relations and identities in Los Angeles. We argue, nonetheless, that a political economy approach informed by both a Marxist and a critical "postmodern" social theory offers the best way to theorize about Latinos in Los Angeles in the context of demographic shifts, changing class formations, and new forms of "global" capitalism. In a recent interview, Stuart Hall echoes our concern with the Left's silence on this issue of class and its failure to articulate sufficiently the relationship between the economic and the political in discussions of global capitalism:

> I do think that's work that urgently needs to be done. The moment
> you talk about globalization, you are obliged to talk about the in-
> ternationalization of capital in its late modern form, the shifts that
> are going on in modern capitalism, post-Fordism, etc. So, those
> terms which were excluded from cultural studies . . . now need to
> be reintegrated . . . . In fact, I am sure we will return to the funda-

mental category of "capital." The difficulties lie in reconceptualizing class. Marx it seems to me now, was more accurate about "capitalism" than he was about class. It's the articulation between the economic and the political in Marxist class theory that has collapsed.[18]

## After "Race" in the Metropolis

Although "race" and "ethnicity" have long been key concepts in sociological discourse and public debate, they have remained problematic. Policy pundits, journalists, and conservative and liberal academics alike work within categories of "race" and "ethnicity" as though there is unanimity as to their analytic value. Racialized group conflicts are framed and advanced as "race relations" problems and are presented to the public mostly in black/white terms.

The dominant image of Los Angeles remains that of a cultural mosaic, a rich tapestry of multinational cultures collected in Angeleno urban space. Through the dominance of its cultural industry—films, television, music, and other forms of entertainment—this image is reproduced for the world at large. This prevailing picture of managed and corporate multiculturalism hides an underlying sociostructural tension running beneath this mosaic image, one more fragmented and fragmenting, divided and divisive, corrosive and corroding. The confusion begins when scholars and media pundits attempt to identify the causes of the fragmentation.

The city of Los Angeles, and Southern California as a whole, both in the popular public imagination and in contemporary academic discourse, is predicated upon a long-established view about "race." Here "races" are fixed and given, unchanging and unchangeable. They are assigned analytic values as determinants of behavior as to how people are and what they do as members of racialized groups. Accordingly, racialized groups are perceived as discrete and homogeneous—the same now as they have always been, their members indistinguishable from each other. Although few scholars today explicitly espouse such a view, the assumption is implicit in works that employ color categories and their ethnic equivalents to explain phenomena unrelated to the possession of certain biological characteristics or membership in a particular ethnic group. This view presupposes as it reinforces the perception that the city is balkanized and fragmented.

Founded upon this image is what we call the zero-sum picture of the great melodrama of "race relations" in Los Angeles: "racial" groups are considered to be deeply at odds with each other, each group "naturally" apart from others and antagonistic toward members of other groups. Benefits to one group are—or are perceived to be—costs to another. This "race relations" paradigm is taken to mark the "racial" divide as much between those presumed "black" and "brown" as between those considered "black" and "white," or "white" and "brown."

Academics, media reporters, and politicians "conspired" to use the vocabulary of "race" to make sense of the 1992 Los Angeles riots because it is a central component of everyday commonsense discourse. And when it became overwhelmingly apparent that it was not a "black/white" riot, the language of "race" was nevertheless unthinkingly retained by means of a switch to the use of the notion of "multiracial" in order to encompass the diversity of historical and cultural origins of the participants and victims. Thus, although the "race relations" paradigm was dealt a serious blow by the reality of the riots, the vocabulary of "race" was retained. But, and here we find the source of the problem, the idea of "race" is so firmly embedded in common sense that it cannot easily encompass a reference to "Koreans" or "Hispanics" or "Latinos," for these are neither "black" nor "white." It is thus not surprising that pundits and scholars stumble over "racial" ambiguity. The clash of racialized language with a changing political economy presents challenges for scholars and activists alike.

If one had begun with an analysis grounded simultaneously in history and political economy rather than with the supremely ideological notion of "race relations," one would have quickly concluded that the actors in any riot in Central Los Angeles would probably be ethnically diverse. Large-scale inward migration from Mexico and Central America and from Southeast Asia into California has coincided with a restructuring of the California economy. As a consequence of the loss of major manufacturing jobs and large-scale internal migration within the urban sprawl of "greater" Los Angeles, the spatial, ethnic, and class structure that underlay the Watts riots of 1965 had been transformed into a much more complex set of relationships.[19]

We aim to demonstrate the shortcomings of this cultural-mosaic image of Los Angeles by excavating the less visible conditions of Angeleno political economy and hybrid culture that this image hides from view. The dominant picture of balkanized Los Angeles, for one, represses the dramatic heterogeneity internal to and across racialized groups in the city. Ghettos are not just poor neighborhoods but are manufactured as self-enclosed and isolated social and residential environments.[20] More emphatically, the zero-sum picture fails to come to terms with the dramatically transformed demographic, economic, and political landscape the city has experienced over the past quarter century.

One purpose of this study is to problematize the notion of "race" and the related concept of "race relations" in social theory and contemporary urban social relations. The ideas of "race" and "race relations" have been questioned analytically for more than a decade within European academic discussion, and it is only recently that some U.S. scholars have begun to consider the rationale and implications of that critique.[21]

In our analysis of racialized urban relations and media representation and discourse, we advocate expanding the contemporary sociological debate by arguing for a complete rejection of the use of the terms *race* and *race relations* in academic and public discourse. In this study, we introduce a conceptual framework of "racialization" as an alternative model to the sociology of "race relations." Following Robert Miles's seminal work,

> racialization refers to those instances where social relations between people have been structured by the signification of human biological characteristics in such a way as to define and construct differentiated social collectivities. . . . The concept therefore refers to a process of categorization, a representational process of defining an Other (usually, but not exclusively) somatically.[22]

By recognizing the process of racialization as the underlying factor in social relations, we can understand the process of signification of one group by another and racialized struggles and tensions. This is important not only in the context of social theory, but also in the context of contemporary politics and social change. This reexamination, stripped of the "race" language, reveals the roles of ethnicity and ethnic politics in shaping the discourse of "race."[23] It further unveils racialized class relations in a changing economy and society shaped by the transition from outmoded Fordist economies and their patterns of politics.

In analyzing these new social relations, we posit, there is no need to employ the concept of "race." Indeed, its retention is a significant hindrance in social theory, politics, and policy. We posit further that class is far more important than the specious concept of "race" in determining the life chances of Latinos in Los Angeles. However, we do not reject the concept of racism, and we maintain that it is necessary for analysts to draw upon the concept of racialization as a tool that will enable them to grasp and map the changing contours of racism(s) and the broad array of structural economic and political inequalities. We explore the implications of this analytic approach in this work. It is with this critical questioning of mainstream assumptions that we wish to theorize about ethnicity, culture, and racialized social and spatial relations in the contemporary metropolis. We explore the strategic opportunities that have gone unnoticed in the language of economic marginalization and social pathology, a language that has been constructed, then reinvented and refined over time, to reinforce and "explain" the social conditions created by a capitalist political economy, with its structural inequalities of income and power. Our discussions of racialized media discourse and of Mexican cuisine in the symbolic economy of Los Angeles illustrate these points.

As Latino leaders and activists contest public space in a changing city, they must fight concrete political battles and also "deconstruct" the elite discourses that promote lopsided, top-down notions of corporate and economic development. In other words, because the symbolic and political economies reinforce each other, political struggles must engage both at once. Thus this book is concerned with labor, capital, city building, and identifying strategic opportunities—a "third way" in the struggle for economic democracy in a city of increasing social polarization.

# 1

# Economic Geography
# of Latino Los Angeles

Finding those snapshots that reveal the human faces of immigrant workers, typically disguised as the late twentieth century's ultimate alien outsider, remains the defining challenge for academics, activists, and journalists interested in explaining and changing our "postindustrial" economy. Sometimes the desired image, or frozen time surface, reveals more than initially intended. This appears to be the case in a 1993 investigative series published in the *Los Angeles Times* on Latino immigrant workers in Los Angeles County's manufacturing workplaces; the article that opens the series begins with three anecdotes of postindustrial Sinclairian death and misery: "One woman was doused head to toe with boiling oil when a machine that laminates menus exploded; a man drowned in a glue vat, and another was struck in the head by a 50-pound chunk of flying metal while tooling a chrome wheel. Some were electrocuted; several were crushed by hydraulic presses or pulled into the gears of other powerful machines."[1]

The final image, which suggests a postmodern version of *Modern Times,* adds a final note of irony to the grim tally: of the forty-three workplace fatalities reported during a recent four-year period, twenty-nine were Latino. The math is chilling, especially when placed in demographic context: although Latinos represented 36.4 percent of Los Angeles County's total labor force in 1990, Latino workers "accounted for 67% of workers who lost their lives in manufacturing-related accidents between 1988 and 1992."[2] The author of the *Times* series, David Freed, justifiably focuses on the causes of Latino workplace deaths and injuries: regulatory neglect, lack of medical coverage, and greedy or indifferent employers who tolerate unsafe working conditions or an ill-trained workforce. And he concludes by suggesting ways to make the status quo work better than it does: greater regulatory oversight and employer accountability, as well as better worker education. Yet, despite his impressive reporting, Freed fails to consider how the reorganization of manufacturing has contributed to workplace injuries, or to explore what other meanings the emergence of a huge Latino industrial workforce might have, beyond the fatal statistics. This chapter begins where Freed's analysis ends. We look behind the image of a worker eaten by machinery to uncover the setting, which has its own story to tell. Its protagonists include a majority Latino industrial workforce, a new social organization of work, and changing processes of landscape formation, all of which have converged in a strange new dialectic. This dialectic, we argue, reveals both strategic obstacles to and opportunities for empowerment available to the Latino community and other progressive sectors.

The emergence of a majority Latino industrial working class in the nation's largest manufacturing metropolis provides the key protagonists of this drama. In 1990, working-class Latinos accounted for more than half of Los Angeles County's manufacturing workforce, although they constituted only little more than a third of its population. A close analysis of government labor data shows that Latinos in Los Angeles County made up 44.9 percent of workers employed in durable goods manufacturing and 66 percent employed in non–durable goods manufacturing. Analyzed by occupation, Latino workers represented slightly more than 50 percent of those employed in the service sector, more than 46 percent employed in craft and precision production, almost 75 percent employed in assembly work, more than 46 percent employed in transportation industries, and more than 60 percent of those classified as laborers.[3] Inside the city limits, the Latino presence in the manufacturing sector has increased to more than 72 percent.[4] All the demographic and economic indicators that we review in this book indicate that these Los Angeles County employment trends have not abated.

Second, the deaths and injuries occurred within a new industrial landscape, or the so-called global factories. Economists across the political spectrum increasingly view the present reindustrialization occurring at the nation's fringes as fundamentally different from previous stages of capitalist development. The transformation of industrial landscapes represents a shift away from large-scale, centralized, mass-production factories employing thousands of well-paid and often unionized employees, otherwise described as *Fordist* industries, toward smaller, high-technology, and craft-oriented manufacturers employing anywhere from 150 to 250 employees, described as *post-Fordist* industries.

Organizational flexibility and an altered relationship to labor markets distinguish Southern California's uniquely eclectic post-Fordist pattern. Rather than maximize profits on the shop floor through efficiencies of scale derived through Fordist mass production, the flexible approach maximizes profit outside the production process by continually discarding its labor force, raw material, and product suppliers to secure cheaper replacements.[5] Organizational flexibility and the search for ever-cheaper sources of labor and materials have led to spatial fragmentation. Faster forms of communication and transportation, and the emergence of international trading networks, have exponentially expanded the world's reserves of surplus labor. Declining labor costs and governments eager to maintain worker discipline have encouraged the globalization of the post-Fordist pattern. In Southern California, the post-Fordist pattern has evolved into two distinct variants, both which rely on the ready availability of immigrant labor. For high-tech industries dependent on highly skilled workers, the region's ability to attract, or "drain," highly educated Asian immigrants provides clear competitive advantages. Not only has another country borne the social costs of educating these workers, their degrees will earn them more in the United States than they can at home, yet those workers still cost employers less than their domestic counterparts. The region's low-tech post-Fordist firms have also replicated the advantages of going abroad, or virtual globalization, by targeting undocumented immigrants, particularly Latinas, as their prime labor source.[6]

The convergence of these new systems of production and social formations demands a reconsideration of the meaning of so-called ethnic workers and their role in the new global economy. The nation's largest manufacturing center is about to become Latinized, a dramatic transformation that has only recently received glib commentary. Part of the underestimation of the role of Latino workers stems from a tendency to view them as a marginalized sector of the labor force. Another reason is the failure to come to grips with the socioeconomic consequences of a postindustrial society.

Two intentions—one descriptive, the other strategic— thus underlie our study. Of the two, however, we emphasize the search for a conceptual language that explains the consequences of the reorganization of industrial production for the global economy. As such, this chapter can be understood as a first step toward the discovery of an epistemology for labor and community organizers in a restructuring economy. Today poor and working communities find themselves in a frustrating struggle to identify and name their enemies and allies. Something has changed. For many community, labor, and political groups, changing conditions have outpaced the language of social and political rewards that once sustained the illusion of an expanding middle class. One of the clearest expressions of this profoundly incongruent moment reveals itself in the way many social scientists, labor organizers, and political activists have either underestimated or ignored the emergence of a majority Latino working class in the Greater Los Angeles area, still the nation's largest manufacturing center in spite of recessions and the elimination of tens of thousands of defense-related jobs.

It is not hard to see why the strategic opportunities hidden in the midst of plant closings, riots, and earthquakes have gone unnoticed. Finding meaning in so much pain must seem the highest form of impertinence. But these conditions themselves cannot be blamed for blinding social scientists, community activists, and political leaders to the important work of reevaluating the Latino community's role in an emerging postindustrial economy. Other factors have contributed to this inattention.

Most social, economic, and political events within the Latino community are framed in the language of economic marginalization or social pathology. Latino poverty and social inequality, it is assumed, reflect an inability to contribute to or participate in the mainstream economy. Latino powerlessness and poverty are also described as the results of a social pathology attributed to racial discrimination. The media, like many labor leaders and sympathizers inflamed by anti-immigrant rhetoric, often portray Latinos as both racialized victims and villains. Their status as undocumented workers exposes them to exploitation, and they are also blamed for lowering wages and undermining the overall bargaining power and social benefits of unionized employees. The average citizen confronts similar ambiguities. The image of the hardworking Latino immigrant both conforms to and subverts the myth of the United States as a democratic ethnic melting pot. These immigrants' stoic work ethic and patterns of reinvestment in the barrios are praiseworthy. But their persistent and increasing illegality and the social and cultural implications of their increasing economic presence undermine a faith in a nation based upon the rule of law and clearly defined boundaries. Each representation, although based on a partial truth, negates or obscures the changing status of the Latino community and the strategic opportunities that flow from that change. We have therefore elaborated a conceptual language by which academics and activists can identify new strategic opportunities. We leave the creation of a fully developed strategy, however, for our final chapters. Instead, we will present strategic opportunities to illustrate the viability of the conceptual categories of description proposed here.

No matter the scale, global economies must still function in local landscapes. Moreover, global enterprises continue to seek comparative advantages provided by the ability of local governments to transfer social wealth into the hands of private capital. Corporate capital's recent victories in deregulating federal policies and power to thwart new regulatory efforts only enhance the local landscape's instrumental value. In contrast to a status quo most often characterized by federal gridlock, corporate capital, whether national or global in reach, takes care of business at the level of state, county, or municipal government. At the local level, it not only has the ability to induce job-starved states, counties, or cities to compete against each other for the next factory, prison, or waste disposal project, it can buy more political influence with less money. Unfortunately, the social and economic transformations needed to facilitate the economies of global efficiency have progressively reduced the control of local communities over their own political institutions. In the name of catchphrases such as "government privatization" and "running government like a business," communities have allowed capital to appropriate more and more of local government's economic planning and regulatory functions.

Capital's increasing co-optation of local government in the name of efficiency has been calculated to appeal to the anti-big-government, anti-tax sentiments of suburban middle-class voters. Often capital has persuaded suburbanites that handing over the functions of government will help to eliminate the social welfare programs they so resent paying for. At the same time, conservative attacks on the evils of "big government" are aimed mostly at the federal bureaucracy in Washington, directing attention away from local government, where capital's intrusions receive far less media scrutiny. We will attempt to show, however, that global capital's economic and political power over local landscapes creates vulnerabilities to new social formations that have the potential to organize local democratic, progressive initiatives. For example, capital's success at cloaking the economic planning and resource allocation functions of local government from public scrutiny has enabled it to speed up economic restructuring, which has, in turn, hastened the Latinization of Southern California's working class.

The demographic reconstitution of the working class is also occurring in other major U.S. industrial cities. Thus the creation of "stealth government" and the emergence of a majority Latino working class must be understood as merely different aspects of a single process of landscape creation and destruction. As a result, any effort to make local government more accountable and democratic must factor in the Latino community as a voting, working, and consuming population upon which Southern California's economic future depends. Fatalistic references to a *Blade Runner* city or yearning for the good old days will not make the present-day configuration of economic and labor forces disappear. Urban immigrant workers, as the recent shift in AFL-CIO organizing policies indicates, must be conceived as load-bearing pillars upon which revitalized labor and progressive social movements will be built.

Whether postindustrial transformation is seen as the result of a shift toward a service economy or as the most recent expression of the continued economic supremacy of industrial manufacturing is not our concern. Rather, we try here to decipher those strategic features of the landscape that marginalized communities might exploit in their struggles for economic justice and political empowerment. We hope that our efforts to identify strategic opportunities for enhancing Latino community participation in the formulation of microindustrial and microeconomic policies will resonate beyond the Greater Eastside and help other urban communities to develop strategies and tactics for redirecting and reducing the most damaging aspects of economic restructuring.

## Constructing Political Space:
## Toward a Language of Cities and Work

The concept of "landscape" that we advance in this volume borrows from Sharon Zukin's recent writings.[7] The novelty of her work stems from the way she expands the meaning of *landscape* beyond the geographic. For Zukin, human landscapes are constructed from the dynamic linkages joining a region's totality of socioeconomic, cultural, and political spaces. Existing social and political institutions and the changing material conditions of the marketplace, she argues, shape a landscape's spatial dimensions:

> In a narrow sense, landscape represents the architecture of social
> class, gender, and race relations imposed by powerful institutions.
> In a broader sense, however, it connotes the entire panorama that
> we see: both the landscape of the powerful cathedrals, factories,
> and skyscrapers and the subordinate, resistant, or expressive
> vernacular of the powerless village chapels, shanty towns, and
> tenements.[8]

Zukin's multidimensional approach to landscape reading provides useful analytic categories for describing the architecture, organization, and loci of power in Los Angeles's Greater Eastside. Her approach also provides us with a method for narrating the Eastside's construction in time by focusing upon the dialectics of capital accumulation and the formation of local political institutions. Explicit in this economic-political dialectic is our representation of the Eastside as a contested terrain where its actors—

indigenous or outside capital, indigenous social classes, and local political bureaucracies—vie for strategic advantages.

The spatial convergence of capital, politics, and class, Zukin argues, can be portrayed as a dialectic of places. The marketplace, the industrial park, and the suburban neighborhood are defined by their distinct roles as places of production or consumption. According to Zukin, these roles take on a revealing character in the transition to a postindustrial society:

> Those places that remain part of a production economy, where
> men and women produce a physical product for a living, are losers.
> To the extent they do survive in a service economy they lack income
> and prestige, and owe their souls to bankers and politicians. By
> contrast, those places that thrive are connected to real estate de-
> velopment, financial exchanges, and entertainment—the business
> of moving money and people where consumer pleasures hide the
> reins of concentrated economic control.[9]

The dialectics of place acquire distinct spatial expressions in late-twentieth-century postindustrial cities. Zukin and others have shown that the spatial expansion of urban landscapes proceed along centrifugal force lines, perpetually moving outward beyond the fringes of previous periods of industrial and suburban development. Eventually, the older urban landscape is left behind to atrophy as each succeeding growth ring moves the benefits of capital further from the original urban core.[10]

At first reading, Zukin's dialectic of places does not appear to favor the Greater Eastside, because Latino barrios are often depicted in popular and academic literature as places of residence for a marginalized pool of surplus labor. Although applicable to certain East Coast Latino barrios, such broad generalizations do not readily apply to the Greater Eastside of Los Angeles. Moreover, such simplistic generalizations should be resisted lest they blind us to the strategic advantages present in specific landscapes. Zukin, for example, recounts several cases in which politically and economically marginalized communities have effectively organized to reverse, or at least moderate, the more noxious effects of postindustrial transformation. Therefore, rather than view the Greater Eastside as part of an imploding inner city, we contend that its spatial expansion obeys the centripetal forces that have created the postindustrial city. In other words, the Eastside's shape and size are direct consequences of its transformation from a collection of semirural "edge suburbs" to an interdependent network of newer and maturing near-in cities and suburbs. Our description of the Greater Eastside as a clustering of postindustrial suburbs contradicts the conventional view of the barrio as politically and economically marginalized territory. In fact, the very forces that have constructed such agglomerations as the Greater Eastside and the San Fernando Valley contain the seeds of emergent confederations that may someday politically validate their economic linkages with new jurisdictional boundaries. Therefore, rather than search the Greater Eastside's landscape for metaphors of inner-city dysfunctionality, we view it as an economically and culturally constructed functional totality. Seen from the ground, the Greater Eastside appears as a random patchwork of uneven developments marked off by freeways, concrete-lined riverbeds, rail lines, and landfills, the Hopewell-like monuments of a throwaway consumer civilization.

However, seen from the air or on a demographer's map, the seemingly convoluted patterning of the landscape reveals the structure of a multicelled organism. Socially and economically differentiated Latino suburban cells, manufacturing zones, and commercial districts radiate eastward from the organism's historic nucleus, or original urban core. Arterial freeways link the nucleus to the expanding edge, facilitating the circulation of goods, people, and information. At the organism's amorphous edges, privileged suburban cells encroach upon places created by older forms of capital accumulation. The newer suburbs wedded to globalized capital are rewarded with more hospitable landscapes, whereas those wedded to obsolete modes of production lose control of the ability to re-create their neighborhoods.

The Greater Eastside was, and continues to be, shaped by the destructive and creative energies unleashed in the competition between older and newer forms of capital accumulation and the ensuing competition between landscapes. Unfortunately, our narration cannot suggest every landscape nuance, as the documentary details needed to recount Southern California's social history are at best fragmentary. The resulting dearth of narrative detail has undermined recent social histories, which have ignored or misconstrued the Latino community's landscape-building role. Yet, despite such narrative gaps, we can salvage enough of a plotline from available sources to retrace the Greater Eastside's sociospatial construction. Rodolfo F. Acuña maintains that the creation of the Eastside's seminal urban Latino core resulted from an economic exodus. As had happened during the 1849 California gold rush, massive white American immigration during the late nineteenth century again overwhelmed the local Mexican population, most of whom lived downtown west of the Los Angeles River in an area known as "Sonora town." Later, by the 1920s, the downtown Anglo elite's rise to economic dominance, led by Harry Chandler's *Los Angeles Times*, further accelerated the Mexican community's eastward flight. The driving forces behind the displacement of Mexicans were the "soaring property values and skyrocketing rents" that the Chandler growth strategy had ignited.[11] By 1929, more than thiry thousand Mexicans had crossed the river and settled in Belvedere Gardens, a planned housing development built over farmland.

At the same time, other Mexicans escaped downtown Los Angeles to establish residential suburbs in El Hoyo Maravilla, Montebello, and points beyond. Prior to their exodus from downtown, the Mexicans of Sonora town had served as a surplus labor pool for local industries.[12] They continued in this role after the exodus as the cluster of Eastside Mexican communities began to coalesce and industry moved east of the river to take advantage of cheaper property values and zoning practices deliberately favorable to the city's and county's rapidly growing industrial sector. In other words, the political and economic elites of Los Angeles early on decided to sacrifice the eastern hemisphere of the city and county to the demands of industrial production, while everything west of the city would become landscapes of recreation and residence. It was accepted that the Mexican industrial labor force, which consisted of mostly unskilled "pick-and-shovel" laborers, some skilled workers, and the micro-middle class of small merchants and professionals who provided services to these workers, would settle in the new Eastside's industrial suburbs.[13] The origins, composition, and residence patterns of an urbanized Mexican labor force are subtleties often lost on non-Latino scholars, who tend to start their studies of urban labor history with the Mexican and Central American migration of the 1970s and 1980s. The fact is, Latino migration, both external and internal, has played a crucial role in the social history of Los Angeles industry since the beginning of the twentieth century. [14]

The urban Latino core east of the Los Angeles River may thus be viewed as an organic demographic unit from which other Latino satellite communities would grow, cell by suburban cell. Uneven economic development accelerated this process. The creation of dozens of new municipalities encouraged the fragmentation of former farmland into a patchwork of residential and industrial places. A key factor in this process of economic gerrymandering was each municipality's ability to create or protect its strategic economic assets. Those portions of the Greater Eastside that could neither capture nor create strategic advantages quickly became dependent upon economically dynamic neighbors.

After World War II, the L.A.-area Mexican population continued its gradual drift east and southeast until it reached the boundaries of an industrial landscape that had drawn most of its workforce from nearby white working-class suburbs.[15] Although it was not yet apparent, the Latino community's arrival at the gates of these white suburbs coincided with the emergence of Southern California's distinctly post-Fordist pattern of industrial development. J. Scott and A. S. Paul contend that during the postwar boom times of the 1950s, "mass production industries accounted for only 7 to 8 percent of all manufacturing employment in Southern California. . . . By 1970, employment in mass production industries in the region had fallen to 4.1 percent of the total, and by 1985 to only 2.8 percent."[16] Southern California filled this void with a growing array of smaller, craft-specific industries differentiated into specialized but interdependent plants producing a diversity of products. Between 1970 and 1985, the ensemble of craft-specialty industries had grown its workforce to more than three hundred thousand workers, or an increase of 81.3 percent.[17]

The fragmentation of industrial production precipitated the decline of unionized, mass-production automotive and steel industries in towns such as Maywood and Bell, which was followed by the rapid emigration of the white workforce from southeastern suburbs in the late 1950s and early 1960s. Eastsiders quickly filled this void. By the late 1970s, it became clear that the expanding Eastside would displace the formerly white southeast while filling in the interstitial spaces left between such older Mexican enclaves as El Monte, La Puente, and Santa Fe Springs. Thus the Greater Eastside is not merely an aggregation of residents of Mexican ancestry; it is a network of neighborhoods, cultural institutions, commercial strips, and suburban manufacturing zones linked by the day-to-day realities of work and play. These linkages, or pairings of places, express deeply embedded relationships between suburbs, or landscapes of rest and consumption, and industrial production that typify the Greater Eastside's spatial organization.

## Constructing the Greater Eastside

Two interconnected transformations were greatly shaped by capital's virtual monopoly over Los Angeles County land-use policies: the spread of post-Fordist industrial development in the eastern and southeastern areas of downtown and the accompanying cycles of suburbanization at the edges of the Los Angeles urban core. "The way the suburban system works," according to Bill Boyarsky and Nancy Boyarsky, is summed up in the gold letters engraved on one wall of the hall where the Los Angeles County Board of Supervisors holds its meetings. It reads, "This County Is Founded on Free Enterprise. Cherish and Preserve It." [18] In areas with large amounts of undeveloped land, such as suburbia, free enterprise means the sale and development of land. L.A. County officials have traditionally encouraged and subsidized this business, even though it is often destructive to the suburbanite's way of life.

As in other forms of suburban government, Los Angeles County has given its elected representatives the power to run their districts like personal fiefdoms. An individual supervisor, for example, can direct the expenditure of discretionary funds in his or her home district. The local political pork barrel has been especially visible to suburban residents because it has been used to reward or punish neighborhoods by granting or denying them such county-funded improvements as street renovations, new library branches, and regional parks. A rapidly declining tax base in recent years has curtailed the redistributive largesse of individual L.A. County supervisors. Even so, these powers, even when not encumbered by federally mandated programs or tax revolts, pale in comparison to supervisors' ability to privatize land-use policies. The various functions of economic government have been privatized through supervisors' cozy practice of appointing friends or political patrons to the L.A. County Regional Planning Commission and other policy-making panels.

It has not been at all unusual for the Regional Planning Commission to allow wealthy property owners and developers to buy zoning exemptions with generous campaign contributions. Not surprisingly, the supervisors' power to appoint or remove commissioners has reinforced their roles as magnets for campaign contributions. From 1981 to 1986, incumbents harvested 91 percent of the campaign contributions made to supervisorial candidates; only 2 percent of these contributions went to challengers.[19] Because supervisors rarely face viable challengers, they can amass huge war chests to advance their own political interests or those of their contributors.

The practice of giving private investors a strong say over land-use policy has tended to outlive individual projects. Over time, capital's cumulative effects have shaped both suburban landscapes and the organization of economic government. The Los Angeles County Regional Planning Commission perfectly illustrates this pattern of privatized government, but it is not an isolated case. All local government agencies charged with managing public resources, such as redevelopment funds and water, air quality, and transportation funds, have been privatized to some degree.

A seemingly endless flow of campaign contributions has paid for the appropriation of government's economic functions. Money given to supervisors by powerful real estate and industrial developers has not only smoothed the way for county-financed storm drains, sheriff's substations, and myriad capital-attracting inducements, it has facilitated the creation of more than thirty cities east of downtown, each one reserving the right to sell its functions of economic government to the highest bidder. The blurring of the political-economic boundaries between the public and private sectors has thus produced its own ironic legacies. After the Watts riot in 1965, the white middle and upper class fled to new edge suburbs to escape growing minority communities and a corrupt, unresponsive Los Angeles city government. Upon arriving in suburbia, however, they encountered a county bureaucracy that made City Hall look virtuous by comparison.[20]

The seeds of cyclical middle-class exodus were sown in political-economic arrangements that reached their clearest expression during the post–World War II succession of real estate and industrial booms that swallowed up the county's remaining reserves of developable raw land. The county's eastern region was hit especially hard by the dual onslaught of post-Fordist suburbanization and industrialization. It was not at all uncommon for cities in and near the Greater Eastside to hand over land planning to private developers, who then proceeded to design whole suburbs, industrial parks, and cities to their specifications.[21]

Here, too, capital's appropriation of the land-planning process shaped the structure and organization of local government. The most crucial of these transformations helped to integrate an array of legal, economic, and political rationales into a single structure euphemistically dubbed the *single-use industrial city*. These cities, populated with businesses instead of people, should be viewed as the equivalent of the post-Fordist center of flexible manufacturing. The degree of flexibility varied from city to city. Some, because they were held back by larger voting constituencies, did not privatize the functions of economic government as thoroughly as did other cities lacking the encumbrance of a voting citizenry.

Still, despite the economic differences and antagonisms among competing cities, a high degree of political coordination emerged among the various functions of intracity and regional economic governments. Such a system of informal and formal intergovernmental cooperation, whether achieved through backroom deal making or umbrella organizations such as the Southern California Association of Government, was designed to protect the political-legal apparatus, which permitted the growth of flexible economic government.

Today, some Greater Eastside flexible suburban cities, such as Vernon, resemble the *maquiladoras* deployed along Mexico's northern border, whereas others, such as Santa Fe Springs, are prosperous Latino middle-class enclaves sustained by post-Fordist manufacturing. Whatever the forms, however, the Greater Eastside's landscape is dominated by the county's most concentrated collection of such municipalities. The traits shared by flexible burgs such as the City of Industry, City of Commerce, Santa Fe Springs, Irwindale, Azusa, and Vernon can be summarized as follows: "It is our thesis that to correctly understand . . . the City of Industry, one must conceive of Industry's basic municipal purpose as one of becoming as much like a private industrial developer as possible while retaining full municipal powers to raise taxes, [to] use the power available to all cities."[22]

Among the functions of economic government most coveted by capital are a municipality's authority to expropriate private property, draw municipal boundaries, and subcontract private firms to provide public services. These powers are typically deployed in the following sequence. First, single-use cities eliminate the inconvenience of citizen rule by carving out city boundaries that exclude voters and, more important, include vital economic assets, such as rail lines, freeway access, or mineral rights. Second, liberal municipal incorporation laws allow single-use cities to contract private firms to provide public services, a technically legal arrangement that often leads to the creation of private monopolies hired to provide public services formerly dispensed by the city. Third, loosely written redevelopment laws permit single-use cities to condemn almost any property, including virgin farmland, as urban blight. When used in combination, these functions of economic government free capital to transfer awesome sums of public capital into private hands, and, as a result, offer numerous opportunities for municipal corruption.

Redevelopment thus has diverted millions of property tax dollars to Greater Eastside economic government, money that would otherwise have gone to the county's general fund. Although this form of economic development arguably flows from redevelopment, its payoffs all tilt toward the state's vast industrial and real estate development infrastructure. To date, taxpayers have had little success in renegotiating the way redevelopment benefits are distributed. The combined might of the redevelopment lobby, California's equivalent of Washington's military-industrial complex, had, until very recently, persuaded state and local governments to divert to it an ever-increasing stream of tax dollars. Ironically, this diversion of public capital continued even as voters staged taxpayer revolts that diminished local governments' abilities to provide basic services.

Despite such massive transfers of public capital into private development, the Greater Eastside's landscape is anything but monolithic. The county's former expanses of raw land, the sheer scale of development, the uneven economic development of local governments, and the diversity of competing economic interests have resulted in anarchic development, which capital exploits by pitting one landscape against others to extract the maximum in public subsidies or policy-making influence. The creation of the Greater Eastside's fragmented and unequal landscape can thus be expressed in the following spatiotemporal terms: the remnants of older forms of capital accumulation have remained close to the urban core while newer, more flexible forms of capital have sprouted on the periphery. The district's southeastern and western extremes illustrate these disparities between newer and older industrial landscapes especially well.

A 1992 survey of two-digit standard industrial classification (SIC) categories for twenty-one Greater Eastside cities shows that manufacturers there employed a total of 121,480 workers. The largest employers in this group of cities, which constitute L.A. County's First District, were firms producing transportation equipment (SIC 37), employing 15.28 percent of the total workforce (see Table 1). The next-highest categories were the related industries of fabricated metal products (SIC 34), at 14.13 percent, and industrial and commercial machinery (SIC 35), at 10.48 percent. Food and other products (SIC 20) employed 11.09 percent of the manufacturers surveyed. Northrop Aircraft in Pico Rivera accounted for 66 percent of the 18,568 employed in the transportation category. But this pattern of highly concentrated employment was the exception, not the rule. As is typical of industries organized upon the flexible model of production, most Greater Eastside manufacturers in the group surveyed employed fewer than a hundred employees.[23]

Our survey data support the thesis that flexible specialty craft industries have fueled the active resurgence of manufacturing in Southern California. They are also consistent with countywide employment data. Although Latinos, Asians, and women form the backbone of the region's post-Fordist industries, with especially heavy Latino and female participation in apparel, furniture, and leather manufacturing, the range of post-Fordist industries employing Latinos is broader than recently acknowledged. Countywide, the printing, transportation, metal, chemical, and petroleum-related industries employ Latinos in consistently high concentrations. A 1994 survey also shows that metal, metalworking, and industrial machinery manufacturers located in or near Latino immigrant working-class communities employed 65,643 workers, or 36.9 percent of the county's manufacturing workforce.[24] In the Eastside's twenty-one-city group, the same metal-related industries accounted for 29.62 percent of jobs in 1992. These metal-related manufacturing jobs pay $500 to $700 per week, in contrast to garment-making jobs, which pay between $250 and $300 per week.[25]

Table 1

**Employment in two-digit industries for the First District's twenty-one-city group, 1992 SIC codes**

| Manufacturing categories | Number of employees | Percentage of total |
|---|---|---|
| 20 Food and other products | 13,430 | 11.09 |
| 22 Textile mill products | 1,438 | 1.18 |
| 23 Apparel and other textile products | 3,714 | 3.06 |
| 24 Lumber and wood products | 1,633 | 1.34 |
| 25 Furniture and fixtures | 5,043 | 4.15 |
| 26 Paper and allied products | 5,982 | 4.92 |
| 27 Printing and publishing | 5,480 | 4.51 |
| 28 Chemicals and allied products | 5,277 | 4.34 |
| 29 Petroleum and coal products | 1,616 | 1.33 |
| 30 Rubber and miscellaneous plastics | 6,635 | 5.46 |
| 31 Leather and leather products | 1,030 | .85 |
| 32 Stone, clay, and glass products | 2,948 | 2.42 |
| 33 Primary metals | 6,099 | 5.02 |
| 34 Fabricated metal products | 17,165 | 14.13 |
| 35 Machinery, except electrical | 12,729 | 10.48 |
| 36 Electric and electronic equipment | 7,402 | 6.10 |
| 37 Transportation equipment | 18,568 | 15.28 |
| 38 Instruments and related products | 2,742 | 2.25 |
| 39 Miscellaneous manufacturing | 2,549 | 2.09 |
| Total | 121,480 | 100.00% |

More-skilled and better-educated second- and third-generation male Mexican Americans have improved their earning power by entering the higher-skilled manufacturing sectors, but at a rate far slower than that of their white male counterparts. Vilma Ortiz argues that the loss of well-paying jobs in Fordist steel, auto, and tire industries and the growth of low-skilled post-Fordist garment, plastics, and electronics manufacturing have pushed immigrant and second- and third-generation Mexican workers into the same industries and, increasingly, the same jobs.[26] Ironically, social compression in the workplace appears to reinforce spatial compression. The working- to lower-middle-class look and feel of such residential neighborhoods as Santa Fe Springs, La Puente, and Baldwin Park are entirely consistent with the socioeconomic resources available to the majority Mexican-origin populations that reside there. In these neighborhoods, a native-born, working/lower middle class of skilled laborers and low-level bureaucrats live side by side with multi-income families of foreign-born, unskilled workers and struggling self-employed entrepreneurs who have saved enough to buy new homes in formerly white middle-class suburbs.

Given the high spatial correlation of Latino employment and residence patterns, one may expect such socioeconomic indicators as income and property values to be reflected in the uneven spatial deployment of post-Fordist flexible manufacturing in the Greater Eastside. The following narratives represent an initial attempt to uncover the Eastside's sociospatial organization and, thus, its strategic power points.

## The Octopus Revisited

As intensely industrial as Vernon is today, it was an "edge" city when it was established in 1905. This first single-use industrial city grew at the periphery of what was then the core of Los Angeles's urban development. But Vernon did not acknowledge its industrial calling until the 1920s, when city founder John Leonis officially transformed it into a "single-use" city. His grandson and successor, Mayor Leonis Malburg, improved upon the single-use concept with a few innovations of his own.

The city bought or condemned existing housing to reduce its residential population, thus eliminating voters who could oppose Malburg's program of unrestricted industrial development. Only the homes of political allies and loyal employees were spared. The effects of Malburg's economic gerrymandering are not surprising. In recent years, an electorate of ninety adult residents, seventy of whom are municipal employees, has maintained the city's industrial status quo. Vernon's voters not only owe their jobs to the city, they depend on it for housing. City employees "live in the town's 32 housing units, receive subsidized rents—as little as $50 a month—for small stucco houses in the shadow of warehouses and factories. All residents must be approved by the City Council."[27]

Eliminating the normal checks and balances of local government freed Vernon's city hall to operate like a business. In 1932, city founder John Leonis requested a special industrial rate from the Edison Company, which Edison refused to grant. The city answered the snub by financing and building its own power plant and electrical grid, all within a remarkably short 150 days. The power plant's five diesel-powered 6,580-horsepower generators went into service in 1933. They were housed inside a massive art deco-style building that came to symbolize more than electrical power. In 1937, Vernon negotiated a truce with Edison and handed over operation of its electrical utility, including its power plant located on East 50th Street. After some modifications, Edison operated the generators until 1972, when rising fuel costs and the aging generators prompted it to mothball the power plant. The city brought its powerhouse out of mothballs in 1980. Rather than buy all of its power from the Southern California Edison Company, Vernon began purchasing cheaper electricity on the open market, importing it from Arizona and elsewhere. Shortfalls in energy supply were filled by the city's power plant. In 1987, the city put two 7,400-horsepower turbines on the foundations originally built for additional diesel engines. The combination of cheaper imports and city-generated power meant that industrial customers paid some of the lowest electricity bills in the state and created major windfalls for the city. City documents show that Vernon Light and Power netted more than $12.3 million in 1989, $12.5 million in 1990, and $23.6 million in 1991. In the following year, however, net revenues earned from rate payers declined. Vernon Light and Power netted only $5.8 million in 1992 and $6.1 million in 1993. The city's golden goose now grappled with the effects of reindustrialization. In the mid-1980s, with the decline of heavy industry, many of Vernon's manufacturing businesses began to leave town. City officials estimated that as many as fifteen thousand blue-collar jobs had disappeared during the 1980s. During an eighteen-month period ending in November 1991, more than sixty companies had left town. [28]

Vernon's pliable government responded to the challenge by facilitating the creative destruction of its industrial landscape. In its most recent role, Vernon has become a platform for post-Fordist, craft specialty industries. The auto, tire, and steel-related mass-production industries and jobs that fled during the 1960s and 1970s were largely replaced in the 1980s by low-wage apparel, food, and furniture industries. Newer flexible industries, together with the older ensemble of low-wage foundry, meatpacking, and metal-plating shops, effectively pushed wages and benefits downward.

Mike Davis cites redevelopment records that show 96 percent of Vernon's forty-eight thousand workers earned incomes so low they would qualify for public housing assistance. At least 58 percent of this largely unorganized workforce falls into the official "very low income" category, making less than half the county median—a dramatic downturn from the area's union-wage norms twenty years ago. [29]

Declining wages and benefits in Vernon were mirrored throughout the region. Scott and Paul note that average manufacturing wage levels in Southern California fell 10.4 percent between 1970 and 1982, in contrast to

Vernon Light and Power, 1999. Photograph by Elliott Johnson.

a nationwide decline of 2.9 percent for the same period. Meanwhile, the unions of Los Angeles County registered a 35.5 percent drop in membership between 1970 and 1983, compared to a 37.2 percent drop registered nation-wide.[30] But even as new craft specialty manufacturers relocated in Vernon, others decided to leave. In the 1980s, apparel and furniture manufacturers left the country in search of Mexican and Asian workers willing to accept even lower wages.

If Vernon provided the prototype for the single-use industrial city, then the City of Industry, with its larger-than-life name, ranks as its most ambitious incarnation. A single-use city founded in 1957, Industry had an industrial infrastructure that was post-Fordist, making it a prime location for both low- and high-tech flexible industries. Through shrewd exploita-tion of the redevelopment process and manipulation of county land-use laws, the city's leaders secured massive transfusions of public and private capital, all achieved at taxpayer expense. During the mid-1980s, Industry repeatedly ran up California's highest municipal debts.

The city, built over once-cheap south San Gabriel Valley farmland, embodies the nation's most potent example of a stealth government. The municipality got its dragonlike shape from the rail lines, freeways, and groundwater reserves included within its boundaries, and from the exclusion of its mostly working-class Latino population. Its fourteen square miles of strategic encirclement, which on a map resembles a griffin with ornate gothic wings, is home to about fifteen hundred mostly manufacturing businesses and a daytime commuter workforce of seventy thousand, but only five hundred residents.[31] But only two hundred or so of its residents are registered to vote. A quick analysis of the city's voter registration records reveals that Industry's voters are connected as blood relations, close friends, employees, or employers to each member of city government. As a result, since the city's council members and mayors are almost never opposed, they routinely win elections by margins of fifty-nine to zero. The Greater Eastside, which suffers the consequences of chronically underfunded schools and social services, can be seen as the county's black hole of redevelopment, and the City of Industry as its dollar-swallowing supernova.

More than $186.2 million, or 51.7 percent of 1989–90 property increments, was diverted to sixty-four redevelopment projects now operating in the Greater Eastside's First Supervisorial District. By contrast, only $25 million, or 6.9 percent of that year's tax increments, was diverted to twenty projects in the Second District, a political jurisdiction that includes South and South-Central Los Angeles.[32] The contrast is especially striking when viewed within the context of the 1992 L.A. riots. Despite millions in property losses in the Second District, the riots failed to inspire government to substantially alter the distribution of public capital. The 1991–92 data show that the First District, represented by Supervisor Gloria Molina, received more than $243 million in tax increments, or 45 percent of the more than $541 million diverted to the county's seventy redevelopment agencies, compared to $40 million, or 7.6 percent of property taxes, diverted to the Second District, where much of the riot damage was concentrated.[33] By the 1994–95 fiscal year, more than $46 million, or 8.64 percent of tax increments, was diverted to the Second District, in contrast to the First District, still the county's leading increment recipient, which got more than $229 million, or 42.2 percent of diverted property taxes.[34] Almost all of these funds, including additional money transferred to the Second District from the Community Redevelopment Agency's Bunker Hill and central business district projects, have been spent on the construction of low-cost housing.[35] But the differing rates at which tax dollars are transferred to these districts show only part of the picture, because these funds are designed to attract private capital and secure debts that cities will incur to pay for their redevelopment projects.

During the mid- and late 1980s, Industry held the distinction of having the state's most indebted redevelopment agency. Today, however, this city of not much more than five hundred residents has a debt second only to that of the Los Angeles Community Redevelopment Agency. In fiscal 1989–90, Industry's redevelopment projects racked up a debt of $1.22 billion and tax increments totaling $4.7 million, compared to the CRA's debt of $1.72 billion and tax increments totaling more than $101 million.[36]

Despite all the public and private capital it swallowed, Industry did give something back—about fifty-five thousand manufacturing jobs plus another six thousand service sector jobs. Payroll data compiled in 1990 by the Stanford Research Institute for the Industry Manufacturers Council showed an average annual salary of slightly more than $20,000.[37] The salary average reflects Industry's mix of manufacturing jobs, newer plants, and the living standards of Industry's workforce.

Industry's largest employers are in fabricated metals products (SIC 34), with 18.4 percent of the city's manufacturing workforce. As of 1992, the average company in this group employed 113 workers, showing the predominance of flexibly organized firms. This manufacturing group takes on greater weight when contrasted with related industries. Manufacturers in the machinery, except electrical, category (SIC 35) employed almost 9 percent of Industry's workforce. These two related categories (SICs 34 and 35) employed 27.2 percent of Industry's workforce, and, as a group, represented the kind of value-added manufacturing that has traditionally paid higher wages than the food or apparel industries. The second-largest employer group was food and other products (SIC 20), with 13.2 percent of the city's workforce. The average company in this group employed 216 workers, with the largest employing 672 workers. The next largest of Industry's employer groups were in the high-technology categories. The transportation equipment category (SIC 37) employed 11.3 percent of Industry's workforce, and electric and electronic equipment (SIC 36) employed 7.39 percent. Together, these employment groups known for paying higher wages accounted for 18.69 percent of the city's workforce.

The contrast with Vernon's workforce is dramatic. Also as of 1992, Vernon's largest employer group was food and other products (SIC 20), which employed 34 percent of the city's workforce. Its second-largest employer group was apparel and other textile products (SIC 23), employing 22 percent of the workforce, compared to 0.12 percent in Industry. The city's third-largest employer group was primary metals (SIC 33), with 13.5 percent, which in Vernon's case often means dirtier and more dangerous foundry and bronze-casting jobs. As in the Greater Eastside, Industry's employment data are mirrored in La Puente's residential landscape. In La Puente, a city of more than thirty-seven thousand residents, 86 percent of them Latino, the median family income was $33,273 in 1989, slightly below the national mean, compared to $23,819 in Bell Gardens, the bedroom suburb to industrial Vernon.[38]

Industry gives back more than relatively higher-paying jobs. It is an especially influential political benefactor. The members of Industry's powerful Industry Manufacturers Council gave more than $130,000 to three state legislators during the ten-year period ending in April 1984. During the same period, council members contributed more than $95,000 to five Republican political action committees and more than $90,000 to former First District Supervisor Peter F. Schabarum. In 1983, the city paid more than $30,400—more than any city in Los Angeles County except Los Angeles itself—to hire former California State Assembly Speaker Robert Moretti as its lobbyist. Recently, Schabarum drew from his traditional base of political support in cities such as Industry to launch his own political initiatives. In 1990, he directed that more than $440,000 of his own campaign funds be spent on passing Proposition 140, an initiative to impose term limits on the California State Legislature. Campaign records show that the funds, transferred through loans Schabarum later forgave, served as seed money to qualify the initiative, which he helped draft, and to raise another $1 million in contributions. Remarkably, Schabarum did this while diverting more than $52,000 to his favorite conservative candidates and causes.[39]

Supervisor Gloria Molina, elected to a First District that preserves much of Schabarum's former industrial base, quickly discovered just how generous her district could be. City and county campaign records show that she raised more than $801,000 in 1991, the year she won the supervisor's seat, a 73.6 percent increase over 1987 fund-raising levels of $461,609, her most profitable fund-raising year as a member of the Los Angeles City Council.[40] After 1991, however, Molina's fund-raising in the First District dropped to considerably lower levels. And like her male Latino political peers, Molina invested her political capital in very modest ways. A review of giving by Los Angeles-area Latino elected officials shows that their investments in Latino political infrastructure have been directed to a tiny handful of organizations such as the Southwest Voter Registration Project and the

Mexican American Legal Defense and Education Fund. These officeholders appear to give slightly larger, although still rather modest, amounts to other candidates running against their various Chicano political rivalries. The pattern seems clear, at least for now. Rather than pooling significantly larger amounts of political capital to encourage the growth of social movements or agendas, Chicano officeholders representing the Greater Eastside appear content to reproduce the turf politics of political patronage long identified with the Democratic Party.

## Toward a Strategic Agenda

Two weeks before the April–May 1992 riots, during an off-the-record dinner gathering with local Latino journalists, Los Angeles County Supervisor Gloria Molina candidly responded to one reporter's comment that local African American political leaders were continuing to deny Latinos their fair share of the city's political and economic pie. Molina said she understood the reporter's frustration. Local African American political leadership, she agreed, had become a prime obstacle to continued Latino political and economic empowerment. Sooner or later, she promised, there would have to be a summit in which leaders like herself would oblige her African American counterparts to face up to the political consequences of demographic reality: Latinos are ready to accept the rewards of being the county's new majority. Her comments were well received. The journalists gathered there complained that the city's African American leaders had used the black/white racial dichotomy to define "minority" struggles for social and political justice to exclude Latinos. Molina empathized with their dissatisfaction. The weeks following the riots would render these frustrations visible. Other Latino community leaders, some elected, others not, would repeat in public what Molina had said in private.

These Latino leaders insisted that because their constituencies had grown in numbers, they deserved a proportionate share of government power. Many African American leaders, who remain convinced that their constituents are entitled to a larger share of government to compensate for past injustices, disagreed. The riots exacerbated these competing claims. The escalating rhetoric surrounding job competition during the ill-fated attempts to rebuild South-Central Los Angeles underscored the quandary in which Latino political leaders found themselves: although they perceived themselves as agents of progressive change, they, like African American leaders, continued to ply the old politics of racial entitlement. Politics, for these Latino leaders, remained a zero-sum, race-reductionist game. Consequently, their failure to look beyond the politics of racial entitlement distracted them from taking inventory of the political and economic power that was and is within reach.

Taking stock of the Greater Eastside's economic and political landscape does not mean that Latino elected officials should drop their demands for more responsive and inclusive government. It merely requires that these leaders put this aspect of political representation in its proper context. Seeking improved social services, for example, for Latino constituents represents only one avenue of political empowerment. This redistributive aspect of local government is becoming less and less important, as continuing budget shortfalls so painfully reveal. Local government has fewer and fewer discretionary funds to spend on alleviating social ills.

Economic government is another matter. Of the two branches, it is now, and will continue to be, the more dynamic, wealth-creating arena for making public policy. That is why Latino leaders simply cannot afford to continue to express their frustrations in ways that reinforce a status quo predicated upon a system of race-based power sharing while ignoring the opportunities that come with understanding the functions of economic government. Yet that is precisely what they do in seeing government as a banquet at which the guests are served according to how loudly they proclaim their appetites.

Margit Mayer argues that the flexibilized world of post-Fordist manufacturing that has resulted from the increasing globalization of capital has fundamentally changed our local politics and urban spaces:

> So-called world cities as well as formerly peripheral cities and regions are becoming direct players in the world economy. . . . The changing division of labor, together with the disengagement of most federal governments from certain domestic programs, has conferred new challenges on the regional and local level and upgraded local politics everywhere. In this heightened inter-urban and interstate competition for growth industries, state funding, skilled workers, and consumer dollars, cities have come to emphasize, exploit, and even produce local specificities and assets. Their planners and politicians confront the task of tailoring conditions to create an environment in which profitable enterprises can flourish.[41]

In Eastside cities such as Industry and Santa Fe Springs, the political economy of place clearly dominates. In these cities, aggressive chamber organizations vie for new investment by advertising their respective access to freeways, sea- and airports, universities, and a trained and exploitable workforce. Only a handful of local functionaries, many of them unelected technocrats who have or will pass through the revolving door of the state's development industry, decide how the Greater Eastside's collection of stealth governments will affect the lives of millions of taxpayers and voters. This feature of economic government is not unique to the Greater Eastside. Increasingly, major questions of industrial policy are being decided piecemeal by such local bureaucracies as the Metropolitan Water District, the California Coastal Commission, the State Agricultural Commission, the county's Regional Planning Commission, and the Southern California Air Quality Management District.

But the hegemony of economic government is far from absolute. The tendency to externalize the efficiencies of production continues to pressure capital to seek markets and production locations that offer real or perceived economic advantages. Mayer argues that the competition between emerging post-Fordist cities and industries has thus created new political space for communities historically disconnected from directing the functions of economic government. As competition among cities and regions intensifies, and localities find their financial resources curtailed as a result of national austerity politics, local and regional political bodies must adopt new roles and a new politics to create these roles.[42]

Theorists such as Mayer argue that local and regional government must begin creating landscapes that foster flexible forms of economic growth that can address social needs, especially the legacies of unequal economic development in the suburbs. Local and regional government must next create new forms of economic government to support and regulate post-Fordist industries. To be effective, such new forms of economic government must also have the power to cut across traditional administrative lines, so as to create a regional coherence that the new flexible manufacturers and services enterprises cannot produce on their own.

Myron Orfield suggests that a way to address metropolitan social polarization and gain democratic control over growth management may lie in a form of regionalism that pools revenue resources to pay for services. According to Orfield, "What's possibly needed is for neighboring cities and suburbs to pool their property and sales-tax bases." Orfield estimates that in the Los Angeles region, "between 65 percent to 85 percent of the metropolitan population would pay lower taxes and receive better local services."[43]

Whether Mayer's or Orfield's vision of a "post-Fordist" regionalism and political organization will help deprivatize the functions of local government or merely complete capital's conquests should not deter Latinos from developing political strategies for the present and future. The evolution

Mothers of East Los Angeles–Santa Isabel in a demonstration to demand an end to environmental racism. Photograph courtesy of Juana B. Gutiérrez, president and cofounder of Mothers of East Los Angeles–Santa Isabel.

toward new forms of overarching oppositional blocs offer local communities, ethnic or otherwise, new avenues for political organizing in a post-Fordist era. Local community groups can organize themselves to shape the policies of new or existing forms of economic government. Groups such as the Mothers of East Los Angeles, the Living Wage Coalition, and a growing array of progressively minded grassroots organizations have demonstrated the viability of this approach, by shutting down noxious plants and prisons and, as we show in Chapter 4, by inserting themselves in the political-economic planning process. Local communities can challenge existing forms of economic government to make its policy-making and planning functions more democratic. That is why the Greater Eastside's concentration of stealth governments can become an asset instead of a liability—all of these agencies are within easy driving distance, which makes them vulnerable to conventional pressure politics.

Latino-elected leaders, when taken as a whole, already represent every inch of the Greater Eastside's political landscape. Their numbers, as we show in chapter 6, are destined to increase as members of the Latino community continue to register to vote and participate in the political process. But even without further increases in Latino political representation at the state and local levels, these elected officials already hold enough political authority to begin a grassroots dialogue on a microindustrial policy for the Greater Eastside. There is no reason groups such as the National Association of Latino Elected and Appointed Officials should not join with local, often Latino-led, labor groups such as the Los Angeles County Federation of Labor and community organizations such as the Los Angeles Alliance for a New Economy and La Hermandad Mexicana Nacional (the Mexican National Brotherhood) to convene a conference to inform and enrich the public debate on the impact of post-Fordist industrial reorganization on Latino workers. The conveners, for example, could invite Los Angeles-area labor leaders to discuss how they have begun to combat the atomization of the post-Fordist workplace and to organize low-wage service sector workers once written off as unorganizable. The leaders of the Service Employees International Union, which, in February 1999, organized about seventy-four thousand low-wage home-care workers in Los Angeles County in one historic election, should top the guest list. In one fell swoop, the SEIU, the nation's fastest-growing union, boosted the ranks of organized labor in Los Angeles County by 10 percent. More remarkably, it succeeded in organizing a workforce that mainstream unionism once stigmatized as too ethnic, too female, and too distant from the factory floor to bother with. The home-care industry is dominated by racialized workers—Latina, African American, and Asian American women—who service their clients, one-on-one, inside the home, a workplace that is the antithesis of the industrial assembly line coveted by labor in previous decades. Not surprisingly, the SEIU's victory was hailed as a landmark event that would elevate service sector workers from a secondary to a primary role. "I believe the history books will show that their triumph . . . will play as important a role in American history as the mass organizing drives in the 1930's," said AFL-CIO President John Sweeney.[44] But these workers could not have been organized if the union had not found a way to create communication linkages to each home-care workplace. In contrast to the Fordist factory's lunchroom, where workers debated issues and strategies, the only threads that connected the isolated home-care workers were the local and state funds with which patients paid the workers' wages. The funding agencies would thus need to be adapted to serve a new social purpose. They would need to double as a communication infrastructure that would permit the unions to trace the funding threads back to the workers' mailboxes.

Legislation would have to be passed to achieve this new objective. By cultivating the support of key lawmakers such as State Assembly Speaker Antonio Villaraigosa, the union lobbied for the enactment of state laws authorizing counties to set up agencies that could assume the role of employers. Next, the Los Angeles County Board of Supervisors voted to establish a fifteen-member public authority to supervise training, run a registry, and bargain collectively with the workers. But because so many home-care workers are renters who change residences often, the registry, by itself, could not guarantee success to the union. The union therefore engaged in door-to-door canvassing to ensure that the final link connecting the organizers to workers was closed. "Between March and November of last year, organizers knocked on the doors of 30,000 workers across the county; 10,600 of those workers signed the cards joining the local and petitioning the agency to hold an election," Harold Meyerson reported in February 1999. "Remarkably, considering that these were all minimum-wage workers, fully half the petitioners agreed to a voluntary assessment on their wages to support the union's political-action program, but then, it was the union's political clout that had brought them this far."[45] Because they are paid from a mix of county, state, and federal funding sources, home-care workers will have a lot to say about what government in general and Latino legislators in particular must do to raise their wages and improve working conditions. Scholars and labor activists, for example, could discuss the feasibility of creating a post-Fordist governmental entity charged with implementing microindustrial policy for the Greater Eastside. If proved successful there, such a model could, in Industrial Areas Foundation fashion, be emulated by other near-in suburbs and towns cut off from their local economic governments. Another panel could discuss a proposal advanced by Roy Ulrich, a public interest attorney, who has argued for a campaign simply to decertify the municipal charters of Los Angeles County's stealth governments. Obviously, decertification would require a major political-legal-legislative undertaking in which Latinos would have to participate. If successful, the Greater Eastside's residential suburban cities could move to annex their stealth neighbors and thus make their post-Fordist industrial landscapes more politically and socially accountable. Undertaking discussion of any of these proposals will require redefinition of the purpose and project of government in a time when the very meaning of government is under attack.

We maintain that the economic forces that have transformed the Greater Eastside into one of the nation's most dynamic industrial landscapes requires a rethinking of Latino political and economic life. Future policy research on the Latino political and economic condition must, therefore, be recast in a more rigorous analytic and theoretical framework. The post-Fordist reorganization of manufacturing and the growing service sector, both heavily dependent on Latino immigrant labor, defy such conventional academic concepts as "race relations" and "urban underclass" and other outdated notions of political citizenship. As many studies have shown, Latinos are widely employed, but within a narrow range of occupational niches, whereas African Americans, especially African American males, struggle to secure any jobs at all. As Roger Waldinger and Michael Lichter write:

> The region's poor African Americans can be seen only as an outclass, however, not as an underclass, as the comparison with their impoverished immigrant brethren makes clear; the former face a penury of jobs and the latter an abundance, albeit at pitifully low wages. Modifying the concept to refer to the "ghetto poor" will not do; the traditional African American ghetto is shared with Mexicans and Central Americans, who enjoy good connections to the employers of low-level help. And the Mexican residents of east Los Angeles—the region's "purest" ghetto for its high degree of ethnic homogeneity—have no difficulty finding work, though securing good jobs is another story.[46]

Moreover, preconceived notions of what constitutes a Latino "barrio" have prevented many from perceiving the actual linkages within and outside of the Latino political and economic landscape. Such a lack of theoretical imagination has, in turn, led many to reproduce the outdated categories of political analysis on subjects such as political redistricting and postriot economic development. Unable to advance an independent policy discourse, Latino scholars and community and elected leaders have been drawn into no-win debates with African American communities on the distribution of economic revitalization funds. But the recent upsurge of Latino voting participation triggered by Proposition 187 and other anti-immigrant initiatives augurs the arrival of a Latino voting majority and, as we will show, an opportunity to reinvent the meaning of local government, political citizenship, and transclass and transcultural coalition politics.

A first step toward this more ambitious goal can begin with an analysis of the dialectics of landscape. Taking a strategic inventory of actual and potential political power in this emergent Latino metropolis requires a mapping of the changing organization of work in postindustrial Los Angeles. Performing this task should prepare Latino leaders to redefine the possibilities of democratic economic reform with consumers, labor, and even the business community. Whether such dialogue can be realized remains to be seen, but the benefits could be enormous—a more democratic and prosperous Latino community.

# 2

# "Policing" Race

## The Media's Representation of the Los Angeles Riots

The firestorm of news media coverage fueled by the Los Angeles riot that erupted April 29, 1992, had a common underlying theme. Whether victims, bystanders, or heroes, the residents of the riot zones were portrayed as actors in a great melodrama of "race relations." Both local and national media promoted coverage that used the concept of "race" as a storytelling strategy. For audience convenience, it seemed, the cast was color coded.

The following example of postriot coverage illustrates the pattern. Days after the riot had ended, a *Los Angeles Times* poll asked local residents, "Do you think *race relations* in Los Angeles are getting better or worse?" With predictable pessimism, 84 percent of the respondents answered that "race relations" had either deteriorated or stagnated.[1] At first glance, it would appear that these poll results naturally reflected the anxieties of a public that had just witnessed the alarming spectacle of a televised riot sparked by the acquittal of the Los Angeles police officers who had beaten Rodney King. After all, the baton blows police landed on King were repeatedly televised during the trial in which jurors weighed whether the police actions were racially motivated.

But the presumption that a cumulative history of racial discrimination against the African American residents of South-Central Los Angeles had sparked the riot was anything but normal. To the contrary, a small handful of social scientists and media scholars, ourselves included, have asserted that the media's racialization of the riot reiterated a socially constructed discourse that preceded the event itself. In a seamless transition hardly detected by media audiences, the coverage promoted racial violence as the preeminent causal link connecting Rodney King's beating by LAPD officers, and the subsequent trial in which the officers were acquitted, to the riot.

With the embers only a few days cold, and at least fifty-one riot fatalities reported, *Times* pollsters concluded that a question on the state of "race relations," typically defined by the media, civil rights organizations, and government agencies as the relative absence or presence of racial harmony between whites and blacks, accurately measured the riot's significance. Like most of the riot news coverage, the *Times* poll reaffirmed what the poll's creators had accepted as true: the single episode of racial conflict captured in the King beating was the prelude to the larger display of racial animosity on the streets. During the riot, the television news media reminded viewers of this linkage by repeatedly contextualizing images of burning and looting with images of the King beating. The fact that Los Angeles residents relied upon television as their primary window on the riot underlines the media's dominant role in the racialization process.[2] Through sheer force of televised repetition, images of King's beating and court trial and, later, images of young black males beating white truck driver Reginald Denny, the riot had been framed between the horrifying bookends of white-on-black violence and black-on-white violence. Worse, these scenes both reiterated a long-established media practice of associating people of color with criminality, either as victims or as perpetrators of violence.[3] In 1997, on the riot's fifth anniversary, the *Times* provided a postscript to its first riot poll. Two-thirds of respondents in the follow-up survey said that "race relations" in Los Angeles are poor, compared to 82 percent in 1992.[4] Despite having had time to reflect upon the criticism of its riot coverage, the *Times* remained trapped by the circularity of racializing logic by continuing to portray the city as "racially split."

Ted Koppel's postriot forays into South-Central for his television program *Nightline* racialized the riot in two basic ways. Like the other local and network newscasts, *Nightline* implicitly framed the riot as a "race relations" crisis. The series titled "Anatomy of a Riot" mostly featured African American civil rights, religious, and political leaders pleading for calm or assessing blame and African American riot zone residents venting their anger about the riot during a "town hall" meeting held in a black neighborhood church.[5] Less than a handful of Latino and Asian sources were interviewed for the series. But the show also reinforced the image of the dangerous black male by turning over two *Nightline* broadcasts to interviews with two former African American gangsters. Although the *Nightline* series acknowledged that members of other races participated in the rioting, and that African American gangs had not devised a plan to riot, Koppel nevertheless asked Li'l Monster, a former Crips member, why gang members had rioted and beaten Reginald Denny.[6] *Nightline* flattered the former Crips and Bloods leaders by presenting them as the riot's most authentic participant/ observers, while presenting civil rights leaders as spokespersons for riot zone residents. The civil rights leaders did not appear to question the media's patronizing power to anoint them the social and moral conscience of urban America. The former gang leaders did not appear to worry that, in acting as ghetto spokesmen, they would be closely identified, at least by some viewers, with the mayhem in the streets. After all, the Crips and Bloods did indeed live in places the media identified as within the riot zone. Moreover, decades of news coverage had shown gang members to be expert in the practices of violence and, in some cases, to have embraced their menacing media reputations as urban savages. In news coverage, on daytime talk shows, in feature films, and on gangsta rap recordings, African American gang members had been represented as active conspirators in the construction of their predatory portraits. In other words, *Nightline*'s explicit representation of the gang members constituted one-half of their potential meaning. The viewers completed Li'l Monster's potential meanings with their knowledge of African American gang members.

There was only one problem. An analysis of court records revealed that only one in ten of those arrested during the riot had gang affiliations.[7] Moreover, the arrest records indicated that the rioters were united more by lives of joblessness, homelessness, and educational failure than by race. Of those Latinos arrested, nearly 80 percent were recently arrived immigrants. Only a third of those arrested were employed, most often as low-paid casual laborers, and nearly two-thirds of those arrested were high school dropouts.[8] Nor were those arrested motivated solely by the Rodney King verdict. Instead, chronic poverty, aggravated by rapid demographic change, economic restructuring, a history of oppressive police tactics, and simple opportunism, contributed to the rioting.[9]

The *Times* and *Nightline* approaches to the riot illustrate a generalized pattern that we propose to examine in this chapter. The media racialized the riot, and that coverage served the status quo. We contextualize our media critique with a post-Fordist analysis of the riot zone, followed by a consideration of the roles that media audiences, government authorities, and Latino leadership played in reinforcing or resisting racialized media representations of the riot. The theoretical questions on race and racialization raised here qualify this as a work of cultural criticism, but with a difference. We attempt to avoid cultural criticism's tendency to overgeneralize from the close reading of a few texts by citing data from more conventional media studies to buttress the qualitative claims of cultural criticism.[10] We also draw upon demographic and economic data interpreted from the perspective of post-Fordist theory to show how events and conditions in the riot zone contradicted the news media's racialized representations.

Two recently published studies provide quantitative data that support an analysis of racialized riot coverage. Erna Smith's is the most comprehensive of the pair.[11] In the second study, Darnell Hunt analyzes a single sampling of televised news coverage, relying upon semiotic, argument, and textual device analyses to detect assumptions embedded in seventeen minutes of verbatim text and video images aired by the Fox-owned Los Angeles television station KTTV Channel 11 on the first night of the riot.[12] He detects at least fourteen major assumptions embedded in the KTTV text and images, all of which support Smith's findings.

Smith's content analysis of televised riot news relies upon "framing theory" to quantify and evaluate the ways local and network television news interpreted the riot.[13] Smith defines news "frames" as themes or story lines that organize facts to give them meaning. "A journalist," Smith writes, "might refer to a frame as the story angle, news peg or hook" suggested by the most important facts.[14] News frames prove especially useful in the coverage of crises or disasters such as riots, because these events generate a daily supply of fresh facts, which reporters must organize into continuing stories. Under such circumstances, news workers are more likely to find facts that validate or conform to news frames used at the start of their crisis coverage.

Whether journalists are reporting a running disaster story or covering a onetime event, framing inevitably leads to selective emphasis. Depending on the news frame, journalists will emphasize some facts while downplaying or ignoring others.[15] As the cultural critics argue, Smith asserts that the reporter's method of creating hierarchies of fact is, like other forms of symbolic communication, socially constructed. Journalists draw their themes, concepts, and narrative devices from the same symbolic well from which society at large drinks. As a result, the prevailing values, assumptions, attitudes, and narrative frames circulating in society offer an ever-available reserve upon which journalists may pattern their stories. Because news framing may reinforce preexisting social and cultural discourses, it is not difficult to appreciate why such studies can elucidate the social construction of racialized news coverage.

To test the validity of her framing analysis, Smith created content categories—victims, sources, and rioters—to quantify the news media's representation of riot causes and participation. First, she defined the victims content category to encompass a broad spectrum of possible behaviors, with violent physical assault at one extreme and the discomfort of "roller skaters being turned away" by police from riot-threatened streets at the other. Second, she categorized on-camera interview sources by ethnicity, race, social geography, and institutional affiliation.[16]

## General Findings

Smith's framing and content analysis offers persuasive evidence of racializing news coverage. The news media cast blacks and whites as the riot's leading actors while almost ignoring Latino and Asian riot performances. "Blacks and whites were centrally involved in over three quarters of the stories about the Los Angeles riot," Smith writes. "In contrast, Latinos and Koreans were the focus of about a quarter of the stories, and much of this coverage was aired on the foreign language stations."[17]

Like Smith, Hunt found that KTTV's coverage never questioned race as a "central factor in these events," but instead relied upon racial labeling to identify riot participants.[18] The media's representation also drew a line separating riot victims by race and ethnicity. Whites and Koreans constituted more than half of those represented as suffering property damages, violent assault, or lives disrupted by the violence. By contrast, 25 percent of the victims were represented as black, and a bit less than a quarter were represented as Latino.[19]

Differences emerged between the framing preferences of national networks and those of local news stations. The networks, which emphasized black/white framing, represented blacks and whites as the central focus of almost 96 percent of their coverage, compared to 80 percent on L.A. stations.[20] Local news coverage emphasized what Smith categorized as character issues, or narrative themes such as lawlessness, the immorality of rioting behavior, and pleas for law and order. The local stations framed 82 percent of their coverage in terms of character issues, compared to 60 percent in the network coverage.[21] Compared to the national coverage, the local stations contained more coverage of violence and efforts to control it. Smith found that "scenes of rioting and the restoration of order 'made up' 72 percent of the dramatic visuals shown on the Los Angeles stations compared with 50 percent on the networks."[22]

Hunt also discovered moralizing assumptions embedded in the local news coverage. Assumption 1 characterized the riot as "undesirable." Throughout the KTTV coverage, Hunt writes, news workers "prefaced or qualified" their reports and commentaries "with expressions of regret."[23] These expressions consistently reminded viewers that the riot represented a threat to the social order. In Smith's study, network news organizations appeared to do a better job of addressing the riot's causes, framing 40 percent of their coverage in terms of public policy issues, compared to 18 percent of the coverage by Los Angeles stations.[24] The networks, however, often framed the riot's cause as a breakdown of "race relations." Overall, 22 percent of the coverage of consequences focused on whether the violence harmed "race relations"; 46 percent of the causal coverage speculated about the riot's impact on the 1992 presidential campaign.[25]

The news media's reliance upon black/white framing also omitted and suppressed narratives and images that either contradicted or failed to support the "race relations" discourse. According to Smith, the media's selection of riot interview sources consistently rendered Latinos and Asians voiceless, but not invisible. Whites, by contrast, were preferred as the authoritative voices of law and order, and the media represented blacks as authorities on the riot zone and the trial verdicts in the Rodney King case. For example, 54 percent of "local, state, and national leaders . . . interviewed were white, one third . . . were black; 7 percent were Asian, and 7 percent Latino." More than 77 percent of official law enforcement sources were white; "18 percent were black; 3 percent were Latino, and 2 percent were Asian."[26]

When the news media sought the public opinions of Los Angeles–area residents not living in the riot zone, they again showed a preference for black and white sources. At least 47 percent of these opinion stories included interviews with African Americans; whites were interviewed in 41 percent of these stories. By contrast, television news included interviews with Latino sources in only 8 percent of their stories, and Asians constituted only 4 percent of such sources.[27] Significantly, when news workers sought African Americans' opinions, they focused their interviews on the verdicts in the King case. Unfortunately, Smith did not create content categories with which to quantify the news media's interviewing practices. Hunt, however, detected a clear tendency on the part of KTTV coverage to link the King beating and the trial verdicts causally to the riot. Hunt's Assumption 4, "The events were caused by the Rodney King beating verdicts," implicitly framed the riot as a consequence of the verdicts, while ignoring other causes for the rioting.[28]

The racialization of the urban landscape intensified when reporters interviewed riot zone residents. Smith found that more "than 77 percent of the riot area residents interviewed were black; 17 percent were Latino, and the remainder were Asians (4 percent), and whites (2 percent)." Visual representation of events within the riot zone reflected the media's sourcing preferences. Almost "half (48 percent) the people shown rioting were black;

31 percent were Latino; 12 percent were Asian, and 9 percent were white. Almost all of the most violent rioters on television news . . . were African American, and blacks comprised the majority of people shown looting."[29] Hunt found that three assumptions also reinforced racialized spatial and temporal linkages: "The events are centered in South Central Los Angeles" (Assumption 2), "The events are riots" (Assumption 5), and "The events are similar to the Watts riots" (Assumption 11).[30] According to Hunt, these assumptions, to the exclusion of others, served to link the social disorder of April–May 1992 with "past riots" that previous media studies have characterized as race riots.

The racialized representation of the riot zone appears logically linked to Assumption 7, "Blacks are 'event insiders,'" and Assumption 8, "Black ministers have a special responsibility to help restore calm."[31] Hunt notes that all of the interview subjects included in the KTTV coverage were black, and all of the news workers conducting the interviews were visibly non-black. Hunt argues that the KTTV news workers "singled out" black sources "as if they were uniquely positioned to" comment on the violence and efforts to restore order.[32] These interviews implicitly cast blacks as riot zone "insiders" with special street-level knowledge of the disorder. Nonblack "outsiders" were represented either as news workers who sought black "insider" interviews or, as in the televised beating of Reginald Denny by black youths in a South-Central intersection, as white victims of black insiders.

The media's power to racialize the riot landscape and its residents must not be underestimated. The relative absence of accompanying contextual explanation and the drop-by-drop coverage of riot violence as discrete events heightened, like water torture, the negative impact of these images. "Although factual and truthful, visuals of people being assaulted and stores being looted and burned are anything but neutral—they send clear messages of lawlessness. Indeed," Smith argues, "research shows that viewers more readily remember" visuals that elicit negative emotions than the information contained in accompanying narration.[33]

Still, the racialization of riot coverage does not become fully apparent until we compare it to the demography of the riot zone. Although Smith's study of news coverage shows that African Americans were represented, whether through images or interviews, as the riot's primary actors, one study estimates that Latinos made up at least 49 percent of the population residing in the most riot-damaged areas, compared to 36.4 percent for African Americans and 7.1 percent for Asian Pacific Islanders.[34] The same study appears to confirm the media's representation of South-Central Los Angeles as the riot's epicenter. Slightly more than 79 percent of the total city damage occurred in the Greater South-Central area, compared to 12.6 in the predominantly Korean Westlake area; only .3 percent of the damage was registered in East L.A.[35] But the coverage failed to account for the dramatic Latino population increases in the high-damage areas of South-Central and Koreatown/Westlake. For example, 67 percent of the Koreatown population was Latino in 1990, despite the high concentration of Korean-owned businesses there. Slightly more than 77 percent of the Westlake neighborhood, which includes the Pico-Union district bordering Koreatown, was Latino.[36]

High Latino population densities also existed in the neighborhoods adjacent to the Koreatown/Westlake neighborhoods once considered majority African American. In the Central Avenue/South Park neighborhood, Latino population had increased to 64 percent; the Latino population in the West Adams/Exposition Park neighborhood was 52.4 percent.[37] Contrary to the area's reputation as an entry point for Central American immigrants, 75 percent of South-Central's Latino community in 1990 was of Mexican origin, followed by Central Americans at 19 percent and other Latinos at 5.8 percent.

Nor was this demographic transformation a recent development. Most of South-Central's Latinos had resided there since 1980, with only about 10 percent arriving since 1985. Moreover, a comparison of census tracts shows that riot-damaged areas were characterized by substantially higher poverty levels, higher unemployment levels, lower per capita incomes, and lower home ownership rates. For example, home ownership rates in riot-damaged areas averaged 25.7 percent, compared to 44.4 percent in non-damaged areas, and more than 41 percent of South-Central's households earned less anually than the federally defined $15,000 poverty level in 1989, compared to the statewide average of 19 percent. In the Koreatown/Westlake area, 44 percent of the households earned less than $15,000. Overall, the proportion of riot zone families living below the poverty level was two to three times the statewide average, and a disproportionately high percentage of riot zone residents subsisted with incomes just above the $15,000 poverty level.[38]

One could defend the riot coverage by noting that demographic factors do not prove riot participation, were it not for the picture suggested by the arrest data and economic losses. Nearly 51 percent of those arrested were Latinos; 38 percent were categorized as blacks, 9 percent were whites, and 2 percent were Asians.[39] The arrest data thus invert the news media's representation of riot participation. In the network coverage, 58 percent of the riot participants shown were black and 24 percent were Latino. In the local coverage, blacks were presented as 48 percent of the participants and

Latinos constituted 33 percent. Both network and local coverage represented Asian participation as slightly higher than is found in the arrest data; the network showed 7 percent Asian participation, compared to 11 percent by the local stations.[40] Televised representation of white participation—10 percent by the networks and 7 percent by the local stations—came within a few percentage points of the arrest data. The participation of property owners tended to confirm the image of Korean Americans and whites as victims, but with ambiguities. Although Korean American store owners (49 percent) and white store owners (11 percent) totaled 60 percent of business owners included in the coverage, Latino store owners appeared in only 10 percent of the coverage.[41] By contrast, city data show that Latino-owned businesses sustained between 30 and 40 percent of the damages.[42]

The sociology and demography of the riot, in other words, were more complex than any of the media representations could fathom. The "two societies, one black, one white, separate and unequal" dichotomy made famous by the Kerner Commission could not contain a "multicultural" riot in which villains and victims defied racial typecasting. Cornel West acknowledges the declining role of race and the riot's underlying complexity when he defines the riot's causes:

> What happened in Los Angeles in April of 1992 was neither a race
> riot nor a class rebellion. Rather, this monumental upheaval was a
> multiracial, transclass, and largely male display of justified social
> rage. . . . What we witnessed in Los Angeles was the consequence
> of a lethal linkage of economic decline, cultural decay, and politi-
> cal lethargy in American life. Race was the visible catalyst, not the
> underlying cause.[43]

Something more in the field of chaotic forces from which the riot emerged frustrated the media's ability to assert its narrative authority. Part of that undefined something could be the distance between the media's preference for framing inner-city events as black/white race discourse and the racial, cultural, linguistic, and political ambiguities implicit in Latino lived experience.

## Category Blindness

Although racism created and led up to the conditions that sparked the Watts riot of 1965, it did not play the same role in the Los Angeles riot of 1992. The causes of social pathology had changed. The structural changes associated with the emergence of a postindustrial economy had somehow reconfigured the city's social relations in ways that were not fully evident in the Watts riot. The most obvious difference between these disturbances is found in the appearance of Latinos on TV screens as looters in the second and third days of the 1992 riot coverage. More than anything else, the Latino presence in "black" neighborhoods resulted from economic restructuring and reindustrialization.

Nevertheless, as Smith's and Hunt's studies show, the news coverage de-emphasized Latino riot participation and virtually ignored Latino public opinion. Smith and Hunt explain the media's inattention by arguing that Latino images did not conform to the media's racialized perception of the riot zone. Smith adds that a pronounced lack of Latino political power in the riot zone, the community's racial ambiguity, and the media's racialized representations of the riot all contributed to Latino silence in the midst of the rioting.[44]

Smith's observations conform to a pattern. Although the field of Latino media studies remains vastly underresearched, several recent studies suggest that Latinos, when compared to African Americans, not only receive proportionately less media attention, but are represented in more consistently negative fashion. Stranger still, Latino images on prime-time, English-language television have either decreased or improved only slightly while the Latino population has continued to grow. The English-language print media reinforce television's disappearing act. A 1992 study of ten leading print publications, including the *New York Times* and *Los Angeles Times*, identified four thousand news items that covered women and minorities. Of these, only 1 percent, or fifty articles, focused on Latinos; more than 25 percent of the stories dealt with African Americans or African American–related issues. So although African Americans receive more negative media representations, they also, by virtue of the greater volume of representation they receive, enjoy a greater variety of depictions, including some that could be characterized as positive. Thus the media coverage criminalized Latino participation with more economy; it reinforced a history of negative representations with fewer images and narratives because these were far less likely to be contradicted by positive images.[45] Future content studies should attempt to isolate and quantify those subtleties that would explain how criminalized representation of Latinos contributes to racialization.

However, even without these studies, the significance that cultural studies theory gives to constructive absence provokes several interpretive possibilities. One very detectable motif in the news coverage of the 1992 riot stressed Latino foreignness. A few local television broadcasts, for example, speculated on the "illegal" status of the Latino looters. During the second day of rioting, KABC Channel 7 anchor Harold Greene asked reporter

Linda Mour, who had returned from a day in the riot zone, "Did you get the impression that a lot of those people were illegal aliens?" "Yes," Mour replied.

The local media also repeated the claims of LAPD Chief Daryl Gates, who said that the "illegal aliens" were among the main agents of the riot. The temptation to take political advantage of the riot also proved irresistible to Congressman Dana Rohrbacher of Orange County. Only a few days after the riot's embers had cooled, the Huntington Beach Republican fired off a telegram to President Bush demanding the quick deportation of illegal aliens arrested during the riot. Only a month earlier, he had called for curbs on health, education, and welfare benefits for illegal immigrants. In the same headline-grabbing speech, Rohrbacher, who found himself facing a tough challenge in the Forty-Fifth Congressional District, suggested that "Pedro" should not expect to get a $50,000 heart bypass for free, effectively exploiting an anti-immigrant motif that contributed to the passage of Proposition 187, the California initiative that sought to deny government services to the undocumented.[46] In other cases, television and newspaper reporters, in dramatizing the plight of those who had escaped burning apartment buildings, reminded viewers that the newly homeless feared deportation. The reporting on this last point was factual. Federal agents did indeed deport Latinos detained or arrested by police.[47] These representations also reinforced the image of Latino illegality—a historically prominent theme of borderlands media coverage. Whether presented as victims of the Immigration and Naturalization Service or as rampaging looters, "illegals" were again shown as "problem" foreigners at the precise moment when state and national policy debates focused upon denying public services to the undocumented.

Despite the black/white framing that dominated riot news coverage, audiences appeared to have reached their own conclusions about the Latino looters. Viewers filled the silence left by these essentially voiceless images with their memories of previous representations of Latinos as "illegals" and inner-city gangsters. It appears that the representation of looting by "illegals" reactivated the image of Latinos as lawbreaking foreigners. Two years later, the passage of Proposition 187 expressed a backlash by the majority of white voters, whose worst fears had been confirmed by the images of Latino riot participation.[48]

However, the long tradition of representing Latinos as alien outsiders must be contextualized. The media have constructed illegal border crossing as more than just a political or economic problem. The image of the illegal is rich in dangerous cultural ambiguities. The undocumented subject threatens simultaneously the conceptual framework that normalizes the state's external political and cultural boundaries and its national system of racial categories. Neither America as a whole nor Los Angeles has yet created a public language with which to conceptualize the mestizos in our midst, for the people who constitute L.A.'s largest population group cannot be strictly categorized as a race, a nationality, or an ethnic group. Rather, Latinos constitute a cross section of Latin American immigrants, most of whom are racially mixed Mexicans and Central Americans. Latinos, as a mixed or mestizo people, are genetically and culturally woven from indigenous, African, Iberian, and European as well as Asian strands. Any attempt to grasp their multiple, overlapping identities must take into account culture, language, and history, in addition to race and class.

During the riot, however, the media's reliance upon static racialized language precluded the use of alternative modes of social description. Like the new virus that the body's immune system has not yet learned to recognize, the media lacked a semantic category with which to encircle Latino ambiguity. The word for that ambiguity is *mestizaje*, which describes the continent's unfinished business of racial and cultural hybridization. In spite of racist urges to forestall five centuries of genetic and cultural dialogue among the descendants of Europe, Africa, and Asia and the hemisphere's indigenous peoples, *mestizaje* continues to insinuate itself in every aspect of Latin American life.

For the moment, then, the media, in collaboration with the state, continue to police the boundaries of Latino hybridity. Not only are Latinos disappeared from the national media at the moment when their numbers are growing fastest, their hybridity, even in those rare moments when Latinos do appear, is either ignored or represented as undesirable. The media coverage of Selena's scandalous murder illustrates the English-language media's difficulty with mestizo images. By narrating the Tex-Mex singer's life and death as an immigrant's rags to riches triumph over humble origins, the English-language media uprooted Selena's identity from its cultural landscape: the overlapping borderlands of her Tex-Mex music—itself a fusion of tejano, rock, pop, and jazz influences—and her Mexican/American biculturalism and bilingualism (she sang in Spanish but often spoke English in private). "Instead," writes Adriana Olivarez, the English-language media "focused on the half that set her apart visually (the color of her skin) and audibly (the Spanish sounds) from the U.S. mainstream."[49] Except for the Latino-targeted media, Latinos get few opportunities to represent their *mestizaje* outside their immediate social or cultural circles.

When Latinos do appear in the national media, they are most often constructed as problem people who either commit or suffer crime. Moreover, Latino criminality and poverty are constructed in two distinct, but mutually reinforcing, dramatic spaces—the inner city and the border zone, both of which are identified with the depredations of poverty.[50] Latino hybridity in both these spaces is either ignored or constructed in threatening terms. The brazen border crosser vilified by anti-immigrant initiatives and featured in local news reports constructs Latino hybridity as Third World savagery. By symbolically running across borders into the safety of major cities, "illegal aliens" willfully mongrelize the rule of law, national borders, and racialized identities while threatening economic stability. They have come for "our (read Anglo, middle-class) women and jobs," some of the more extreme representations insist. Whatever the degree of racialized hysteria, these representations of the "illegal" emphasize an intractable criminality, which is attributed to an underdeveloped civilization and thus suppressed at all costs. This crisis of signification is institutionalized. The Latino presence in U.S. newsrooms remains low. A 1998 study conducted by the American Society of Newspaper Editors found that people of color made up 11.47 percent of print journalists, although people of color composed about 26 percent of the U.S. population. Latino journalists accounted for only 2.8 percent of editorial employees in the nation's newspapers, although Latinos constituted more than 10 percent of the national population. Moreover, the proportion of print journalists of color had increased by only 1.21 percent in the preceding five years, although the overall size of U.S. populations of color grew by 2.5 percent during the same period.[51] With numbers as low as these, it is hard to imagine Latinos having much of an impact on the culture of mainstream journalism. The U.S. Census Bureau, for its part, has had an especially difficult time trying to figure out how to classify Latinos by color. In the 1940 census, Latinos were classified as "black" or a "racial" nonwhite group. In the 1950 and 1960 censuses, the term "white person of Spanish surname" was used. In 1970, the classification was changed to "white person of Spanish surname and Spanish mother tongue." Then in 1980, Mexican Americans, Puerto Ricans, and other Central and Latin Americans of diverse national origin were reclassified as "nonwhite Hispanic." Latinos were back to square one. Because the Census Bureau uses a "white/black" paradigm to classify citizens, it has shuttled Latinos back and forth between these two extremes. In each case, the organizing principle behind the labels has been the perceived presence or absence of color.

## Discourse Discipline

Several critical theorists argue that the media gain control over public discourse by making their version of the social order appear natural, and thus transparent. By rendering the ideological assumptions of journalistic "facts" invisible, the media encourage the audience to adopt these news "facts" as public knowledge. The media perform this sleight of hand by making the "facts" appear objectively true, thus normal and beyond dispute or contestation. That is how the version of the social order constructed by the media acquires credibility and thus exchange value. Ideology normalized as public knowledge can be commodified and disseminated in discrete units of consumption, otherwise called news. Over time, media audiences also become conditioned to the media's normalizing methods. They not only believe the version of the world the media construct, they come to rely upon it. By enculturating audiences to become consumers of news, the media produce a disciplinary effect: they enculturate audiences to accept the values and norms of the media as their own.

The media, however, cannot suppress all competing knowledge systems or anticipate all discourse challenges. The media reiterate individual semantic victories to maintain their narrative authority over time. As the 1992 Los Angeles riot demonstrated, with few exceptions, the media neither anticipated nor controlled the challenges to the status quo expressed by subordinated social formations. In such a war of position, the media reiterate their narrative authority in order to maintain the exchange value of news. But the act of reminding audiences that the news is believable and authoritative also exerts a subtle disciplinary effect. The methods that normalize the production of public knowledge also strengthen the dominant social order by promoting the desirability of the status quo. Reporting inner-city crime not only conveys the notion that certain racial or ethnic groups are more prone than others to commit antisocial acts, it delineates the threshhold that distinguishes normal or civilized social behavior from antisocial or savage behavior. In a sense, one can say that the idea of normalcy requires or depends upon the transgressions of violent crime. It is in this way that crime stories reinforce the desirability of the status quo; they not only emphasize the likelihood of punishment, but, more fundamentally, construct the meaning of social deviance and civilized behavior. The racialization of crime news is an especially powerful means, but not the only means, of marking the boundaries of deviance because it associates dark skin color with savagery and whiteness with civilization. However, the means of producing crime news hides the symbiotic power relationship between the media and the state. As Thomas S. McCoy explains:

> Mass media order society's discourses by structuring the thresholds of thought, knowledge, and communication. [Media] institutions strategically, if unintentionally, collude with corporate and governmental interests in the pursuit of policies that maximize control over populations, as well as individual members of society.[52]

The symbiosis is particularly strong between the news media and the police and other institutions of law enforcement. The news media seek to reduce frictions with law enforcement in order to secure a steady supply of crime narratives, and law enforcement needs the media to show the public how its services maintain law and order. Neither Hall's nor McCoy's thinking here is not deterministic. As the Los Angeles riot demonstrated, chaos destabilized the hegemonic order by offering scenes it could not quickly interpret or explain. At such moments the media's inability to assert their narrative authority becomes detectable. Power relationships that had seemed anonymous and systematic suddenly become visible when mobilized to reassert authority over the production of public knowledge. The more profound the social upheaval, the more the media must struggle to reassert their narrative authority. The first hours of televised coverage of the rioting showed how the media's discursive reflexes were called into action, and how the media faltered before reasserting their narrative authority. A crucial part of that failure preceded the riot itself. The increasing corporatization of news meant that both print and broadcast news outlets had reduced or failed to increase their coverage of inner-city audiences, whom advertisers still perceive as less lucrative compared to the residents of the upscale suburbs. Television news anchors and reporters tried to fill the contextual void by calling the rioters "hooligans" and "thugs" when it became clear that the violence being broadcast from helicopter video cameras would not be contained by the police.[53]

The despairing commentary of KABC Channel 7 anchor Paul Moyer thus expressed more than indignation. It expressed a crisis of inscription. Conventional reporting practices could not normalize the rioting as it flamed out of control. Lacking a perspective from which to render the scene meaningful, Moyer had no choice but to fill the void by attempting to uphold the values of the status quo. Without prompting from such primary definers as the police, or, rather, because the police had momentarily abdicated their roles as primary definers during the first hours of the riot, Moyer filled the vacuum. Like the World War II–era journalists who racialized Chicano youths by calling them "zoot–suiters" and "pachucos," those television news workers who called the rioters "hooligans" or "thugs" assumed the primary definer's role to speak on behalf of the state, and so initiated a moral panic with both immediate and long-term consequences.[54] But the role reversal revealed an instability. The local media did not construct a chorus of outrage in the usual way. Rather than build up to the ventriloquism of consent in stages—reporting the facts, followed by a law enforcement response demanding a swift and ruthless restoration of order—the local media immediately escalated their rhetoric to moral outrage. By jettisoning the language of "objective" reporting, Moyer broke his professional composure and momentarily cracked the normalizing facade of his usually affable and paternalistic TV persona to uphold the "morality" of the status quo without having constructed the illusion of consent. His normalizing reassurances could not hide his medium's discursive impotence. The media's service to the social order suddenly became visible.

The crisis of signification was brief. Within hours of the first evidence of rioting, the media had mobilized to regain their narrative authority by representing the riot as a racialized conflict and as a law-and-order melodrama. This took several forms. Some law-and-order coverage focused on police maneuvers and plans for imposing marshal law. Other coverage focused on damage to property and then, later, on efforts to repair or rebuild the city's smoldering businesses. Yet we cannot ignore a third, less prevalent, but no less damaging theme in the coverage: that the images of Latino looting reactivated the representation of Latinos as "illegal aliens."

Taken together, all these discursive responses reinforced the desirability of the status quo, which is understandable. Television stations and newspapers function in local landscapes. News coverage that encouraged residents of the riot zone to respect the police, stop destroying private property, and participate in rebuilding efforts could recommit them to the dominant social order. When the coverage escalated to "moral panic," some citizens, including suburbanites who faced no danger, rushed out to buy guns in record numbers; others demanded that the governor mobilize the National Guard. Some took to the streets in efforts to contain the violence, images that the news media used to bolster the status quo. The image of actor Edward James Olmos sweeping up the glass of shattered shop windows also illustrated the news media's complicity in the fabrication of hope. It seized upon Olmos's brigade of sweepers as evidence of a populace heroically recommitted to the social order.

But the media did not maliciously conspire to racialize and criminalize the rioters or enoble the sweepers. Instead, institutional arrangements and market forces conditioned the media's racializing responses. "Journalists most often speak the same language as their sources, those in control," McCoy notes.[55] Their authoritative sources condition them to speak the discourses of power and to derive credibility from such an association. The media thus reiterate the dominant discourses to maintain access to power and all the benefits that flow from such access. Discourse reiteration under such circumstances protects the media organization's immediate self-interest and enhances the credibility of its news products. Over time, however, repeated discourse mobilizations produce long-term effects. By emphasizing the need for racial harmony, law and order, and "rebuilding" efforts, the local media in effect asked inner-city and suburban residents to ignore the social inequalities that contributed to the riot and instead rally together to protect the status quo. Meanwhile, the images of looting Latinos, and Latinos' corresponding silence as riot subjects, helped to trigger a series of "moral panics." Proposition 187, followed by Proposition 209, an anti–affirmative action initiative, and Proposition 227, an anti–bilingual education initiative, should all be seen as delayed responses to the riot coverage and a steady stream of anti-immigrant representations, all of which have transformed Latinos into the most recent incarnation of the alien savage.

The media's version of the 1992 riot thus differed only slightly from their coverage of the 1965 Watts riot. In 1967, the Kerner Commission's report criticized the media's failure to explain the underlying social and economic causes of the rioting that had swept through the nation's major cities two years earlier. In 1992, although the television networks made a greater effort to address the riot's causes, their coverage misunderstood the event in two basic ways. First, it focused on the state of "race relations" as either a cause or a consequence of the rioting. Second, even when the coverage addressed economic causes, it failed to show how globalization, economic restructuring, and automation had transformed the Los Angeles industrial landscape. Had the media been more vigilant, had they monitored conditions in South-Central and Pico-Union, they would have realized that the Watts riot of 1965 signaled a massive transformation of the city's economic and social order. That transformation dealt both liberating and devastating blows to South-Central and neighborhoods immediately southeast and southwest of downtown. On one hand, the repeal of restrictive housing ordinances in 1964 finally gave the black working and middle class the freedom to obtain better housing outside the ghetto boundaries created by decades of de jure discrimination. On the other hand, economic restructuring began to transform L.A.'s core industrial sectors.

Corporate land development, the movie and television industry, light and medium-sized manufacturing, warehousing and distribution, and, most important, mass-production industry had constituted vital sectors of the old economic order. Less than a decade later, large corporate industries would begin to falter in the face of domestic and offshore manufacturing based on flexible, craft-based production dedicated to small-batch outputs and ever-greater investments in laborsaving manufacturing technologies.[56] Although Japanese manufacturing would later be recognized as the preeminent center of flexibilized manufacturing, key sectors of Southern California manufacturing also emerged as elements of a post-Fordist industrial regime. As Mike Davis recounts, the plant closures that resulted from "economic restructuring" hit those Fordist industries that had only recently begun to employ African Americans in significant numbers. These plant closures, in turn, set in motion a chain of demographic and technological events that radically transformed L.A.'s urban landscape:

> This outward seepage of the Anglo population in the 1960's (36,510) became an exodus in the 1970's (123,812) and the 1980's (43,734). Racial hysteria, abetted by "blockbusting" in the city of Lynwood, was followed by a second wave of plant closings in the late 1970's. Much of the trucking industry, escaping gridlock and land inflation, migrated to new industrial zones in the Inland Empire, fifty miles east of L.A. And disastrously, within the short space of the "Volker recession," local heavy industry including the entirety of the auto/tire/steel complex collapsed in the face of relentless Japanese and Korean competition.[57]

The second round of plant closures triggered the flight of as many as seventy-five thousand working- and middle-class African Americans from South-Central during the 1970s and 1980s.[58] Like their white counterparts, they abandoned old neighborhoods for jobs in San Bernardino and Riverside Counties, or returned to the southern hometowns their parents had left during World War II, when they sought defense industry jobs. Still other workers of color, as Davis notes, were simply left "stranded in an economy that was suddenly minus 50,000 high wage manufacturing and trucking jobs."[59] The newly emerging black middle class migrated to near-in suburbs such as View Park and Baldwin Hills. The exodus of an established business community not only hollowed out South-Central's once-thriving small business community, it removed a key component of its political leadership. Left behind were those segments of the African American community with the fewest social resources or work skills.[60] The Watts riot did not set the exodus in motion, but it did make the departure of the black working and middle class irreversible, and thus set the stage for the 1992 riot.

To be fair, some elements of the media tried to retrace the economic chronology that linked Watts to Rodney King and the arson and looting on the afternoon of April 29, 1992. The *Los Angeles Times,* for example, in a series that began running less than two weeks after the riot had been contained, attempted to summarize the history connecting the Watts riot to the "Rodney King" riot.[61] Contributors to the series identified the riot's "fundamental causes" as demographic change, chronic unemployment, police brutality, poor schooling, and the delay in sending in the National Guard. But they ignored the public policy failures of the city's ruling elite and the global economic forces that had produced these symptoms. The most direct acknowledgment of postindustrial decline the series mustered was found in three one-sentence captions noting the closure of plants that had employed South-Central residents.[62] The series also reported the publicly financed redevelopment of the downtown cityscape of high-rise banks and hotels, but did not explain how this diversion of local tax dollars affected the historically neglected areas of South and Central Los Angeles.

Most of the news coverage, as Smith's and Hunt's studies suggest, was far less ambitious. The media isolated the riot within a racialized frame, much of which it personalized with human-interest angles or evoked through law-and-order stories that emphasized individual responsibility for wrongdoing. Either way, the media's habit of moralizing or personalizing the riot coverage, to the degree that it was also racialized, effectively framed the "race relations" discourse in the language of popular racism. In contrast to elite or institutional racism, popular racism is a belief system held and expressed by individual community members.[63] It is, by nature, ubiquitous, reactive, and not the expression of deliberate corporate programs or government policies. The coverage that played upon Rodney King's "can we all get along" plea shows how the media personalized the riot for its audiences. The media's representation of the riot as the consequence of popular racism freed the audience to either ignore or accept blame for the disaster. The human-interest stories, because they reduced complex events to the scale of individual emotions, avoided asking if certain social classes were disproportionately responsible for the rioting. Thus the atomizing power of the "race relations" discourse, even when it wore a humane mask, further strengthened the hegemonic order by extricating social institutions and elites from the crime scene. Yet a question remains: Did audiences accept the representations of the riot as the news media had encoded it? As Hunt stresses, the media's power to racialize does not prevent an audience from rejecting all or part of such representations. For Latinos, at least, the answer is an ambiguous maybe.

Hunt, who compared media content analysis to structured focus group interviews, concludes that the black study groups he interviewed were the most likely to challenge hegemonic media conceptions, followed in order of oppositional intensity by Latinos and then whites. Hunt notes that the Latino informants from South-Central Los Angeles "generally accepted the textual assumption that the black raced community owned the events, that its members were the event insiders," and that the rioting "was indeed 'wrong.'"[64] South-Central's Latino informants also tried to disassociate themselves from Latino rioters. These informants claimed that the Latino rioters shamed their community by using the riot as a pretext for looting. None of the Latino study groups challenged KTTV's news-gathering methods until prompted to do so.[65] Hunt also found quantitative and qualitative differences in the ways black, Latino, and white study groups expressed oppositional tendencies:

> Black raced informants exhibited a consciousness qualitatively different from that exhibited by Latino raced and white raced informants. Although several Latino raced and white raced informants questioned the textual assumption that the [riot was] undesirable, when the dust settled, Latino raced and white raced informants generally understood the events as they were depicted in the KTTV text as crime.[66]

Hunt, however, conditions his assessment by adding:

> It is significant that certain Latino raced and white raced (as well as black raced) study groups challenged the textual assumption that the news media are fair and factual. That is, this finding at least holds open the possibility that news representations of the world if not the events in question might be received by viewers with some measure of skepticism.[67]

Like Hunt's Latino informants, Latino political leaders responded to the riot in a manner that appeared to be motivated by shame, evasiveness, and narrow self-interest. Some, in attempts to deflect anti-Latino rage, quickly noted that members of the larger, mostly Mexican American Latino community east of the Los Angeles River sat the riot out in their homes. In efforts to distinguish rioting Latinos from the peaceful ones, Javier Hermosillo went so far as to attribute the relative peacefulness on the Eastside to superior "cultural values." Weeks later, Los Angeles County Supervisor Gloria Molina felt obliged to acknowledge that, "by commending the residents of East L.A. for their restraint, we were attacking the people of Pico Union."[68] Other Latino leaders, such as Los Angeles City Councilman Richard Alatorre, responded with disturbing candor. "I try my best to be an advocate for [immigrants'] concerns," said Alatorre, whose Fourteenth District includes the communities of Eagle Rock, Lincoln Heights, and Boyle Heights. "But I didn't get elected to represent them. I have a responsibility to the people I happen to represent."[69] The councilman's comments spoke volumes about the parochialism of Latino political leadership in Los Angeles. Up until the riot, local Latino elected officials, who are almost all second- or third-generation Mexican Americans, publicly invoked the Latino community's rapid demographic growth when it served their purposes. But when the riot erupted, Alatorre and many of his colleagues showed that they actually define their constituencies as conquered turf. For Alatorre and his peers, it was the voting fraction of the Latino community that shaped their politics. That is why Alatorre judged the city's recently arrived Central American immigrants as superfluous. After all, these newer Latinos did not live in his district, nor had they yet voted in sufficient numbers to be of interest to him.

Caught unprepared, Latino leaders and everyday residents could not discern any self-interest in identifying with their brothers and sisters in the riot zone. And, as subsequent studies would show, the Central Americans in the riot zone had difficulty imagining the city's Mexican American leaders as their spokespersons, or Eastsiders as their brothers and sisters. The sense of political disconnection in the face of cultural commonality underscored a paradox. "Study after study has demonstrated that while there is a commonality of experience among Latinos, there is a low level of knowledge and ethnic solidarity among Latinos of different ancestries," Popkin, DeSipio, and Pachon note. "Instead, Latinos in Los Angeles, . . . who are predominantly of Mexican ancestry, have little knowledge of or a belief in a common culture with" other Latinos.[70] For the most part, neither the news coverage nor local leadership attempted to address this discursive need. There was one notable exception to this picture. A month before the streets of Los Angeles burned, members of Local 11 of the Hotel Workers and Restaurant Workers Union released a video documentary that predicted social disaster if the city's growing inequalities of wealth and power were allowed to widen. The video, titled *Los Angeles: City on the Edge,* did not point to a crisis in "race relations" but to an economy based upon low-wage service sector jobs as the underlying source of social injustice. As it turned out, the video anticipated the moment when the Latino community, led by progressive elements and the Latino-targeted media, would give a resounding answer to the media-constructed moral "panics" of the 1990s.

# 3

# Mexican Cuisine

## Food as Culture

The following passage, written by Charles Fletcher Lummis and published in 1903 in *The Landmarks Club Cook Book*, captures a revealing moment in Los Angeles cultural history:

> While a few other cities are as "cosmopolitan" as Los Angeles, no other city in the world is made up of so many intelligent and well-to-do people so far from their old homes and from homes so widely scattered. Without going outside their own yard or their own "social set," [housewives] may exchange recipes for English puddings, New England pies, French sautes, Italian pastes, Swiss hassenpfeffer, Virginia corn pone, Mexican chocolate—in fine, the dishes of every land, and from typical housekeepers thereof.[1]

In many ways, Lummis's chapter titled "Spanish-American Cookery" anticipates the marketing tactics of superstar chefs who today write cookbooks and go on cable TV to promote their restaurants. In both epochs, culinary texts created by a workforce that specializes in cultural criticism express ideologies of cultural incorporation that underlie the creation and perpetuation of urban landscapes and cultural spaces. In early-twentieth-century Los Angeles, sales of *The Landmarks Club Cook Book* represented one of several schemes Lummis devised to finance the preservation of California's old Spanish missions. But California's most influential booster-journalist peddled more than recipes. Lummis also used crumbing missions as tangible symbols to claim Southern California as a homeland for a displaced and alienated Anglo middle class. As others have argued, Lummis provided the narratives and symbols with which Mexican Los Angeles could be revalorized as a fantasy landscape of Spanish romance.[2] In contrast to the blatantly anti-Mexican discourse of the mid-nineteenth century, Lummis's more subtle Hispanic fantasy appropriated those Mexican cultural images that could be interpreted as "Spanish" (read white and European) or dependent on Anglo leadership and protection while excluding others. And he succeeded, with the backing of the city's WASP elite, who saw in his books, articles, and civic leadership a way to give Los Angeles the cultural respectability it lacked. The city's infant tourist and restaurant industry, complemented by the mass merchandising of food products, produced an especially powerful means of constructing Lummis's new urban imagery. Like the theatrical re-creations and pageants so favored by Lummis and his contemporaries, the dining experience provided a visceral means of giving the mission-based Hispanic fantasy the flavor and aroma of a full-fledged simulacrum.

The Hispanic fantasy discourse continues to play a role in the design, construction, and marketing of Los Angeles landscapes. At the Border Grill in Santa Monica, for example, the jagged, angular lines of a metaphorical border fence suspended from above symbolically divide the restaurant in half. In a city where tourists and an international business set experience dining as simulated cultural travel, the Border Grill capitalizes on the most ubiquitous aspects of the city's Mexican landscape. Like the Taco Bell commercials of the early 1990s, the restaurant commodifies *la frontera* as thrill-seeking threshold preceding contact with the exotic Other. The patronizing multiculturalism implied in the restaurant's interior design and its menu is overtly expressed by its owners, Susan Feniger and Mary Sue Milliken, in their cookbooks and their first cable television show, *Too Hot Tamales*. The show prefaced its neocolonial appropriations of world cuisine by reviving a gendered variant of the Hispanic fantasy discourse. Since the early years of Hollywood, the female stereotype of the Latin "hot tamale," or half-breed harlot, has conveyed the image of a lusty, hot-tempered, sexually promiscuous, racially mixed, and therefore degraded mestiza subject.[3]

In the end, both Lummis and the "hot tamales" uproot Mexican cuisine from its cultural and social contexts, but with different technologies and aesthetic strategies. The elite chefs of Los Angeles use a postmodern aesthetic to appropriate and incorporate Mexican recipes and ingredients, and then disseminate their appropriations nationwide through cable television, radio shows, and Web sites, as well as through the cookbooks and magazine features Lummis would have recognized. In the global city, these methods of cultural appropriation, image construction, and dissemination are aided by the transformation of urban cultural industries. In today's Los Angeles, the circulation of the public, its physical opportunities for social or cultural contact, whether indoors in private malls, theme parks, movie theaters, video stores, or restaurants, increasingly revolves around the consumption of cultural products. Hence the importance of what Sharon Zukin defines as the critical infrastructure, which designs production and consumption of cultural products. Zukin's concept of critical infrastructure covers a broad spectrum of knowledge workers, beginning with the "high-culture artists and performers" typically identified with the cultivation of urban taste, but also including cultural service workers such as museum curators, advisers to corporate art collectors, cheese sellers at gourmet food stores, restaurant waiters, chefs, restaurant owners, and "restaurant critics whose reviews are eagerly read for vicarious cultural consumption."[4] The critical infrastructure expresses a new global division of labor that requires the internationalization of investment flows and the power to commodify local landscapes and traditions. But it also reinforces that division by normalizing the policies of economic and spatial restructuring in global cities and by producing critiques that cultivate self-aware, status-driven consumption among its urban denizens. To Zukin, restaurant reviewers epitomize the critical process that constructs the imagery of the global city:

> They visit restaurants, writing up reactions to dishes and comparing them with the composite menu of their collective experience. By these activities, the critical infrastructure establish and unify a new perspective for viewing and consuming the value of place—but by doing so they also establish their market values.[5]

Zukin's conception of critical infrastructure and her analysis of cultural production offer an especially powerful means of contextualizing the incorporation of Latino workers and the appropriation of Latino menus in the Los Angeles restaurant industry. Restaurants, particularly such style-setting restaurants as the Border Grill, embody those spaces where the critical infrastructure and immigrant Latino workers produce and market the multicultural cuisine that defines Los Angeles as a global city.

That restaurants help manufacture the edible multicultural texts and symbols upon which a global city's pluralistic self-image is constructed is not surprising. The metropolis of the industrial age has long been identified as the style center that generates cultural models emulated in the suburban and rural periphery. In the postindustrial global city, that function has intensified as cultural production has become its chief economic activity. Building upon her earlier studies of gentrification, Zukin advances the concept of the symbolic economy in her latest book to explain this transformation more thoroughly. She argues that urban elites appropriate the images, narratives, and symbols of multiculturalism and then inscribe these into the built environment, to communicate their tastes, values, and desires to their cultural peers and to the citizenry at large.[6] The exterior form and contents of a new museum are the metaphorical sheets of paper upon which elites represent their visions of a culturally pluralistic city. It is the critical infrastructure's job to make sure these texts are read correctly so that international investment flows without hindrance.

Although urban elites use the critical infrastructure to dominate the means of symbolic production and distribution, there are several reasons they do not control it absolutely. To begin with, the huge costs of constructing their grand narratives depend upon the consent of the culture-consuming, taxpaying, and voting public. Moreover, their texts are continually contested, and thus subject to the give-and-take of a cultural dialectic. Zukin thus coins the term *symbolic economy* to frame this multisided cultural dialectic. The creative destruction of landscape formation is more than a material process; it is the language of power, the means by which elites include and exclude symbols to construct and communicate the urban images, narratives, and visions they hope to make real. To Zukin, the symbolic economy speaks especially clearly in restaurants. These quasi-public spaces allow us to gauge a city's globalizing reach through "the quality of life a city offers" its corporate executives. "High-class" restaurants, she adds,

> suggest an aura of sensual excitement akin to the latest financial information, publishing coup, or fashion scoop. Indeed, restaurants have become the public drawing rooms of the symbolic economy's business and creative elites. The more corporate expense accounts are concentrated in a city, the greater the resource base to support both haute cuisine and *nouvelle* alternatives.[7]

Restaurants also function as important gateways and clearinghouses for global labor recruitment. The size of a city's restaurant workforce, "the countries of origin of participants, and the volume of monetary transactions that pass through" them, Zukin writes, make "restaurant work an important transnational activity—and one that is mainly undocumented."[8]

Zukin's analysis of New York's elite restaurants can be applied to restaurants in Los Angeles, but in different ways. For reasons of history and geography, New York's elite restaurants lean more toward classic European standards. Not surprisingly, as many as twenty-five four- and five-star restaurants operate in New York, compared to only five in Los Angeles.[9] But the economy of stars does not mean that Los Angeles and Hollywood, the Vatican of celebrity glamour and popular culture, lack elite restaurants.

Rather, for what they lack in lacquered mahogany, silverware, white table-cloths, and haute respectability, they more than compensate with copious servings of glamour, multicultural exoticism, and nouvelle chic.

Like ethnic enclaves repackaged for tourists as nostalgia or exotic Otherness, restaurants, particularly those that set the standards and images imitated by other restaurants, represent the global city's quintessential discursive space. Zukin maintains that style-setting restaurants' pairings of architectural and culinary design with cultural tourism and culinary performance produce "a city's visual style." At the center of this space stand the restaurateurs, who "often appear as a cultural synthesis of the artist, the entrepreneur, and the social organizer. The restaurant itself is both theater and performance. It serves and helps create the symbolic economy."[10] Like the city officials and developers who promote cultural development and the architects who design office towers, the menu-designing chefs function as public intellectuals. The local critical media, which are particularly dependent upon and identified with their audiences, normalize elite culinary representations by translating them into popular vernaculars. When echoed by the local critical media, a city's political, economic, and cultural elites negotiate a city's "look and feel," designating which cultures "should be visible" and which should remain invisible.[11]

In Los Angeles, the multicultural style-setting restaurants straddle a paradox. Throughout the restaurant industry, but especially in the style-setting nouvelle restaurants, Latino immigrant workers play the role of unskilled physical labor while college- and academy-trained chefs play the role of culinary artists. In such an intellectual division of labor, a cadre of mostly non-Latino elite chefs appropriates and reinterprets the Latino ingredients and recipes their Latino staffs assemble into nouvelle creations. That the ubiquitous contradictions of multicultural commodification do not seem more jarring is due in part to the cultural discourses that obscure them.

Our goal in this chapter is to deconstruct the symbolic representation and material production of Mexican cuisine in Los Angeles to reveal its hidden gastronomic culture wars. For most of the twentieth century, culinary symbolism and metaphor have served as important tools for constructing racialized Latino images and, later, for appropriating Mexican culture, and later still, for constructing the city's image of multicultural pluralism. And now, as Latinos emerge as the Los Angeles area's majority population and workforce, particularly in the growing service sector, the dialectic between representation and production of Mexican cuisine offers a critical means of gauging Latino cultural power, or, more precisely, the relative lack of such power. Because of the domestic, feminized connotations and decentralized production of restaurant work, and because of restaurants' classification as secondary production centers dominated by immigrant workers, the study of culinary representation and production has not been a priority of social science research. That oversight should give way to new realities. The various forms of food service constitute the fourth-fastest-growing industry in the United States; waiting tables ranks sixth among the nation's fastest-growing job categories.[12] These trends underscore the need for a serious assessment of restaurant work in general and of Latino restaurant workers in particular. The U.S. Census Bureau estimates that as many as 209,741 people were employed in Los Angeles County's eating and drinking places in 1994, compared to more than 173,000 in New York in 1998.[13] Latino immigrants, when compared to Anglos, are also overrepresented in Los Angeles County's food services industry by a ratio of more than two to one, and make up as much as 70 percent of this workforce.[14]

By themselves, however, statistics provide few clues that would explain the operations of the symbolic economy in the city's restaurant industry. That is why we have examined two discrete types of social texts to help us in our analysis of culinary representation and production: the more widely read literature of urban landscape formation and the city's lesser-known body of culinary literature. With this triad of demographic, landscape, and culinary texts, we will attempt to show how the city's elites have tried to remarket Los Angeles as a "multicultural" metropolis by simultaneously incorporating and marginalizing Latino cuisine and low-wage culinary workers.

Changes in the political economy and the technological environment have increased the importance of cultural production. To be sure, goods solely defined by their cultural use and meaning have long been crucial components of industrial production. Beginning in the late nineteenth century, a series of technological and marketing innovations created a mass-media revolution that permanently altered production of cultural goods and services. Equally important, a mass-culture revolution occurred in the largest cities. Today, a comparable revolution in cultural production is under way in the new global cities. New digital technologies now encourage the proliferation of industries based solely upon the commodification of cultural artifacts, information, and spaces. In addition to the city's old content-based industries, such as the print and broadcast media, film and sound-recording media transformed by the digital revolution, and the new cultural industries that operate in cyberspace, we add those industries that commodify cultural landscapes, goods, services, and images, such as movie studio theme parks, restaurants, hotels, guided movie star tours, and clothing and food manufacturing. Recent data show that lost aerospace jobs, casualties of the Cold War's end, have been replaced and superseded in Southern California by new jobs in the cultural sector. Between 1990 and 1997, the number of people employed in the core businesses of motion pictures and television jumped from 143,000 to 262,000, or 83 percent. Servicing this growing industry in turn generated another 50,000 culture-based jobs, from music recording to on-location gourmet catering.[15] Such displacements signal structural changes in the economies of global cities.

As manufacturing reorganizes in the suburbs and cities suffer recurring financial crises, culture emerges as the principal "business of cities." That transformation, which Zukin sees in the "growth of cultural consumption (of art, food, fashion, music, tourism) and their industries," fuels "the city's symbolic economy, its visible ability to produce both symbols and space."[16] Since Southern California's emergence from its recent economic downturn, the investment of huge sums of public and private capital in the arts and entertainment infrastructure of Los Angeles continues to sustain and expand the region's elite cultural institutions, including its restaurants. Despite their seeming pluralism and populist disdain for class snobbery, the style-setting multicultural restaurants of Los Angeles are its most representative elite institutions. Like the city's other spaces of cultural production, these restaurants have benefited from massive cultural infrastructure investments. Capital funneled into museums, such as the new Getty Center on the Westside, the conversion of Hollywood studios into amusement parks, and the planned construction of computer-age DreamWorks studios in the Ballona Wetlands will require a complement of elite culinary spaces.

Once inside the restaurant, the tourist and overseas businessman experience a safe and highly aestheticized encounter with the multicultural city before heading off to an evening at the Dorothy Chandler Pavilion, a private screening on the Universal Studios lot, or an afternoon at the Museum of Contemporary Art. In other cases, dinner at Patina Restaurant is the evening's theatrical event. The multicultural style-setting restaurant thus functions as an entertainment niche in its own right or as a prelude to another cultural experience. Either way, investments in culinary entertainment remain intimately linked to local and global economies of scale. Not only do the critical infrastructure's journalists, public relations operatives, and marketers create and perpetuate places of "multicultural delectation," tens of thousands of immigrant workers ensure that these places operate profitably and smoothly. But as economic life in the global city gravitates toward cultural production and communication systems converge and their technologies blur, new spaces for cultural contestation appear.

Los Angeles, a veritable tangle of culture industries, exemplifies the global city as arbiter of cultural meaning and investment, but also as a postcolonial territory subject to the reinterpretation by its Latino majority.[17] The nearness of its postcolonial past thus presents certain risks to elite efforts to incorporate, reconfigure, and commodify the city's multicultural landscapes. Its culture industries must create narratives and images that render harmless whatever oppositional tendencies its inhabitants preserve in their memories. The elites know they cannot fully control and exploit the landscapes of the present without also patrolling the landscapes of the past. In a city such as Los Angeles, that postcolonial moment occurred only yesterday, when Charles Fletcher Lummis set about inventing a cosmopolitan identity for Los Angeles in the course of a very long walk.

While walking west from Ohio in 1884 and writing about his journey in installments for the *Los Angeles Daily Times* (as the paper was then called), Lummis delivered his first account of Mexicans and their food at Cucharas Creek in southern Colorado. After portraying the plaza's "greasers" as "snide-looking, twice as dark" as Indians, and ineffably lazy, he took his first shot at Mexican cooking. "Not even a coyote will touch a dead Greaser, the flesh is so seasoned with the red pepper they ram into their food in howling profusion."[18] Lummis's characterization reiterated a well-established anti-Mexican discourse. Throughout the Southwest, publishers of dime novels, travelogues, and newspapers used culinary analogy to illustrate Mexican savagery and depravity to mark a community as racial Others. The newspaper story reproduced here, which was published in the 1899 edition of the *Los Angeles Record*, illustrates the pattern. Efforts to hunt down the seller of the tamale in question proved fruitless. But a lack of evidence did not hinder the *Record's* reporter from leveling accusations: "Bad meat is often used in the manufacture of tamales, the offensive taste being disguised by the fiery condiments which are used." The next paragraph, written with a man's lustful eye, establishes the other side of this good-versus-rotten narrative: "Miss Hufford is a most pronounced blonde. She has beautiful flaxen hair, a pearly complexion and large expressive blue eyes. She is about 21 years of age." The reporter's effort to convict a cuisine by means of racist analogy is transparent: a flaxen-haired beauty, the image of Anglo racial purity, succumbs to a putrid tamale made with spices and chiles to disguise the flavor of rotten meat. The reporter did not need to remind his readers that tamales were made by Mexicans, a word already cloaked in negative connotations. Words such as "bad meat" and "rotten"

# SHE EAT A TAMALE
# AND NOW LIES AT
# THE POINT OF DEATH

## Miss Maud Hufford Is Suffering From Ptomaine Poisoning

### THERE IS LITTLE HOPE OF HER RECOVERY

The Victim of the Tamale Is Employed at the People's Store and Is One of the Handsomest Shop Girls in Los Angeles

Miss Maude Hufford, one of the handsomest girls in Los Angeles, has been lying at the point of death since early last Sunday morning. Her condition is due to ptomaine poisoning, produced by a tamale that was composed of putrified meat.

Miss Hufford has been employed at the People's store for the past year and a half, and her friends are legion. She was in the department devoted to wools.

Last Saturday noon Miss Hufford and her fellow clerks sent one of the boys out to purchase some tamales. Miss Hufford partook of one of them. A little later she began to complain of feeling ill, but she remained at work until the store closed at 9 o'clock.

Accompanied by her roommate, Miss Lawrence, Miss Hufford went to her apartments at 421 Temple street. She complained of a severe pain in the region of her stomach.

About 2 o'clock Sunday morning Miss Hufford was seized with a violent vomiting spell which lasted for several hours. The following morning one of the leading physicians of the city was called to attend her. Miss Hufford then exhibited symptoms of acute indigestion. The physician emptied her stomach and found portions of a partly digested tamale. Miss Hufford fell into a comatose condition and remained in the stupor during Tuesday, Wednesday and Thursday.

On Wednesday night Miss Hufford was removed to the home of her brother, Guy D. Hufford, who lives with his wife at 1622 South Los Angeles street.

Miss Hufford suffered terrible agony, even though unconscious. Every joint in her body became stiffened, and it was necessary constantly to massage her with hot alcohol and move every joint each two hours.

Yesterday morning she emerged from the comatose condition and was able to speak a few words.

She is still delirious, however, and the crisis has not yet been reached.

The patient is visited from two to four times daily and everything in the physician's power is being done to save her life.

The attending physician took consultation with another physician, and both declare that the putrified tamale is responsible for the girl's condition.

An unsuccessful effort was made to ascertain where the poisonous tamale was purchased.

Ptomaine poisoning is caused by eating shell fish, canned game, milk and meat, which have become decayed.

Bad meat is often used in the manufacture of tamales, the offensive taste being disguised by the fiery condiments which are used.

Miss Hufford is a most pronounced blonde. She has beautiful flaxen hair, a pearly complexion and large expressive blue eyes. She is about 21 years of age.

*Los Angeles Record* story from 1899 illustrating the pattern of the use of culinary analogy to indicate Mexican depravity.

reminded readers what they already knew—that Mexicans were dirty and deceitful.

By the time Lummis, a native of Lynn, Massachusetts, got to New Mexico, however, his opinion of "greasers" had undergone a transformation. In his 1892 travelogue *Tramp across the Continent*, Lummis excused himself for his "silly" Anglo-Saxon prejudices before painting Mexicans as a "quaint, kindly people, ignorant of books, but better taught than our own average in all the social virtues."[19] It was while writing this book and serving as *Times* city editor that Lummis built his home just north of Los Angeles, on the banks of the usually dry creek bed called Arroyo Seco, where he developed a fondness for Mexican cooking. In the home he dubbed El Alisal (the place of the Sycamores) he held court, entertaining artists and intellectuals with dinner parties that featured Mexican cooking and pontificating on the southwestern Hispanic legacy.[20]

From his fortresslike home, Lummis wrote articles, books, and edited magazines such as *Out West (Land of Sunshine)* that wrapped sun worship, health fadism, and nostalgia for bygone Spanish days in a single package. His patronizing view of Mexicans was entirely consistent with his Brahmin upbringing. He intended his publications for people like himself, the middle and upper classes he adeptly beckoned to the city. In Los Angeles, he founded the Landmarks Club, a group that worked to preserve the missions from further decay and established the Southwest Museum to house the region's Native American artifacts and Californio history.[21] But the character of Lummis's work would be dictated by the cultural and economic alliances he would make in Los Angeles.

Like other eastern intellectuals of his generation, he'd become disillusioned with the ideals of American democracy; the capitalist robber barons didn't need reform-minded do-gooders and middle-class self-improvers to run the Republican Party. Feeling left out, as well as disgusted by the greed of monopoly capitalism exposed by the muckrakers, he and other disenchanted intellectuals known as mugwumps searched for a new homeland. They found it in California and the greater Southwest, a landscape that Lummis imagined as "enchanting" rather than simply savage.[22]

Refashioning the past to their personal advantage, they now saw themselves husbanding a fallen Hispanic civilization. Lummis, for his part, assumed the pose of a Spanish grandee, going so far as to call himself Don Carlos, a conceit, writes historian James W. Byrkit, that evokes the imagery of the southern Lost Cause: "Indians toil happily in the fields for Padre Agustin or Don Jose, rather than blacks for Ol' Massa; caballero is just another name for cavalier; sprawling ranchos . . . replace the colonnaded mansions." Both mythologies, Byrkit adds, glorify the "loftier aspects of Western civilization: traditions, leisure, refined literary tastes, sartorial formality, and well-bred social graces, including courtliness."[23]

And what better symbol of loftiness than California's abandoned missions, given that crumbling adobe could evoke a time when gentle padres presided over vast pastoral domains in idyllic splendor. Lummis understood the myth's bankability, writing at one point, "The Missions are, next to our climate and its consequences, the best capital Southern California has."[24] Lummis's strategy for selling California impressed his boss at the *Times*. Colonel Harrison Gray Otis needed more than sunshine to compensate for the natural harbor and water that Los Angeles did not have. Behind the booster grandiosity lurked insecurity over Southern California's image as a cultural wasteland good only for convalescing tuberculars. That is why Otis stressed the patrician side of the Lummis myth but suppressed the facts that the Franciscans had flogged runaway Indian laborers and that Yankee freebooters had lynched and swindled the Mexicans less than a century before. Lummis wanted to reassure the affluent Babbittry of the Middle West, so sought after by Otis as real estate investors, that Los Angeles offered Spanish-flavored European refinement.[25] And anything, including Lummis's cookbook, could be transformed into a symbol of bourgeois gentility.[26]

However, in turn-of-the-century Los Angeles, very few Mexican homemakers dreamed of sharing recipes with the "social set" to which the book appealed. A deep social chasm separated their worlds. But for a handful of wealthy ranchero families trotted out at fiesta time, most Mexicans were miserably poor and socially invisible.[27] The profoundly unequal relationship between communities not only precluded the housewifely recipe exchanges Lummis imagined in his cookbook, but maintained the social distance that protected him from comparing his fantasies to the Mexican community's social isolation. His selective inclusions and exclusions freed him to incorporate mestizo Mexican culture into his romanticized conception of Spanish culture and so create a sophisticated origin myth for the patrician class of Los Angeles.[28]

Lummis, however, cannot take all the credit for reinventing California. In 1884, Helen Hunt Jackson published *Ramona*, a novel she wrote to denounce Native American exploitation; *Ramona* became, in the hands of D. W. Griffith, the perfect libretto for selling his vision of Spanish California. Griffith's 1910 film version of the novel deployed the Hispanic fantasy discourse to elevate *Ramona* to the level of respectable art for middle-class audiences. Jackson had originally made her protagonist, whom she identified as Mexican, the offspring of a Scottish father and an Indian mother, which Europeanized the character for readers who perceived mestizos as degraded "half-breeds." Griffith transformed the novel's half-white "Mexican" protagonist into the "daughter of the noble Spanish house of Moreno." And with Mary Pickford cast as Ramona, Griffith encouraged the male members of the audience to fantasize about a "Spanish" beauty and yet still portrayed Mexicans and Native Americans as innately inferior beings too powerless to impede progress, represented as white conquest and capitalist expansion.[29] By 1916, the novel had generated as much as $50 million in publishing, stage, and screen revenues (a sum equivalent to the amount generated by a Spielberg blockbuster today) as well as provided the mythic rationale for landscape transformations already in progress. "In Southern California a town (home of the Ramona Pioneer Historical Society), streets, businesses ('Ramona's Chile Rellenos'), and real estate developments have been named after Ramona."[30]

Los Angeles area restaurateurs and cookbook writers swept up in Lummis's mission revival movement thus made their enchiladas and tamales more palatable for non-Mexican diners by affixing a "Spanish" label. The Spanish Kitchen, run by Ismael Ramirez and located at 127 North Broadway, in the heart of downtown, advertised to English-language readers its "Beef & Chicken Tamales" in the March 16, 1912, edition of the *Los Angeles Record*. The ad promised, "The only place in the city where you can get a genuine Spanish Dinner," followed by a rather un-Spanish-sounding list of dishes: "Special Chicken Tamales / Spanish Tamales / Enchiladas / Spanish Beans / Tortillas."

Published in 1914, Bertha Haffner-Ginger's *California Mexican-Spanish Cook Book* appears to rationalize the misrepresentation of Mexican cuisine by asserting that the "majority of Spanish people in California are as devoted to peppery dishes as the Mexicans themselves, and as the Mexicans speak Spanish, the foods are commonly called Spanish dishes."[31] It would have been more honest for Haffner-Ginger to write that the term *Spanish food* was simply wrong, and left it at that. But she could not deny the midwestern housewives who bought her book and attended her in-person culinary presentations a taste of the romantically imagined landscapes that had lured them to California. So she went along with Lummis and friends. Aside from her cookbook's "Regular Spanish Dinner" menus of enchiladas and "carne con chili" lifted from local restaurants and photos of genteel "Spanish" señoritas, Haffner-Ginger invoked mission revival mythology by including a photo of the dome-shaped oven next to which Ramona, the tragic Indian protagonist of Jackson's novel, was allegedly married.

# REGULAR SPANISH DINNER

## 60c

### Including Table Claret

SOUP

SALAD

ENCHILADAS

CARNE CON CHILI

SPANISH BEANS

SPANISH RICE

FRUIT AND COFFEE

---

## Special Spanish Dinner

## $1.50 per plate

"Regular Spanish Dinner" menu reproduced from Bertha Haffner-Ginger's *California Mexican-Spanish Cook Book*, 1914.

Culinary reinvention paralleled the ongoing landscape transformations. In 1896, the Landmarks Club prevailed upon the Los Angeles city attorney to render an opinion against the use of the city's historic plaza as a marketplace, despite the plaza's long tradition of food sales and the common Mexican practice of using plazas for trading purposes.[32] But Lummis decided what was best for the people who used the plaza. His Landmarks Club argued in an unsigned *Los Angeles Daily Times* article that the produce and food vendors who sold their goods to Mexican shoppers each week represented a "perversion and practical obliteration of the most important landmark in the city."[33] The intervention of Lummis, a Landmarks Club founder and a former *Times* editor, and Otis, *Times* publisher and a club director, makes this a classic example of news management. The *Times* portrayed Lummis as saving the plaza from the people who had built and maintained it for more than a century. Like his fiestas, Lummis's incursion into the plaza more than boosted the city's tourist industry. His "civic" interventions later helped city elites to exclude and silence groups such as the Wobblies and syndico-anarchist Magonistas, who used the plaza to agitate and organize.[34]

Despite the tremendous power of city elites to reconfigure landscapes, members of the Mexican community found ways to defend their own cultural spaces. After 1900, the yearly arrival of hundreds and then, in the 1920s, tens of thousands of Mexicans instigated a nostalgia for home cooking. New restaurants opened, menus became more elaborate, and restaurant owners tried to cash in on the immigrants' nationalist sympathies by running ads during Mexican national and religious holidays promising "authentic" Mexican fare. In 1921, two days before the sixteenth of September, the holiday celebrating Mexico's independence from Spain, the Gran Restaurant Mexico offered "one of those Xochimilco meals that shall remind of better days back home." The menu listed "real mole poblano," enchiladas with cream, fried chicken, breaded pigs' feet, *champurrado con piloncillo* (a hot drink made with chocolate, milk, and raw sugar), tostadas topped with meat and vegetables, *queso fundido* (chiles melted into Mexican cheese), chile verde stew, and huevos rancheros. It is hard to gauge the authenticity of the cooking from these Spanish-language newspaper ads, but they clearly catered to a working-class immigrant clientele. Many of these eateries qualify as "third" places, or establishments that blur the boundaries between private and public space, serving as living rooms for the homesick, archives of culinary memory, and cozy places for politicos, artists, and journalists to arrange their affairs.[35]

Despite low-paid work and the loneliness of exile, Mexicans now at least had enough spare time and spare change to enjoy something akin to their own Harlem Renaissance.[36] This rebirth reflected the immigrant's cultural transformation. Paradoxically, these strangers from different corners of Mexico now hungered for their roots, but also for a sense of community. Their search led them into the streets, the squares, the shops, and the theaters, where they shared experiences of a popular culture that chronicled their struggles and adjustments to their new home. In downtown bakeries, *tortillerias,* pool halls, dance halls, music halls, music stores, restaurants, bars, theaters, and even art galleries, the exiled immigrants found places where they could be Mexican in public. The theaters, the most well attended of these venues, were probably more popular than the churches. In 1927, for example, about a half dozen downtown Los Angeles theaters regularly featured Spanish-language plays, musical revues, and silent movies, including Spanish-language films produced in Mexico.[37] Newspapers such as *La Opinión* provided information that helped the members of the Mexican community adapt to their new home while maintaining a link with their homeland, and a handful of music stores recorded local Mexican artists, many of whom sang *corridos,* or story songs about the revolution they had fled and the new country they had found. Pedro J. Gonzalez, formerly Pancho Villa's telegraph operator, persuaded a local radio station to give him his own early-morning show. His program, the nation's first Spanish-language radio broadcast, quickly attracted advertisers who recognized the Mexican community's growing purchasing power. Gonzalez's singing group, Los Madrugadores, or the Early Risers, performed his popular tune "El Corrido del Lava-platos," or "The Dishwasher's Ballad," a humorous account of Pedro's first work experiences after he crossed the border.[38]

Restaurants such as La Misión Café, which capitalized on mission revival imagery and advertised "Exquisite Mexican Dishes," were thus more than mere purveyors of food and drink. Consuelo Bonzo, who founded La Misión in 1924, not only hired musicians and dancers to entertain her customers, she also invited the city's political leaders to hear the concerns of the Mexican business community and hosted special celebrations for visiting artists.[39] A May 13, 1927, story in *La Opinión* announced that Virginia Fabregas, touted on playbills as "the pride of our race," would dine with the members of her company at La Misión Café on the last night *Divorciémonos* (Let's divorce), the play in which she was appearing, ran at the Capitol Theatre on Spring Street. The article noted: "Mrs. Bonzo, proprietress of the well-known 'La Misión' Café, has been entrusted with preparing an exquisite dinner with which to honor the aforementioned persons. An orchestra shall enliven the genial gathering."[40] Bonzo also joined the

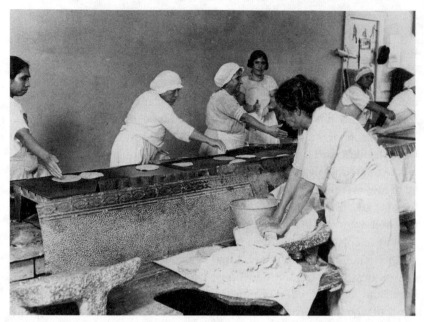

Woman grinding flour for tortillas, circa 1920s or 1930s. Photograph from Security Pacific Collection, Los Angeles Public Library; reprinted with permission.

*mutualistas,* or mutual aid groups, that fed and clothed the indigent among her countrymen and later paid their train fares back to Mexico during the repatriation hysteria of the 1930s.[41]

Consuelo Bonzo's contacts with the Los Angeles political and cultural elite paid off. In 1924, *Times* editor in chief Harry Chandler, the most influential member of the city's ruling elite, built upon Lummis's mythologizing. Chandler, at the insistence of Christine Sterling, persuaded the City Council to convert the plaza and an adjoining alley into a historic monument celebrating the city's Californio founders. Sterling envisioned the alley running between buildings previously owned by Italian and Chinese shopkeepers as a Mexican shopping bazaar with restaurants that would cater to the tourists who visited the Lummis-restored mission across the street.[42] She therefore interceded on Bonzo's behalf after learning of Chandler's plans to demolish the businesses along Spring Street, where La Misión Café was located.[43] While other Mexican-owned businesses were pushed south of the Los Angeles River by a Chandler rebuilding campaign designed to raise downtown property values, Sterling invited Bonzo to open a restaurant in the former alley, now transformed into a mythical street that had never really existed, so that she might serve a style of cooking the city's Mexican founders

La Misión Café on North Spring Street, Los Angeles, circa 1920s. Photograph courtesy of William Estrada, curator, history division, El Pueblo de Los Angeles Historical Monument.

had never tasted.[44] The city offered Consuelo Bonzo and her Italian husband, Alfredo Antonio, the old Pelanconi House, built around 1855, which was situated next to the old plaza in the middle of the new tourist destination.[45] The restaurant, which opened in a building formerly owned by Italians and served a style of Mexican food designed to please Anglo tourists, was renamed La Golondrina, after Mexico's sentimental farewell song. Like other Mexican restaurants of that time, the restaurant's name made connections with sentimental romance and immigrant yearning.

The deportation and repatriation of as many as a million Mexicans, which began in 1931 with a raid in La Placita, just yards from La Golondrina, initiated a frontal assault upon the Mexican presence in Los Angeles.[46]

The city would have to wait until the 1980s before it would witness a revival of the Mexican community that would exceed the levels of cultural influence attained in 1930. But even at its height in the late 1920s, and for decades afterward, the Mexican community in Los Angeles lacked the power or focus to prevent the WASP elite from dominating the city's symbolic economy. Aside from a handful of Spanish-language newspapers, radio stations, recording studios, and assorted politically committed media, the Mexican community relied upon popular cultural forms to construct a sense of group identity and maintain control over neighborhood cultural spaces.

That picture would change after the 1940s, when Mexican American activists would begin to win important social victories in the local labor movement and a few local elections during the 1950s. After the 1960s, these modest gains would be bolstered by the emergence of Chicano political activism, a burst of mainstream and grassroots book and magazine publishing by and about Chicanos, the rapid expansion of Spanish-language television, and the grudging admittance of a handful of Mexican journalists into the mainstream English-language media.[47] In East L.A., a resurgence of Mexican cultural pride hastened the disappearance of "Spanish" restaurants. The numerous *puestos* (food stalls) of the First Street Mercado, the introduction of *pescaderías* or seafood restaurants serving steaming bowls of *siete mares*, Mexico City-styled *taquerías* serving *tacos al pastor*, and *birrierías* serving slow-roasted kid would offer new spaces for the social construction and expression of Chicano and Mexican identity. Neighborhood eateries such as Manuel's Tepeyac in East L.A., La Golondrina in Olvera Street, Lucy's El Adobe across the street from Paramount Studios, and Barragan's and La Villa Taxco on Sunset Boulevard continued to serve as third places for political discussion and deal making between an emerging Mexican American middle-class political leadership and the Democratic machine. Meanwhile, the spread of Mexican restaurants followed the movement of Mexican Americans into the suburbs. Central and South American restaurants would continue a slow but steady acquisition of cultural space in the Pico-Union/Westlake area, Hollywood, and Echo Park. Incremental increases in Latino political, economic, and media empowerment accompanied these conquests. But after the 1970s, the government and media diluted them by reviving the term *Hispanic* and other aspects of the "fantasy legacy."

The quality and quantity of the culinary publishing record, and the subordinate role to which it assigned Mexican cuisine, illustrate the persis-

Restaurant on Fourth near Evergreen, circa 1930s. At that time, the term *Spanish* was used instead of *Mexican* to describe the food. Photograph from Shades of L.A., Los Angeles Public Library; reprinted by permission.

tence of this discourse. A 1994 national search of library databases found more than nineteen hundred citations of books on California cookery. Of these, only forty-four, or about 2 percent, are dedicated in part or in full to Mexican or Spanish cuisine, and only eight are written by authors with identifiable Spanish surnames.[48] Most of the forty-four so-called Mexican cookbooks were compiled by Anglo women's church or other social groups, with sections dedicated to "Spanish" recipes, or else published in trade books, such as *California's Mission Recipes,* that stress the romantic "Old Spanish" days. Mark Preston's *California Mission Cookery,* published in 1994 and based upon Haffner-Ginger's book mentioned earlier, represents one of the latest versions of the fantasy legacy:

> And as I read her [Haffner-Ginger's] recipes, I was transported back to the "Land of Sunshine," a golden state of fiestas and rodeos lasting for many days. It was a time when there was clean air, clear water, orange groves, and cattle grazing on a thousand hills. It was a time of charros, Mexican gentlemen farmers in the mold of Thomas Jefferson and flashing dark-eyed senoritas with roses held between their teeth as they danced the jota.[49]

In using the phrase "Land of Sunshine" Preston acknowledges Lummis's magazine, which was created to extol Southern California's weather, missions, and Spanish romance.

Although the Los Angeles critical media could not match Preston's Hispanicizing nostalgia, food writers and restaurant reviewers, particularly those at the *Los Angeles Times*, left much of the city's Hispanic fantasy legacy intact while constructing the city's image as the nation's capital of Third World cuisine. For example, Ruth Reichl, the foremost chronicler of nouvelle cuisine in Los Angeles during the 1980s and early 1990s, wrote a *Los Angeles Times* feature tracing the origins of California cuisine to such newly discovered texts as Encarnación Pinedo's *El Cocinero Español* (The Spanish cook), published in 1898 in San Francisco. Reichl correctly notes that many of the stylistic qualities identified with California cuisine—a love of fresh fruits, vegetables, edible flowers, and herbs, and aggressive spicing and grilling over native wood fires—were elements of Mexican cuisine documented by Pinedo's recipes nearly a century ago. But Reichl overlooks the colonized subject behind the text. More than a fine cook, Pinedo was a direct descendant of the Berreyesa family, one of Alta California's wealthiest and most tragic of the elite ranchero families. From 1846 to 1856, Yankee miners, soldiers, and vigilantes lynched or shot a total of eight Berreyesa men. The family was also beset by crooked land lawyers and squatters who reduced one of the most land-rich Californio families—an estimated 160,000 acres of Santa Clara Valley ranch land—to humiliating landlessness. To the other disillusioned Californios, the Berreyesa tragedy symbolized the measure of their defeat. But Reichl mentions nothing of these inconvenient postcolonial memories.[50] Intended or not, her omissions leave much of the Hispanic fantasy legacy intact, which is not surprising, given the critical media's reasons for rediscovering California's culinary history.

Beginning in the San Francisco Bay Area in the 1970s, and then later in Los Angeles, the West Coast staged a culinary revolution called California cuisine. The new label acknowledged recipes and ingredients from European and Pacific Rim culinary sources. Soon afterward, Los Angeles began to emphasize its Mexican and Native American influences. But despite its international scope, a single culinary aesthetic, nouvelle cuisine, dominated this explosion in culinary innovation. The new cuisine perfectly suited such emergent global cities as Los Angeles in their transition to economies of cultural production.

Like the European modernists of previous decades, the elite French chefs who initiated the nouvelle revolution in the early 1970s utilized the images, flavors, and associations of the exotic Other to critique a preceding generation of French haute chefs. There were differences, however. The nouvelle came after modernism had reached its cultural zenith; it also lacked modernism's aggressive assaults on middle-class sensibilities. The new style instead reflected a gentrifying sensibility produced by changing social conditions at home and abroad. Increased nutritional awareness, the availability of more leisure time, and faster transportation combined to deconstruct the haute menus of the Île-de-France. Whereas the haute tradition had constructed its social exclusivity by faithfully reproducing a hidebound culinary canon, the nouvelle chefs made the haute aesthetic the object of consumption. Whereas the old haute recipes evoked pomp and prestige with such aristocratic titles as *ducs de Bourgogne* and *noisette d'agneau Edouard VII,* the new chefs emphasized ingredients and cooking procedures with titles such as *ravioles de truffes à là creme de mousserons.*[51] The revolution in transportation expanded French vacation and dining habits. For example, new wine regions were added to the tried-and-true destinations in Côte d'Or. The nouvelle chefs of Paris followed their patrons on holiday, and thus rediscovered regional cuisines while inaugurating five- and four-star restaurants in new locations. Meanwhile, the increased availability and speed of refrigerated rail and air transportation meant that chefs could demand the best in seasonal produce from the provinces, and from the world. The nouvelle style also emphasized the chef's personal artistry over the old school's selfless obedience to tradition.[52] The new chefs thus challenged discerning patrons to read the old haute values in the edible text of the nouvelle recipes. The nouvelle method's symbolic hierarchies deconstructed and reassembled haute and regional French cuisine in a way that prepackaged that cuisine for international export. The French superstars of nouvelle cuisine thus took their show on the road, performing their style with new ingredients in major cities around the world. They established their own restaurants and academies at home and abroad, training thousands of non-French chefs to speak the nouvelle culinary language. But whereas classical haute cuisine had established its hegemonic dominance over regional cuisines by military and political means during the formation of the modern French state, nouvelle cuisine relied upon the market and cultural forces to establish its hegemony over global cuisine, particularly in the United States.[53]

Like the nouvelle chefs, who had rediscovered and reinvented France's regional cuisine, the American nouvelle disciples applied their techniques and aesthetic to local ingredients and recipes, a gentrifying impulse that explains an initial interest in regional culinary history. The practitioners and promoters of California cuisine, nouvelle cuisine mexique, and Cal-Mex,

Southwest, and Tex-Mex cuisines, as well as other variants of the new American cuisine, mined the past to feed a commodifying aesthetic. But few of these chefs felt compelled to engage in a comparable critical dialogue with Mexican and other so-called Third World cuisines. The appropriation and rejection of local ingredients and recipes gathered from around the world represented, at a symbolic level, the rhetorical assertions and counterassertions of an argument occurring within a culinary tradition. The haute and nouvelle partisans did not seriously attempt to engage the practitioners and advocates of non-European, nonnouvelle culinary discourses in their dialogue.

The same went for Los Angeles, which emerged as a hotbed of nouvelle experimentation in the 1980s. With rare exceptions, the city's nouvelle disciples were not interested in incorporating Mexican cuisine as a fully realized cultural or aesthetic subject. Instead, the poststructuralism of the nouvelle style appeared to vanquish historical memory and freed chefs to fill their tamales with smoked salmon or caviar without having to worry too much about the cultural ramifications of how they had appropriated recipes or combined ingredients. The nouvelle chefs also discovered that they could make Mexican cuisine more palatable to their upscale clientele if they called it *southwestern,* a term that simultaneously evoked New Age appropriations of Native American mysticism and the Hispanic fantasy legacy and de-emphasized overtly Mexican influences.

John Rivera Sedlar, founder of the trend-setting Los Angeles restaurants St. Estephe's, Bikini, and, recently, Albiquiu, expressed this neocolonial attitude in his book *Modern Southwest Cuisine,* a gastronomic tour de force fraught with discursive contradictions. Rivera Sedlar, among the first Latinos to join the ranks of the French-trained style-setting elite, nevertheless expresses the ambiguities that come with being the lone pioneer in a new professional culture. On the one hand, his cooking shows a real knowledge and appreciation of New Mexico's regional cuisine. On the other, his writing reiterates European culinary hegemony by characterizing his native New Mexico cooking as "earthy," a "common people's cuisine" that offered "a limited palette," while portraying French cuisine as a refined, aristocratic, and modernizing influence.[54] Rivera Sedlar appears to have succumbed to the Hispanic fantasy that imprisoned preceding generations of New Mexican cookbook writers in a tangle of conflicting discourses. In the 1930s, cookbook writers like Fabiola Cabeza de Baca and Cleofas Jaramillo attempted to protect their local culture from appropriation by Anglo artists while asserting fictional Spanish, more European, ancestries so as to pass as second-class whites. But before we judge these writers too harshly, Genaro Padilla warns us that

> our antepasados were not fools. They had moments of clarity . . . in which they knew they were lying to themselves, and they certainly knew they were engaged in a battle in [which] lies were crucial to survival. In intercultural discourse between a dominant and sub-ject group, survival is predicated upon strategically voicing one's presence. Often, simply being able to open one's mouth signals a moment of affirmation.[55]

In the 1980s, the chefs who invented southwestern cuisine echoed the neocolonial narratives of the 1930s, but with different objectives. By striking poses as heroic westerners, these chefs ennobled an earthy cookery and, in the process, invented themselves as culinary artists, a creative sta-tus that inscribed a new division of intellectual labor in the city's style-setting restaurants. Today, their neocolonial stance has been institution-alized in culinary academies nationwide, including at the Los Angeles Culinary Institute in Encino. Although the institute's Web site suggests a global reach, its European-trained staff and course curriculum focus upon the haute and nouvelle style. The institute's handful of courses in Hispanic cuisine are also less than they appear to be—the emphasis is Iberian, not Latin American.[56]

The food writers who fussed about "exotic" new ingredients and the ingenious ways nouvelle chefs painted on plates legitimated the chef's cul-tural appropriations. Few of the critical infrastructure's members noted the imperial way a new generation of European-trained chefs had detached Mexican and so-called Third World cuisines from their social and cultural histories. More important, the one-way conversation of a postmodern French aesthetic imposing itself upon New World foods and ingredients was held up as a sophisticated urban metaphor of "salad bowl" multicultur-alism. David Rieff, the New York writer and son of Susan Sontag, takes the culinary metaphor quite literally when he writes:

> Indeed, it was on the . . . far more basic level of what people ate that this multiculturalization of the Southland had progressed the far-thest. Ethnic restaurants and fast-food restaurants, only recently . . . confined to particular neighborhoods or immigrant-owned mini-mals, seemed to be sprouting up everywhere. . . . A generation of Anglo kids whose parents had been raised on steak and baked potatoes could comfortably tell the difference at a glance between

Thai and Cantonese food. A previously exotic prospect like, say, a Szechuan dinner now seemed almost tame, a Mexican burrito as American as a hamburger. In other words, their bellies were growing up multicultural.[57]

The local and regional media also romanticize the nation's growing appetite for Mexican food as a premonition of multicultural communion. Latino cultural critic Richard Rodriguez echoes both the imperial pose of the nouvelle chefs (he describes Mexican cuisine as "peasant" cooking) and the romance of multicultural culinary communion:

> In California, where our borders are not holding, there is an even more interesting development, mixed-race cuisine. Down the block is a restaurant that features Chinese-Italian. A skinhead I know hates Mexicans—but loves tacos. While blue-rinsed grannies and inept politicians are marching under the SOS (Save Our State) banner, demanding firmer borders, Americans are switching from ketchup to salsa.[58]

Several trends contributed to L.A.'s decade of culinary fame. One began in the 1970s with the dramatic increase in dining out, reinforced by the gentrifying return of Reagan-era yuppies, who practiced multicultural dining in formerly abandoned urban enclaves. Southern California's exploding culture industries, typified by the proliferation of Disneyland-like theme parks, also rediscovered and repackaged the city's ethnic enclaves, including their restaurants, as multicultural tourist destinations. The arrival of billions in Asian investment dollars and increased Asian immigration led to the expansion of Little Tokyo in downtown Los Angeles, as well as to the creation of a Chinese metropolis in the San Gabriel Valley city of Monterey Park and a Vietnamese suburb in Orange County. These, among other demographic changes, produced dramatic transformations of Southern California's cultural landscape, which included the proliferation and improvement of Asian and Latino restaurants.[59]

After several frustrating decades of trying to reinvent the city as a metropolis of high Euro-American culture, Los Angeles's elites went with the demographic flow. Beginning in the 1980s, elites, led by the downtown "blue bloods," latched onto the city's ethnic mosaic to sell Los Angeles to the national media as a "world-class" multicultural city. In the 1960s, the downtown elite used the construction of a new music center to spearhead the redevelopment of Bunker Hill, a twelve-square-mile core of dilapidated hotels, homes, and apartments, for larger real estate development schemes.[60] The late Dorothy "Buffy" Chandler, wife of *Times* publisher

Harry Chandler, had, by dint of political shrewdness, overcome the rivalry between the downtown elite, which had dominated downtown since the late nineteenth century, and the Westside's Jewish movie moguls and savings and loan bankers; she persuaded both sides to compete to raise the money to build the Los Angeles Music Center.[61] But renewed leadership competition between the city's Westside and downtown elites delayed the removal of Bunker Hill's working-class and minority residents from land targeted for redevelopment. Later, even after the downtown elites had everything in their favor—a compliant county government and a $50 million donation from Lillian Disney—their poor planning and arrogant mismanagement of the Disney Hall project would also delay their reinvention of downtown.[62] By the early 1980s, with land clearing completed and the pro-development agenda reconsolidated under Mayor Bradley's administration, the downtown elites would resume unfinished projects by sinking unprecedented sums into high culture.[63] This time around, however, the cultural rationale for enhancing downtown property values, and attracting new buyers and tenants to the high-rises constructed with huge sums of public financing, underwent a modification.

In addition to showcasing generic high culture at the Music Center and other newly constructed museums, the downtown elites would market L.A. as the capital of the Pacific Rim.[64] The city's hosting of the 1984 Olympic Games, preceded and followed by two Los Angeles Arts Festivals, which included artists from the Pacific Rim, and redevelopment projects rationalized as cultural improvement, drew upon multicultural motifs to engender wider public support. Toward this end, Davis writes, the downtown elites recruited an army of "mercenary" intellectuals and artists to construct the image of a global city worthy of international investment. These elites

> patronize the art market, endow the museums, subsidize the regional institutes and planning schools, award the architectural competitions, dominate the arts and urban design task forces, and influence the flow of public arts monies. They have become so integrally involved in the organization of high culture, not because of old-fashioned philanthropy, but because "culture" has become an important component of the land development process.[65]

The city's style-setting restaurants, and the food writers who reviewed them, played a prominent role in the "revalorization" of L.A. culture. The critical infrastructure fostered the convergence of Hollywood-style glamour with poststructuralist "multicultural delectation." Prominent architects designed culinary theaters where Reagan-era yuppies and nouveaux riches could flaunt their success. Meanwhile, style-setting chefs—the preeminent urban intellectuals of the global city—were constructing dishes from exotic ingredients that mimicked architectural postmodern design. The chefs at Patina, Citrus, and Chinois constructed crispy, edible cookie triangles standing upright upon sumptuous chocolate mousse rectangles all criss-crossed with Miró-like raspberry squiggles and powdered sugar to produce the visual delights of jewelry. Restaurateurs, chefs, architects, and interior designers marshaled music, lighting, celebrities, attractive waiters and waitresses, as well as taste and aroma to simulate and normalize the experience of consuming the multicultural Other. These new culinary spaces, in other words, symbolically fetishized a kind of cultural cannibalism. The style-setting restaurant's mode of cultural production ran on more than symbolic appropriation, however. Its commodification of multicultural cuisine reinforced and relied upon a division of labor that trapped Latino immigrant workers in the role of brute physical laborers.

In Los Angeles and New York, the nouvelle restaurants exploited a two-tiered employment structure that consumed vast quantities of immigrant Latino workers as well as unemployed or underemployed artists and actors. In the 1990s, a sobering recession prompted the elite chefs of Los Angeles to reevaluate and modify their recipes, but not the division of labor that had transformed the style-setting restaurant into a transnational institution. Today, as we near the end of a so-called economic recovery, immigrant workers in the style-setting multicultural restaurants labor behind kitchen doors in unglamorous steam and heat while underemployed artists perform in public view, seating patrons, explaining menus, and presenting food. Emphasizing the performative quality of their labor, these waiters and waitresses, Zukin writes, resemble "Disney World performers." They "project an air of knowing or personable authority . . . and speak proper English to middle-class customers without being either servile or surly."[66]

Immigrants, by contrast, have their reasons for seeking out the industry's low-paying, often dead-end jobs. Lack of English-language skills and U.S. educational credentials, willingness to work unusual and long hours at subminimum wages, "and the restaurant industry's traditional barriers to unionization, make this a pliable" labor force preferred by employers.[67] In her ethnographic survey of New York restaurants, Zukin also found that those immigrant workers allowed direct contact with the public were more European in appearance and had mastered English and urbane middle-class manners. By contrast, Mexicans dominated "the lowest-skill kitchen positions," a fact she attributes to the rural origins of immigrant workers who have not yet acquired "urban job skills."[68]

Available data suggest that the division of labor Zukin observed in New York may be more accentuated in Los Angeles. In 1990, 108,921 persons in the L.A. area were employed in creative occupations (actors, directors, dancers, musicians, and so on), compared to 114,231 in New York. However, such creative occupations are growing at a faster rate in Los Angeles than in New York; much of this growth is generated by L.A.'s television and film industry.[69] Los Angeles is also home to far larger Latino and Asian communities than are found in New York, and an economy that historically has depended upon undocumented Latino labor.

Unfortunately, gaps in restaurant workforce data make it difficult for us to elaborate upon these numbers.[70] Still, available workforce data and anecdotal evidence allow us to make preliminary generalizations about the Los Angeles area's restaurant industry. For example, data on occupational concentration in Southern California show that in 1990 Latinos were more than twice as likely as Anglos to be employed in food service jobs, a broad category that covers the full spectrum of restaurant service and food preparation.[71] This pattern holds for that portion of the Latino workforce classified as cooks. Compared to Anglos, Salvadorans are 3.1 times as likely to be employed as cooks; Guatemalans are 3 times as likely and Mexicans are 3.3 times as likely as Anglos to be working as cooks.[72] Data provided by Local 10 of the Hotel Employees and Restaurant Employees International Union confirms the pattern. In 1996, Mexican American and other Latino employees constituted 58 percent of the New Otani Hotel's 388-member service workforce, a proportion consistent with the slightly more than 50 percent of Latinos employed in Los Angeles County's more than 1.14 million service sector jobs.[73] Moreover, in 1990, 72 percent of Mexican immigrant men in Los Angeles were concentrated in a handful of occupational niches, which included restaurant work.[74] In 1990, 75 percent of these workers had not graduated from high school. Moreover, they averaged annual salaries of $18,000, compared to $30,500 earned by native-born Mexican Americans.[75] Anecdotal evidence appears to confirm the job bifurcation implied by the statistical data.

During a guest cooking engagement at a Southern California restaurant, Rick Bayless, award-winning owner and executive chef of Chicago's Frontera Grill, was "flabbergasted" to see an entirely Latino prep crew replaced by white line cooks when the restaurant opened its display kitchen in the evening. "I had someone tell me that you could not get a line position if you were Hispanic," Bayless later told a writer.[76] Another restaurant and travel writer who has years of experience writing about Southern California's restaurants recounted the case of a light-skinned Argentinian who started working in the kitchen of a Los Angeles-area gay restaurant:

> After about four days of working there, the owners told him, "You are too good looking to work in the back." They turned him into a waiter, then he went off to Citrus [the epitome of a Los Angeles style-setting restaruant], where he's making hundreds of dollars. It's indicative of what happens in all restaurants. He had a good capacity to learn English. He was surrounded by busboys from Mexico. The others were not learning English, while he was aggressively learning English.[77]

Although Bayless and celebrity nouvelle chefs such as Wolfgang Puck have trained and promoted Latinos to more creative and visible positions, several structural factors explain why style-setting restaurants prefer to employ Latino immigrants in unskilled and less visible positions. First, the celebrity chef and assisting sous and line chefs represent the biggest part of the style-setting restaurant's kitchen labor costs. Industry insiders note that restaurant owners do not spend money to increase the education or training of immigrant Latino workers, aside from the on-the-job training these workers receive. And the language barrier between the skilled, generally non-Latino chefs and the unskilled Latino dishwashers and busboys reinforces the social distance that separates these groups. Executive chefs tend to handpick the other skilled staff from among their social peers, which includes colleagues with whom they have worked or trained at other elite or style-setting restaurants.

A recent trend has further heightened the social bifurcation of skilled and unskilled restaurant workers. Traditionally, most skilled restaurant employees received their training and experience on the job. Today, however, the preferred pathway to becoming a style-setting chef begins with a university degree, followed by vocational training in one of many European-styled culinary academies and an apprenticeship in a style-setting kitchen.[78] By contrast, few Latinos receive elite professional training, although they represent the majority of Southern California's restaurant workforce. Latinos made up 10.4 percent of 556 students enrolled in the chef's program at San Francisco's prestigious California Culinary Academy in 1996, compared to 65.3 percent for white students and 13.3 percent for Asians.[79] Even this low percentage of Latinos receiving elite culinary educations represents a significant advance. More than a decade ago, the number of Latinos enrolled in elite culinary academies would have been almost undetectable. Still, the majority of immigrant Latino workers enter the restaurant industry by the back door, through referrals or recommendations from other Latino immigrant workers. These immigrant workers, moreover, get their on-the-job training at middle to low-end full-service and fast-food restaurants—a career path that does not prepare workers for the style-setting restaurant. The high restaurant failure rate and the undocumented status of many of these immigrant workers also increase their vulnerability. When seen from the immigrant worker's perspective, the obstacles to advancement are indeed discouraging.

"It is very hard for [immigrant Latinos] to conceive of learning English, finishing high school, and then going to college" in order to become a chef, one industry insider observed. "It's hard enough for them to stay employed." The restaurant's intellectual division of labor ghettoizes unskilled Latino workers, many of whom remain in the same positions for ten to twenty years.[80] That many of these midrange and fast-food restaurants serve Mexican food and are Mexican or Latino owned does not significantly alter the social relations of production.

The success stories of Latino chefs who have opened well-reviewed restaurants also confirm the pattern. Jose Rodriguez, chef and owner of La Serenata de Garibaldi in Boyle Heights, and Felipe Cabrera, owner and chef of El Emperador Maya in south San Gabriel—both of whom received early training in French and North Italian restaurants—say they would have appreciated the opportunity to receive formal training, especially in Mexican cuisine. Rodriguez has also noted that it strikes him as ironic that the largest population of Mexicans outside of Mexico City does not have its own institute of Mexican gastronomy.[81]

The low levels of Latino academic achievement and professional training represent other factors suppressing Latino representational power in the symbolic economy of Los Angeles. Too few Latinos are academically positioned to receive professional training at elite culinary schools and institutes, and too many are overrepresented in the vocational schools that lead to careers in midrange and low-priced fast-food outlets. One recent study found that only 4 percent of California's Latino high school graduates are fully eligible for admission to the University of California. In fact, Latino enrollment in the UC system declined from 2,991 in 1989 to 2,218 in 1992, although the state's Latino student population continued to expand steadily. Only 6.2 percent of students of Mexican origin, and only 10 percent of Latinos, complete four or more years of college, compared to 22.3 percent of non-Latinos.[82] By contrast, 58.2 percent of the students who graduated in

1995 from Los Angeles Community College with vocational degrees in food service management were identified as Latino; 36 percent of food service management graduates were white, and 7.6 percent were listed as Asian.[83] Advanced training in restaurant management, which offers another route to the style-setting restaurant, again shows low Latino participation. Mexican Americans graduating in 1996 from California State Polytechnic University, Pomona, with MBAs in hotel and restaurant management constituted 8.5 percent of the class, whereas whites made up 33 percent of the class. Chinese students accounted for 20 percent of these graduates, and only 1.9 percent of the MBA recipients were listed as black.[84]

Granted, the bifurcation that typifies the style-setting restaurant is more the exception than the rule in mid- to low-priced restaurant chains. These mostly corporate-run restaurants offer slightly better pay, more opportunities for advancement, and greater economic stability and are more egalitarian than the style-setting restaurants. And as second-generation Latinos continue securing low- to mid-management positions and Latino union representation increases, Latinos stand to increase their social influence within this sector. But the lack of occupational mobility for immigrant Latinos continues to limit their representational opportunities in style-setting restaurants and the critical infrastructure. Although they make up more than 22 percent of the nation's populace, Latinos represent only 2.6 percent of the nation's newspaper editorial staffs, 3.2 percent of radio news staffs, and 6 percent of television news teams. In Los Angeles in 1990, Latinos constituted 40 percent of the population but only 6.46 percent of the *Los Angeles Times* news staff.[85]

Their near exclusion from the critical infrastructure and their structural subordination in the workplace articulate Latino restaurant workers' functional relationship to the symbolic economy. The social relations of restaurant production and the representation of Mexican cuisine mutually constitute Latino immigrants as a subordinated workforce while normalizing the commercial and aesthetic appropriation of Mexican culture. Structural factors such as inadequate educational preparation discourage these workers from effectively contesting the representation of their labor and their cuisine inside the restaurant, while racialized media representations of Mexican culture devalue immigrant restaurant workers in society at large. This structural-cultural symbiosis explains why the Latino flavor of Los Angeles—a city with a Mexican population second only to Mexico City, with more than thirty thousand restaurants where Latino cooks prepare myriad cuisines, and with a Latino workforce large enough to shut down the city's restaurants if it stayed home—remains marginalized in the city's culture wars.[86]

Some scholars see a growing Latino middle class as the solution to Latinos' cultural silence in the city they will soon dominate numerically. They expect upward social mobility, which they confuse with the ability to earn middle incomes, to resolve the paradox. Either Latino assimilation will reinforce the current hegemonic order or majority political and consumer buying power will allow Latinos to construct a mainstream version of Latino culture. We believe this optimism is misplaced.

The Latino community has yet to create a cultural class that is sufficiently independent and self-informed to represent itself publicly, let alone challenge the present hegemonic order. A visit to Rodriguez's *La Serenata* illustrates our point. Most of Rodriguez's customers are white professionals who visit the restaurant as if taking a minitour to the Eastside's borderlands. In fact, Rodriguez complains that he has had only modest success in attracting the kind of middle-class Latinos who can afford the restaurant's prices.[87] Josephine Ramirez, a Getty Research Institute project associate who studies community-based cultural projects and knowledge systems, believes she knows why. Experience has shown her that the city's growing Latino middle class equates high culture with European fine art and cuisine far more than with Mexican culture or cuisine. Nor do those in this stratum of Latino Los Angeles yet see themselves as constituting a cultural class, or as art patrons; instead, they defer to the city's elites for received notions of high culture—which, Ramirez notes, should not be surprising. Given their recent immigration, their strong ties to working-class culture, their weak ties to Mexico's elite cultural classes, their relatively low levels of formal schooling in Latin America, and the assimilationist assaults of U.S. public education, Latinos' silence in high-culture discourse is understandable. Consequently, the Latino middle class and immigrant nouveaux riches have just begun to consider the possibility of organizing a Latino cultural class, of becoming a class for themselves.[88] Meanwhile, the anti–Latino immigrant, anti-bilingual, and anti–affirmative action backlash of the 1990s has hardened an educational status quo that has rarely served Latinos well, and that still retards the development of Latino cultural classes.

If Latino majority numbers are to lead to the formation of a cultural class, the core of that class will emerge from the community of working-class immigrants and the popular culture they create and consume. We offer a few reasons. First, Spanish remains the language of the service sector. Behind restaurant kitchen doors, immigrant workers relying upon well-established social networks that maintain their access to restaurant jobs ensure the dominance of Spanish in the workplace. Second, the purchasing power of a growing immigrant population has expanded Spanish-language media and provided the Latino community the resources to satisfy its cultural appetites. An expanding economy of nostalgia supplies these im-migrants with the raw ingredients they need to maintain and elaborate upon a vibrant culinary culture within the home and in the neighborhood. The memory-driven side of the market is sustained by the region's indige-nous Latino cultures, new immigrant arrivals, and the second- or third-generation retro-Latinos trying to recover what they have forgotten.[89] When Latino immigrant children are factored in, it is easy to see how the cultural side of this demographic equation drives the Latinization of consumer ap-petites and the growth of Spanish-language media and popular culture.

The vitality of Latino popular culture, with all its contradictions, rep-resents an important strategic resource. As recent organizing efforts in the service and craft-based industries have shown, culture-based networking can be used to break immigrant workers out of their social isolation and build class awareness. As we will show in chapter 4, the use of guerrilla theater, performance art techniques, and photographic testimonials as or-ganizing tools in service unions have already proved successful enough to try in the city's kitchens. By consciously adding cultural benefits to their or-ganizing agendas, union organizers may someday find themselves bargain-ing for higher wages, medical benefits, and discursive power for immigrant workers. Developing unions as cultural institutions would begin to invest the immigrant majority of restaurant workers with the intellectual authori-ty to represent their own cuisines. Although such a future may seem far off, a variant of this model already exists. In France, the best chefs come from the working class and acquire mastery through on-the-job apprenticeship. Such a system cannot work here as long as the service sector divides work-ers into first- and second-class wage earners. But the unions could pursue their own institution-building strategy to make service sector work more economically and culturally rewarding.

The unions, while increasing their Latino and Asian memberships, could assume more of the responsibility for cultural training and draw upon the expertise of neighborhood arts organizations. At the same time, these Latino-led unions could mobilize voters to both strengthen and reorient their local educational institutions. The schools would have the task of building a worker-oriented culture class that, on the one hand, challenges and opens the local critical infrastructure and, on the other, democratizes the restaurant's social organization and allocation of representational power. As we will show in the chapters that follow, the first steps toward these objectives have already been taken. Organizations such as La Her-mandad Mexicana Nacional have taken a half step in this direction. In re-cent years, this immigrants' rights organization has obtained federal adult education funds to prepare several hundred thousand Latino immigrants for citizenship while maintaining discursive control of the pedagogical process. The organization's success has produced a vicious backlash from the Right, which, at this writing, has threatened La Hermandad's access to continued funding. La Hermandad's vulnerability underscores the need for Latino self-determination over local public educational institutions dominated by Latino students.

# 4

# Contesting "Showtime"

## Latino Leaders in Downtown Development

> Las ciudades despliegan suntuosamente un lenguaje mediante
> dos redes diferentes y superpuestas: la física que el visitante
> común recorre hasta perderse en su multiplicidad y fragmentación,
> y la simbólica que la ordena e interpreta, aunque sólo para
> aquellos espíritus afines capaces de leer como significaciones los
> que no son nada más que significantes sensibles para los demás.
>
> **Angel Rama, *La Ciudad Letrada*, 1984**

As Angel Rama noted in 1984, cities can be read as texts.[1] In urban land-scapes today, the completion of a high-rise or a sports stadium can serve as a bookmark in the ongoing story of city making. New structures of concrete and glass not only reshape the urban landscape, they can symbolically close an argument, one in which power has temporarily silenced its rivals to impose its version of what a city should become, or mark a moment when an older narrative gives way to a new story line. The debate that raged over the construction of a state-of-the-art indoor arena in downtown Los Angeles points to such a discursive turning point. The aging elites who had recently lost control of the city's story in the early 1990s would, in building the arena, regain control of the downtown narrative, but only after making concessions to angry home owners and a revitalized, Latino-led labor move-ment. A founding member of the blue-blood family, the *Los Angeles Times*, also suffered a blow to its credibility when, under new corporate leadership, it reverted to the boosterism that had once earned the paper a reputation for ruthlessly advancing its antiunion, growth-at-any-cost agenda. Ironi-cally, the blue bloods suffered this reversal after the arena had opened its doors and the arena controversy had nearly abated.

Flanked on the west by the Harbor Freeway and on the south by the Santa Monica Freeway, and built upon the former grounds of the Los Angeles Convention Center's North Hall, the arena never lacked visibility. Even before construction began, this space for commidifying athletic competition already functioned as an ideological arena where different political and economic blocs competed to fix their urban narratives upon the downtown landscape. To the city's aging Anglo elite, building a $400 million arena represented a chance to regain control of the city's present and future. Publicly, the blue bloods (William Fulton's apt term for the downtown elite) argued that the arena, together with other nearby projects, would once and for all transform downtown Los Angeles into a "world-class" tourist destination, because it would attract new infusions of capital.[2] The arena would more than accomplish their goal. Multibillionaire Philip Anschutz, chairman of Anschutz Corp., vice chairman of Union Pacific Corp., and a major shareholder of Qwest Communications, Edward P. Roski Jr., California's biggest developer, and later, media mogul Rupert Murdoch invested millions downtown to become honorary members of the blue-blood elite.

The blue bloods also hoped the arena, eventually christened Staples Center thanks to a $100 million naming deal, would accomplish something more elusive: it would become a sports temple with which area residents could identify, and that they would rally around. The recent flurry of downtown development projects might even mend the elites' fractured political leadership, or at least defend established methods of "privatizing" the functions of local government. City officials encrypted their modest dreams in characteristic hyperbole. The arena would be "a catalyst for the development of Hotel, Retail, Dining and Entertainment facilities in downtown Los Angeles by creating new jobs, enhancing the viability and financial performance of the Convention Center, revitalizing the Central Business District, attracting more visitors to the downtown area and generating increased activity at hotels, restaurants, and other businesses in the area." Translation: they hoped that investing millions more in public subsidies would stanch the flow of losses at the adjacent, money-losing Convention Center, restore investor confidence in downtown's depressed property values, and fill up downtown hotels and office towers. The city also produced financial reports predicting a $120 million spending boost in the city and the creation of 1,200 permanent arena jobs, plus another 850 new permanent jobs generated by arena-related business.[3]

Blue bloods, developers, and city officials, however, would not realize their objectives without a contest. The strongest and most visible challenge came from a familiar quarter—disenfranchised suburbanites, particularly San Fernando Valley home owners represented by Los Angeles City Councilman Joel Wachs. The Valley's emergence as one of several economic confederations that ring downtown reveals the same centripetal forces that created the Greater Eastside, but with a different result. In contrast to the Greater Eastside, which the downtown elite had jettisoned beyond the city limits to facilitate the area's development as an industrial sacrifice zone, the blue bloods took a proprietary interest in the Valley. The downtown elites owned the land, controlled the water, and managed the planning process that made the Valley's overdevelopment possible. The blue bloods engineered a suburban landscape and tried to populate it with their kinds of folks— white, middle-class consumers, and preferably Republican voters. Their sense of neocolonial entitlement produced a grudging resentment from Valley residents that, over the years, has expressed itself as opposition to court-ordered school desegregation, home owner support for Proposition 13, and the slow-growth revolt against uncontrolled suburban development and more city-subsidized development downtown. Charter reform plans for devolving political authority to neighborhoods and expanding the City Council to twenty seats represent the latest efforts to give the Valley a greater voice in City Hall. Yet many analysts say such compromises will not prevent the inevitable. Sooner or later, the Valley will incorporate as a new city. It is too early to tell how Latinos and Asians, who make up 40 percent of the Valley's 1.3 million inhabitants, will fare if such a municipality is formed. Some Latinos predict continued minority marginalization if a new Valley city is formed; others note that it will merely delay the day when Latinos achieve majority status.[4] But there is one certainty: the new arena, combined with the Metropolitan Transit Authority (MTA) budget overruns and delays in constructing the city's subway system, reenergized the latest Valley secession drive.

Los Angeles, however, does not face its suburban revolts in isolation. Like other major urban centers, it has had to contend with the complex social, economic, and technological forces that have pushed white, middle-class home owners to the urban periphery. Other major cities have also struggled with de- and reindustrialization, automation, revenue losses brought on by middle-class taxpayer flight, and the emergence of new urban multiethnic majorities. It is the number and scale of these transformations, and the responses to these new conditions, that distinguish Los Angeles.

The reorganization of the city's economy around culture- and information-based modes of production represents one transformation. In an effort to entice global investors and suburban consumers to aging land-scapes, city leaders have repackaged ethnic neighborhoods for multicul-tural tourism and built modern art museums and luxury hotels to spruce up downtown financial districts. Movie studio back lots have been recycled into multithemed amusement parks. Universal Studios, for example, has reenacted movies such as *Jurassic Park* and *Back to the Future* as amuse-ment park rides. Each themed landscape is based upon a cultural narra-tive, whether blockbuster movies or multicultural tourism; each localizes an industry that manufactures stories, ideas, fashion, and other cultural products for national and global audiences.[5]

Building a state-of-the-art sports arena downtown represented the next increment in the development of a culture-based economy. The city's old urban elites, however, would have to build a consensus to continue "theming" the downtown landscape. Their efforts to represent the con-struction of sports arenas as natural and necessary would require both dis-cursive assertions and strategic silences to discredit knowledge, arguments, and place memories that might undermine their development schemes.

Whether the blue bloods can arrest the decay of downtown remains to be seen, but it is already clear that the global city's culture-based and information-based mode of production is premised upon a surplus of low-paid, mostly immigrant labor. Los Angeles, an employment pyramid that creates a few high-wage information-based jobs at the apex of the struc-ture and a vast majority of low-wage culture-based service jobs at the bot-tom, also leaves a huge revenue and income gap in the middle. Prior to the hollowing out of the city's urban economy, white- and blue-collar workers, who earned middle incomes in professional services and unionized Fordist manufacturing, paid for needed social services and capital improvements. Under the present restructured wage regime, the resulting revenue and in-come gap will remain, even with the attainment of full employment.

The third team to join the arena contest advanced its own remedy to the conflict between the newer suburbs and an aging city. Like the blue bloods and their developer allies, the alliance between organized labor and liberal Democrats had been a familiar fixture at City Hall since the 1960s. And true to its pro-development history, the labor side of this partnership came out early in favor of the arena. Yet much had also changed from the time when the unions blindly backed any development that promised more jobs. By the time the arena debate drew to a close in late 1997, the liberal-labor alliance had mutated into a labor-Left alliance with a new agenda, new allies, and new leaders. A quiet revolution inside Local 11 of the Hotel Employees and Restaurant Employees Union set in motion transformations that would acquire definitive form by the time arena construction began.

Despite the Latinization of Los Angeles County's workforce, Local 11's leaders insisted that meetings be conducted in English; they discouraged further contact with their members by closing the local's office doors at 4:00 P.M. The local's Anglo leaders ignored Latinos at their own peril. The major hotels were replacing union employees with nonunion immigrants while the local expended its energies in protecting member benefits. In 1987, the rank and file, led by Maria Elena Durazo, the local's worker representative, filed a lawsuit challenging the leadership's refusal to conduct meetings in Spanish. The local elected Durazo president on the strength of that challenge, but the international retaliated; it placed the local under trusteeship. Two years later, the membership reelected Durazo president, and the result was allowed to stand.[6]

From the start, Durazo's commitment to organizing immigrant Latino workers went against conventional wisdom. Prior to the 1990s, national labor leaders remained convinced that the fear of deportation prevented undocumented Latinos from joining unions. Many also assumed that because Latinos were concentrated in the so-called service industries, those industries had less strategic value than the manufacturing industries that relied on skilled workers.[7] Business unionism had failed to realize that the line separating primary manufacturing and secondary service industries had blurred. The post-Fordist factory worker not only manufactured multiple products, but performed services as well. Moreover, the conditions that made labor unions strong in the 1950s began to vanish in the 1960s. The corporations did what they could to break their social contract with labor. They refused to pay social benefits and exported or erased millions of manufacturing jobs typically represented by unions. The low-wage, so-called low-skill, and nonunionized service sector outgrew the manufacturing sector as the manufacturing sector became polarized from within. Automation and computerization eliminated the old skilled jobs from which unions had drawn their strength, and employers sought immigrant workers for the low-skilled jobs that remained. By the time Durazo and other Latino organizers rose to union leadership, the proportion of organized workers in Los Angeles County had dropped from 25 percent in the 1950s to 15.5 percent in 1993. Meanwhile, the proportion of Latinos employed in the manufacturing and service industries increased until it reached about half of both sectors by 1990.[8]

Where their predecessors saw weakness and decline, Durazo and other Latino organizers saw potential strength. They proposed to reinvent the county's service sector unions as a social movement. Under Durazo's leadership, the thirteen thousand–member local thwarted hotel owners' efforts to crush it while protecting existing contracts and winning new ones in the midst of a recession. Inside the union hall, meetings were opened up to passionate, multilingual debate. Outside, the local's professional staff focused their energies on organizing instead of handling member grievances. The local complemented its customary financial support of national political campaigns by putting rank and filers on the street to register recently naturalized Latinos to vote and to canvass the homes of union members and new citizens at election time.[9]

Durazo, operating in one of the world's most media-saturated environments, also demonstrated a pragmatic grasp of the symbolic role culture plays in the organizing process, starting with the linguistic needs of an immigrant workforce. Besides conducting meetings in Spanish and English, she encouraged once-silent immigrant workers to practice the militant organizing skills learned in Mexican and Central American labor struggles. The local's previous leaders had failed to value the long history of militant Latino labor organizing in the United States and Latin America. Durazo also resisted calling a strike, because doing so would give hotel owners an excuse to fire workers and replace them with other immigrant workers. Instead, the local expanded its community networks and changed its discursive strategy in order to bring new social forces to bear upon the hotel owners. One such countervailing force appeared in the early 1990s, when hotel occupancy rates in Los Angeles dropped to 30 percent.[10]

Bad public relations could be a powerful union weapon in an industry that increasingly relied upon symbolism and imagery to market its services. The tourist industry's marketing of the city's cultural landscape contributed directly to the appeal of upscale hotels.[11] Hotels also invest in cultivating images of hedonistic fantasy, social and spatial exclusivity, and policelike security to entice their customers. Tourists do not visit hotels to be reminded of the social inequalities and violence of everyday life. The sight of angry pickets runs counter to these expectations. A picket line or well-timed counteradvertising campaign can change a hotel's fantasy landscape from a theater of private consumption to a theater of class conflict.

A month before the 1992 riot exploded, and in the midst of contract negotiations, Local 11 released a video documentary titled *Los Angeles: City on the Edge* to convention planners nationwide. The video predicted that a tourist industry that had grown rich by increasing social inequality would push Los Angeles to the brink of a "disastrous confrontation." The documentary outraged business leaders. A union had had the temerity to do what the tourist industry has always done—represent a city in a way that was advantageous to its interests.[12] The video was no fluke. The local has since collaborated with local artists on an English/Spanish *fotonovela* that gives the union's views of its boycott of the New Otani Hotel. This work is an agitational narrative in the form of a pulp crime story about a Latina house-keeper falsely accused of stealing a laptop computer. Its wild-eyed narrator explains at one point that the local tourist industry that sells Los Angeles "as a tourist Mecca" also fosters the "social conditions" that hurt tourism. Paying the lowest wages possible fuels the poverty and despair that produce crime.[13] Local 11 and other Latino-led unions also made their discursive influence felt statewide by mobilizing labor in California to reject Proposition 187's anti-immigrant provisions.[14]

Then, in 1993, Durazo's local invested about $100,000 to found what eventually became the Los Angeles Alliance for a New Economy (LAANE), the strategy-making head of an increasingly vibrant alliance of grassroots organizations that formed today's Living Wage Coalition. "She was the visionary," Madeline Janis-Aparicio, LAANE's executive director, has said of Durazo. "She recruited me, she brought me on staff, and paid my salary to set up LAANE."[15]

The pair made a dynamic match. Durazo has a law degree from People's College of Law in Los Angeles, and her résumé before she arrived at Local 11 included organizing stints with the Center for Autonomous Social Action (CASA) and the International Ladies Garment Workers Union (ILGWU); she was among the first Latina leaders to organize undocumented immigrant Latino workers. Before heading LAANE, Janis-Aparicio had graduated from UCLA's law school and served from 1990 to 1993 as director of CARECEN, a Central American immigrant-advocate group. Prior to and after leading CARECEN, Janis-Aparicio worked for Latham & Watkins under George Mihlsten, the region's leading developer lobbyist. Janis-Aparicio, one might say, is also Latina by marriage and culture. A Los Angeles native of Jewish ancestry, she learned Spanish when her parents moved to Mexico City. She is married to Salvadoran artist Edgar Aparicio. And like Durazo, Janis-Aparicio has cultivated Latino and Latina leadership.[16]

Eight of LAANE's thirteen directors, starting with its president, are Latino; nine are women. The alliance has its own sources of support and draws its members from more than sixty progressive, multiethnic community groups, labor organizations, and church groups, such as Clergy and Laity United for Economic Justice (CLUE). Durazo is LAANE's president. Miguel Contreras, Durazo's husband and executive secretary of the powerful Los Angeles County Federation of Labor, and Councilwoman Jackie

Goldberg also sit on LAANE's executive committee. Each has played an important role in the movement to improve life for immigrant workers and in crafting the city's new labor-Left agenda; Janis-Aparicio, however, is credited with bringing the coalition's pieces together.[17]

Under her leadership, LAANE abandoned the slow-growth agenda advanced by progressive and environmentally minded liberals to focus on building a coalition around the class issues of the 1990s, specifically, raising the wages of the county's fastest-growing and largest job sector—the low-wage service jobs generated by culture-based industries. Although Los Angeles County's unemployment rate has dropped to 6.1 percent with rapid growth, many of the jobs being created are in such culture-based industries as the restaurant and garment industries, which pay workers minimum and subminimum wages to produce "style-" and "fashion-based" commodities and services.[18] Harold Meyerson writes that "L.A.'s vast immigrant influx has enabled low-end employers to depress wages throughout entire industries and sectors—so much so that native-born Mexican American men were making a lower percentage of the average white-male wage in 1989 than they were in 1959."[19] A comparative study of tax returns for a two-year period beginning in 1994 indeed shows that the number of middle-class households in Los Angeles County continued to shrink. The proportion of households making between $40,000 and $100,000 each year suffered a 7.7 percent decline, shrinking this upper-income bracket from 30 percent of county residents to 26 percent during the two-year period. The proportion of households making between $100,000 and $500,000 annually grew by 29.7 percent, although these households constituted only 7.3 percent of the county's populace. Likewise, households earning more than $500,000 grew by 40.2 percent, although they constituted only .5 percent of county residents. The fastest rate of income growth affected the least people, whereas the majority of families living at or near the bottom of the income pyramid showed the slowest progress. Lower-middle-class households, which made between $20,000 and $40,000 annually, increased by 6.7 percent to make up 25 percent of the county's total population. The proportion of households earning less than $20,000 annually, a solidly blue-collar income bracket, grew by 13.5 percent, swelling to 41 percent the proportion of county residents living under the poverty level.[20]

Much of that 41 percent lived in the newly Latinized Westlake, Pico-Union, and Central Los Angeles neighborhoods arrayed in a semicircle of poverty surrounding the arena. A survey conducted by the city's redevelopment agency found that the average income of families living closest to the arena earned less than $15,000 annually.[21] Contrary to popular perception,

From left, Richard L. Trumka, secretary treasurer of the AFL-CIO; Maria Elena Durazo; and Miguel Contreras at "Stars and Strikes Dinner," March 9, 1996. Photograph courtesy of the Southern California Library for Social Studies and Research; reprinted by permission.

low wages earned in the downtown garment industry, toy factories, and produce warehouses, and in Westside gardening and housekeeping jobs, and not welfare abuse, fuel poverty in this sector. In addition to enduring the highest levels of overcrowding and the lowest levels of educational preparation, Latinos there had suffered some of the lowest levels of political participation. For example, in 1992, Mark Ridley-Thomas's Eighth Council District was 30 percent Latino, yet only 3 percent of registered voters in the district were Latino. In Rita Walters's Ninth District, which includes that corner of downtown where the arena was eventually built, Latinos made up 63 percent of the population in 1992, but less than 8 percent of registered voters.[22]

With neighborhoods such as these in mind, an array of groups, including LAANE, allied themselves to pass a living wage ordinance in Los Angeles. The proposed ordinance required employers contracted by the city to provide city services and firms that receive municipal subsidies to pay employees $7.39 an hour with benefits or $8.64 without. The arena debate, which coincided with LAANE's living wage campaign, gave the coalition its first chance to test its strategies and discover its weaknesses.

In April 1997, about nine months after most Los Angeles residents

Ed Roski, left, and Mark Ridley-Thomas pushing Coliseum proposal. Photograph courtesy of the *L.A. Business Journal*; reprinted with permission.

learned of the plan to build an arena downtown, LAANE, under City Councilwoman Jackie Goldberg's leadership, rallied the votes to override Mayor Richard Riordan's veto and pass the law known as the living wage ordinance.[23] A month earlier, Riordan had vetoed a previous council vote on the measure, arguing that it would make Los Angeles less welcoming to business. Members of the Chamber of Commerce and the Central City Association, still a blue-blood mouthpiece, claimed the ordinance would bankrupt businesses and cause the loss of thousands of jobs. LAANE said its studies showed the ordinance would benefit about eight thousand jobs, a far cry from the numbers claimed by opponents. The Living Wage Coalition, led by LAANE's strategy and research on the economic disparities in the Los Angeles job market, prevailed in the end, but not before the coalition's internal divisions were revealed.

The Los Angeles County Federation of Labor, the coalition's most powerful member as the representative of 240 member unions, confused its allies when it endorsed the reelection campaign of Mayor Riordan, who opposed the ordinance. Complicating matters further, federation president Miguel Contreras and Local 11's Durazo signed on early with the mayor's arena project, expecting union jobs in return for his support.[24] LAANE members pressed Contreras to clarify his loyalties. He responded with an open letter to Riordan stating that the Federation of Labor would oppose the mayor's efforts to weaken the ordinance. Two weeks later, after LAANE's strenuous lobbying and fence-mending, rank-and-file federation members voted to take a neutral position on Riordan's reelection bid.[25]

Meanwhile, LAANE took a page from Local 11's media tactics. Actor David Clennon, playing Dickens's Jacob Marley, dragged death's chains into the City Council chambers to appeal to the consciences of council members by portraying Mayor Riordan as the city's new Scrooge. LAANE videotaped the moment for use in future organizing, and the council passed the ordinance with a veto-proof majority, winning last-minute support from Councilman Wachs, the arena's most vocal critic. Contrasting what he had heard during the arena and living wage debates, Wachs signaled LAANE's plan to slip a living wage provision into the final arena agreement:

> Your heart tells you that something is terribly wrong when a person who is willing to work day in and day out can't make a living wage. Nowhere has that been made more clear to me than on the recent [arena] debate. . . . I sat here and watched one prominent businessperson after another . . . beg this council to give tens of millions of dollars to the developers who are going to own the arena, and to the millionaires who are going to play in [it]. . . . The least they can give is a living wage to the people who are going to live [near] the arena.[26]

Although the local media characterized the vote as symbolic, the Living Wage Coalition's arguments and data had won the City Council's support and softened the mayor's opposition. But again, the interests of coalition member organizations diverged.

The Federation of Labor's members still remained wedded to business unionism's pro-development philosophy, prodding member unions to back the mayor's subsidy package by contributing to key City Council members. "The strategy there was to basically ensure, by supporting the project, that they would provide good jobs for the community," Janis-Aparicio has noted. But early union support for the arena trumped LAANE's ability to pressure developers to win ironclad commitments on such issues as job recruitment, job training, and minority business contracting.[27]

In May 1997, a month after the passage of the living wage ordinance, the arena project won the second in a series of City Council approval votes. The council's early support for the arena, particularly among members who had supported the living wage ordinance, further restricted the coalition's bargaining options. Even if the coalition had wanted to, persuading council members such as Hernandez and Ridley-Thomas to reverse their votes would have been difficult. Like the unions, the council's more progressive members had given their support away early and pressured developers to hire, train, and subcontract local residents and business owners, implement the ordinance, and fund replacement housing for 250 residents displaced by the project. At moments when negotiations stalled, Councilwoman Goldberg made behind-the-scenes threats to withhold her vote if certain conditions were not met.[28] But in the end, only Councilwoman Rita Walters reversed her vote—not nearly enough to topple an eleven-vote pro-arena majority.[29]

LAANE's leaders had little choice but to trust their council allies to do the right thing as they bargained for a union-friendly, living wage arena. Their only potential leverage came from Councilman Wachs, who threatened to qualify an initiative to let voters decide whether the developers should receive millions in public financing. But LAANE's decision to pursue a low-profile negotiating posture meant it had no direct way to benefit from Wachs's initiative drive. According to Janis-Aparicio, the coalition realized that instead of bargaining from a position of strength, it would have to pressure the developers and the city to honor promises after the project was completed. At that point in the debate, LAANE "hadn't developed the power base or the language to frame the debate."[30] The media coverage reflects Janis-Aparicio's assessment. We could not find any news stories in the local press coverage that detailed LAANE's reasons for pressuring arena developers to honor the living wage law.[31] From the start of the arena debate, blue bloods and developers maintained the discursive initiative.

As early as May 1995, newspapers in Denver, Colorado, ran stories describing Philip Anschutz's plans to build a new sports arena in downtown Los Angeles in a joint venture with Edward P. Roski Jr. By October of that year, the Denver papers reported that Anschutz and Roski, after having concluded their takeover of the Los Angeles Kings hockey team, were already developing plans to build a multithemed arena in Los Angeles for the Kings and the NBA's Lakers. In the months during and following these reports, Roski, Anschutz, and their representatives quietly presented their ideas to L.A. city officials and the blue bloods before officially announcing their plan the following year.[32]

Public records show that between March 1996 and March 1998 Anschutz and Roski—through their L.A. Arena Co. partnership and Roski's Majestic Realty—paid nearly $580,000 to lobbyists and public relations operatives to orchestrate a multifaceted pro-arena public relations campaign. Majestic and the L.A. Arena Co. paid Latham & Watkins almost $149,000 for its lobbying services. Except for a 134-word wire brief, the developer's largesse received no media coverage.[33]

Janis-Aparicio has had firsthand experience working for George Mihlsten, the chief strategist at Latham & Watkins. She has described him as "a consensus builder in the worst way" because he used organizing tactics that created the appearance of widespread voter support. He filled the City Council chambers with pro-arena constituents whom the council members, because of debts owed and promises made, could not afford to ignore.[34] And, when all else failed, Mihlsten resorted to economic blackmail. The lobbyist, who had sparked a bidding war between Long Beach and Anaheim over a Disney water theme park and had extracted millions of dollars in concessions for the DreamWorks studios in Playa Vista, told the council that his clients would build the arena in Inglewood if they vacillated. The threat pitted needy community against needy community. "Now which community is in greater need?" Greg Nelson, a Wachs aide, has put it, posing the choice Mihlsten offered the council: the African Americans and Latinos "who live within a three-mile radius of Inglewood, or the mostly Latino community that lives around the Convention Center?"[35] The neighborhoods surrounding the arena have suffered some of the city's highest poverty levels. Meanwhile, Inglewood, a working-class city that is 50 percent African American and nearly 40 percent Latino, was expected to face job losses and a $1.5 million drop in annual tax revenues after the Kings and Lakers left the Great Western Forum in 1999.[36] Massive cuts in aid to housing, schools, and social services, the growing inequality in both individual earnings and family income, and scapegoating initiatives such as Proposition 187 had further intensified competition among all cities. That climate of competition perfectly suited a developer like Roski, who built his empire by using the scarcity of jobs and investment capital to bargain for more public subsidies. Author and urban planner William Fulton has noted:

> A lot of the big guys who own major league teams are also developers. Guys like that know how to hold government hostage, how to grease things politically. That's why they're so good at extracting things from government when they become sports team owners. The sports facility simply becomes another aspect of the political economic game the developers and local government are already playing.[37]

Meanwhile, the developers and the unions directed campaign contributions to the receptive council members. Whereas council members Wachs, Walters, and Nate Holden voiced opposition early, Hernandez and Ridley-Thomas expressed a willingness to listen and to deal on behalf of their job-starved districts. The arena developers, the blue bloods, the unions, and building trades groups made sure the council members did not lose interest. That interest was especially evident in Ridley-Thomas, who, from the beginning, viewed the arena as a means to advance his own quest to return a National Football League franchise to the Los Angeles Memorial Coliseum.[38] Nor could the pro-arena lobby risk antagonizing council members who might mobilize the impoverished neighborhoods surrounding the arena against the project. After all, residents there could justifiably argue that the arena represented another example of downtown gobbling up subsidies that could be better invested in outlying neighborhoods.

City Council campaign contribution records for 1995, 1996, 1997, and 1998 show that arena developers, their corporate operatives and blue-blood allies, together with unions and construction trades groups that hoped to benefit from the project, funneled about $13,430 to Hernandez and $16,765 to Ridley-Thomas, for a total of $30,195. More than half of the contributions came from arena developers, lobbyists, and blue bloods. Riordan, a staunch arena backer and major downtown property owner, was himself a player in the contest. The law firm hired to lobby on behalf of the arena project contributed $6,750. The political action committee controlled by Riordan's law firm, his law partners, and the Central City Association, an organization of developers, construction firms, leasing agents, and real estate companies that remains a mouthpiece for downtown property interests, contributed $2,100. Federation of Labor members, such as Durazo's Local 11, and construction trades organizations, such as the Engineering Contractors Association, which publicly supported the arena project, contributed $12,580.[39] Although not excessively generous, these contributions represented an integral part of the pro-arena campaign.

Moreover, Mayor Riordan had already begun to cultivate close ties to Ridley-Thomas and Hernandez by placing them on important city panels, such as the Community Redevelopment Agency. By the time the arena lobbying began, both council members understood the kinds of rewards the mayor could deliver if they backed the centerpiece of his downtown development plan. Hernandez stood to bolster his credibility and progressive credentials by delivering jobs, job training, and business contracts for his constituents. Ridley-Thomas had even more to gain from supporting the mayor's pet project. Ridley-Thomas had found a champion who might yet summon the roughly $800 million in private and public funds needed to secure an NFL franchise and modernize the aging Coliseum, which is located in his district. Campaign contributions cannot hold a candle to a highly visible development in his district, the idea of prolonged access to the developers who want to return an NFL team to the refurbished stadium, or the power that comes from serving on government panels that regulate these investments. Ridley-Thomas benefited early from this special access. In October 1996, Roski, responding to a request from Ridley-Thomas, contributed $10,000 to the opponents of Proposition 209, the anti-affirmative action measure.[40]

Mihlsten's simulated consensus building inside City Hall also coincided with the rebirth of boosterism at the *Los Angeles Times*. For most of the twentieth century, the paper was, among other things, a shamelessly blatant supporter of the Chandler family's business interests and virulently conservative Republican politics. As David Halberstam writes: "The friends of the Chandlers were written about as they wished; their enemies were deprived of space, or attacked. What was not printed was as important as what was printed." The *Times*, Halberstam adds, when judged according to journalism's democratic ideals, "was a manifestly unfair newspaper; it appealed to ignorance and prejudice and it fanned passions."[41] And it was powerful, not only dominating California's Republican Party, but filling the discursive vacuum left by the decline of both parties before television made party organizations almost irrelevant. The family built the paper's power base by pursuing business interests first, primarily in real estate development, and publishing interests second. Experience had rewarded the Chandlers for using the paper to promote projects that increased the value of their sprawling real estate holdings. It is not surprising, given the family's vast property and business holdings, that keeping conflicts of interest out of the *Times* was a full-time job for the paper's editors.

However, starting in the 1950s under Norman Chandler, and continuing in the 1960s, when his son, Otis Chandler, took over as publisher, the paper's boosterism was moderated. Norman began to restrain the family's inclination to use the *Times* overtly to promote its business interests, and Otis appointed new corporate managers and editors at the paper to foster a new kind of professional journalism. In time, Otis succeeded, winning awards for the *Times* and the respect of his competitors by redefining the paper's journalistic culture. His new managers and editors pursued the greater corporate good, which included the corporation's interests, under the protective mantle of professionalism and journalistic impartiality. The corporation's interests encompassed not only the obvious—promotion of Times Mirror media enterprises and products—but the development of a billion-dollar real estate business through continued support for the politics of growth, which included publicly subsidized redevelopment. For example, Times Mirror properties located inside the Bunker Hill redevelopment project have seen their values soar thanks to millions of dollars in public and private investment. In 1959, the year the redevelopment of Bunker Hill started, the assessed value of its twenty-five city blocks was $20.3 million. After thirty-two years of redevelopment, Bunker Hill's assessed property value had soared to $2.8 billion. The twenty-two parcels of Times-owned property inside the Bunker Hill project area, which were worth $52.4 million in 1982, reaped their share of redevelopment's rewards.[42] The corporate discourse of professional journalism allowed the Times to continue promoting freeway, water, and redevelopment projects, but expressed through the neutral optimism of the California Dream. The expanding new suburbs produced legions of new middle-class readers and the nightmare of uncontrolled growth. Beyond Southern California, meanwhile, new forces were quietly reorganizing the newspaper industry.

By the 1980s, the next phase of the "corporatization" of the newspaper industry was well under way. Giant media conglomerates gobbled up profitable newspapers while discarding economically marginal papers. To maintain profit margins of as high as 20 percent, the new corporate managers demanded results. Newsrooms were restructured, and the competition to improve share values increasingly shaped editorial agendas. At first, the *Times* had been successful enough to resist the worst of these trends, but declining profit margins took their toll. By the early 1990s, the paper initiated its first round of downsizing, cost cutting, and pandering to advertisers, but the Chandler family, which continued to hold a controlling interest in Times Mirror, remained dissatisfied with the results.

Mark Willes, former chairman and CEO of General Mills, was appointed chairman and CEO of Times Mirror in 1995 to accelerate the process. In order to reverse falling profits and lift stagnant stock prices, Willes vowed to finish the job of pulling Times Mirror's media businesses into the mainstream of corporate media. He betrayed not a twinge of guilt when he vowed to introduce the "brand-management techniques he learned at General Mills to boost circulation and attract advertisers." *Brand management* means several things to Willes. Like the broadcast media, which decades earlier had redefined network and local news programs as profit centers instead of public servants, every part of the Times Mirror empire would be accountable to the bottom line. And like the technological proliferation of media that revolutionized media marketing to target the most lucrative market segments instead of mass audiences, nothing ensured profitability more than focus. Every media product would provide a clearly defined service for a targeted demographic market segment with plenty of disposable income. Each section would set its own editorial and advertising goals, and then try to reach them. To ensure coordination,

Willes pledged to blow up the wall that had traditionally separated editorial from advertising departments.[43] That wall, which had been erected over the decades to reduce advertiser influence on editorial coverage, and thus ensure editorial independence, now represented an obstacle to the complete dominance of market ideology in the newsroom. That barrier would have to be battered down. Like the world's media conglomerates, Times Mirror would seize every opportunity to execute its marketing plans and cross-promote its editorial products. Readers would be constructed as consumers first and citizen readers last, further weakening the paper's already shaky commitment to socially responsible journalism.

Willes began to impose his disciplinary regime in 1995, when he cut 700 jobs at the *Times*, 150 of them from the editorial staff, and closed its unprofitable sections. He also eliminated a few thousand more jobs at the other Times Mirror media enterprises and shut down the *Baltimore Evening Sun* and *Newsday*'s Manhattan edition. At the *Times*, he appointed a business manager for each section to make sure his strategic plan would be implemented. The Willes strategy eventually produced dramatic results, boosting Times Mirror stock prices to record levels. Not surprisingly, it also sparked controversy. Journalists inside and outside the *Times* said they feared that advertisers would now be able to dictate the kinds of coverage they wanted.[44] Willes's critics, however, ignored his return to boosterism.

If pre-Willes *Times* reporters and editors had already earned a reputation for "preferring big investigations about small fry," and of being too smugly middle-class to care about the city's working-class underdogs, then expecting an outbreak of populist sentiment in the newsroom after his arrival was inconceivable.[45] "If you still think that we are the ink-stained wretches of yore, you are mistaken," said one *Times* reporter, who spoke on the condition that her name be withheld. "We are all upper-middle-class and college-educated. We are no longer the working-class heroes of the past. I think this a social reality that influences all of journalism, which is why you don't see more critical coverage of corporations. We share similar assumptions, the same ideas as the business community. This is a gradual evolutionary process that has changed the nature of journalism." Another highly regarded veteran reporter who asked not to be identified agreed with his colleague's assessment: "I don't think it ever gets to the point where the reporter proposes a story the editors will later decide to kill. The reporter may not even think they're censoring their own ideas. Instead, they assume that the paper's corporate perspective is the same as the public's perspective."[46]

Willes's contribution was to make *Times* editors and reporters more prone to corporate discipline when he implemented his downsizing and restructuring plans. "People don't feel motivated to take risks, and everybody is overworked," one reporter said. "We are so thinly spread that everybody is doing the work of three people." These conditions, she believes, encourage a subtle form of self-censorship. "I think it's more like, maybe I won't go after this story. Why? Because all they hear from their editors is, 'Can you make this shorter?' Who wants to invest a big effort in an investigative piece just to see it end up on the cutting room floor?"[47] Other staffers said that the hegemony of market-oriented journalism inside the newsroom caused the defection of thirty of the paper's best reporters and editors to the *New York Times*.[48] Willes's critics also overlooked the new civic role he envisioned for the paper. The man *Times* employees dubbed the "cereal killer" promised to take the paper's civic involvement to another level. Focusing media attention on a problem and then waiting for government to address it was no longer enough. The *Times* would again play a fixer's role. "We are not talking about running things. But we are talking about using the platform and the spotlight of a great newspaper to help others who have the desire and focus to make change."[49] The "others" Willes sought to help included arena developers, his blue-blood colleagues, and the Chandler family itself. He dispensed that help in several forms.

Like other publishers who have used their editorial pages to lead crusades, Willes set the agenda for the paper's opinion pages. He boosted the arena in the name of downtown development, which benefited Times Mirror's still major real estate holdings there, and reasserted the blue-blood historic entitlement to dictate downtown development policy. Willes also resorted to the news management techniques of earlier days when he personally promoted the arena as a news story. At the same time, *Times* news coverage of the project was characterized by an astounding lack of curiosity and narrowness of focus. The *Times* essentially reported the city's biggest downtown development project as sports and local-government stories, a deployment of resources that suited the Willes agenda. Predictably, the sports reporters, with their adolescent pro-sports bias and ignorance of the political economy of downtown development, implicitly favored a new arena, while the paper's Metro reporters contented themselves with following the City Council debate and developer responses and press releases. A survey of fifty-five *Los Angeles Times* arena stories published during the period leading up to the project's final official approval shows that 36.36 percent of them were generated by the City Council and the developers. Sports reporters wrote another 36.36 percent of the arena stories. In other words, 72.72 percent of the arena stories were either generated by the City Council-developer debate or were written by the paper's sports reporters. The remaining fifteen opinion and editorial commentary pieces were either strongly supportive or moderately critical of the project. About 12.72 percent of these stories were strongly favorable; 14.54 percent of the editorials criticized the project over such procedural issues as developer secrecy, not the merits of the project itself.[50] In the end, *Times* reporters let the pro-arena publicity juggernaut dictate where and how the arena debate would unfold. For the most part, only arena opposition expressed from within the City Council chambers would be heard, limiting the contest to a more controllable one-front engagement. But it would take the arena's completion and a scandal to show just how timid the *Times* reporters had become and just how bold the boosters had grown.

Campaign contributions, lobbying, and media management could not erase a particular vulnerability. The power and wealth wielded by the pro-arena forces in promoting another downtown project made the San Fernando Valley's alienated voters more receptive to arguments that privilege fiscal prudence and demands for open government. Councilman Wachs capitalized on these typically middle-class resentments early, targeting that part of the arena proposal that required $70.5 million in city subsidies to build a new twenty thousand–seat home for the NBA's Lakers and NHL's Kings. Borrowing from the Left's rhetoric, Wachs, a centrist Democrat, described the deal approved by the City Council in May 1997 as a corporate welfare package that gave the arena developers subsidies that would saddle taxpayers with more debt.

In the deal initially approved by the City Council, arena developers were not required to repay the city's subsidies or to pay for the use of city property for twenty-five years. The city, in turn, promised to collect parking revenues from the city-owned Convention Center and assorted ticket, utility, business, and sales taxes to repay the bond the city would float to underwrite the project. The city, in the meantime, promised to guarantee the bond with money from its general fund, but acknowledged financial risks. The arena, the city estimated, could raise as much as $11.4 million a year in annual revenues, or lose $32 million over a twenty-five–year period if exorbitant ticket prices and frightening neighborhoods drove fans away.[51]

Seventeen prominent academics sided with Wachs, arguing that building state-of-the-art arenas in inner cities will not halt the inexorable outflow of investment capital and white-collar jobs to the suburbs. None of the downtown arenas built in the 1990s, they argued, have come even close to delivering the economic or image boosts their promoters had promised.

Staples Center. Photograph by Rodolfo D. Torres.

In every city where a new arena has been built, the number of new jobs created has accounted for only a fraction of the region's job market.[52] Despite
this unimpressive record, cities guaranteed team owners, developers, and
players millions in tax subsidies while slashing welfare budgets for the poor.
According to one estimate, taxpayers will end up paying almost 60 percent
of the $12 billion invested in building arenas for the four major profes-
sional leagues between 1987 and 2000.[53] Professors Robert Baade and Alan
Sanderson conclude that the benefits of a publicly subsidized sports industry flow in one direction: the "owners and players are the primary beneficia-
ries of stadium and game spending, and their wealth and earnings are
largely spent in the communities in which they reside, or even out of
state—not in the communities where their team plays. Without direct
spending around the stadium, there is nothing to multiply." To the contrary,
they argue,

> constructing a stadium at public expense creates a reverse Robin
> Hood effect—taking from the poor and giving to the rich. Tax-
> payers in general end up increasing the wealth of franchise owners
> and players, and subsidizing the entertainment of fans who fill the
> stands on any given Sunday. And we know without question that
> owners, players, and NFL season ticket-holders are more affluent
> than the public at large.[54]

Prophetically, the critics also insisted that new arenas modeled upon multitheme parks are simply too profitable to require public subsidies. These sports cathedrals of the future, aside from earning revenues from ticket sales and TV rights, profit from luxury box seats, indoor shopping, hotels, and building-sized electronic signs blinking ads to freeway commuters. Taxpayers rarely vote on whether their cities should subsidize these projects or entertain competing bids from other teams or arena developers, because major league franchising rules discourage cities from hosting more than one team. As the arena debate in Los Angeles wore on, the fiscal arguments criticizing the project began to resonate with voters, and so increased Wachs's ability to exact concessions from the developers and their elite allies.

But LAANE's low-key lobbying and the pro-development bias of its union members prevented the Living Wage Coalition from exploiting Wachs's fiscal critique. LAANE could have filled in the gaps in Wachs's argument. It could have framed the arena as an object lesson in corporate welfare, putting the city's downtown development history on trial to show how Roski represented the latest in a long line of developers who have privatized the city's planning and policy-making power. It didn't. With no vocal progressive opposition, the arena debate thus devolved into a contest between downtown boosterism and fiscal conservatism.[55] The blue bloods emphasized the arena's potential payoffs and avoided probing the developers' biographies. Mayor Riordan and the downtown boosters claimed that spending millions for a downtown arena was essential to the city's survival. "Downtown is the heart of Los Angeles, and if we let it die, the whole city dies too," City Council President John Ferraro told the *L.A. Times*.[56] The *Times* delivered its message with urgency. One sports columnist advised the city to "hurry." Roski and Anschutz were losing patience, the sportswriter warned. "This deal is about as good as it can get."[57] The *Times* also criticized the city's bureaucratic sluggishness, echoing arguments Riordan made to get his way at City Hall.

The *Times*, still dominant among the blue-blood elite, had narrowed the debate leading up to the City Council's May 23, 1997, project approval vote. In its editorials, the public statements of corporate brass, and editorials by scholars such as Kevin Starr, the paper reverted to its role of downtown booster, but strenuously avoided reconsidering the arena's political significance in light of the city's rapacious downtown development legacy. One editorial advised the council members that the "grinding debate over social and political concerns" had "obscured the many potential benefits that an arena offers to Los Angeles."[58] Meanwhile, Mark Willes used his special media access to explain the arena's larger significance to a compliant *Times* reporter:

> We have an almost historic opportunity, with the cathedral, with Disney Hall, to literally start to make a significant impact on the economic vibrancy of downtown. In a way, it doesn't have anything to do with music, it has everything to do with the kind of city we live in.[59]

Willes, who had recently joined the board of the Disney Hall's fund-raising committee and pledged $5 million to keep the project alive, conveniently overlooked the millions of public dollars already invested in the project and the blue bloods' failure to push the long-stalled project forward after a decade of setbacks.[60]

The first of these came in April 1992, when a televised multiracial riot shattered the city's carefully constructed image as the multicultural capital of the Pacific Rim. The next came in 1993, when the courts halted the Community Redevelopment Agency from diverting any further property taxes to downtown projects. The courts ruled that the agency had violated the terms of a 1977 decision that set a $750 million cap on the amount of tax dollars the agency could invest in the 1,549-acre redevelopment zone known as the Central Business District, which includes the infamous Bunker Hill development. The City Council tried to override the court's ruling, passing an ordinance that lifted the spending cap and extended the CRA's life for another fifteen years. The courts rescinded the council's action, but only after more than $1.6 billion of property tax money—or more than twice the amount stipulated in the 1977 court ruling—had flowed into the CBD.[61] By the time the courts turned off the CRA's spigot in 1995, the blue bloods, who had counted on their ability to subsidize their favorite developers, were left with a poorer and weaker agency. As the CRA appealed the decision, the blue bloods discovered that the Walt Disney Concert Hall project, which started so brilliantly in 1987 with $103 million in Disney family gifts, was in disarray and desperately short of funds. Urban policy analyst William Fulton concluded that the blue bloods so bungled the project that they risked losing their viability as a ruling elite.[62]

By May 1997, however, Fulton's epitaph seemed premature. A year before, Eli Broad, a Southern California billionaire real estate and insurance magnate, joined Mayor Riordan on the Music Center board. Broad, a recent blue-blood recruit, took charge of fund-raising. Eventually he raised the more than $225 million needed to break ground in late 1999.[63] Rumors also circulated that the arena developers would sell part of their facility, teams included, to Rupert Murdoch, who had previously announced his desire to buy the Dodger Stadium and baseball franchise. Selling a piece of the arena and its teams to Murdoch, some sports fans and sportswriters feared, would put the city's soul in the hands of a global media magnate with a poor record of hometown loyalty. "Are Anschutz and Roski really owners, or merely developers who will flip their team—or teams—to the highest bidder once the arena is built?" asked *Times* sportswriter Bill Plaschke. "It's a shame they don't have more on their resume than two years of bad hockey."[64] Despite initial denials, Murdoch confirmed the rumors when he bought Dodger Stadium in April 1998 and disclosed that he had, after all, bought a 30 percent stake in the new arena.[65]

At the time the Murdoch rumors surfaced, the idea that Roski and Anschutz might be hiding something from the public did not raise suspicions. All but one member of the City Council bowed to Roski and Anschutz's demands that their agreements with the arena tenants, the L.A. Lakers and Kings, remain secret. But a deputy city attorney who had read the lease agreement affirmed that the Lakers and Kings had not made ironclad commitments to stay in their new home.[66] Now Wachs criticized the council for undermining the principle of open and honest government: "If they want public money, they have to play by our rules. . . . we've got to play by the public's rules. . . . It is a litmus test of honest and open public discourse."[67] On local radio talk shows, outraged callers pointed out that a Kings or Lakers departure would stick taxpayers with a debt of more than $70 million and a second, money-losing white elephant next door to the Convention Center, which the city subsidizes to the tune of $19 million a year.

The Wachs-led opposition began to take its toll. In late July, the City Council announced that it had begun to negotiate with the developers to determine which part of the agreement could be made public. Then, in mid-August, the city grappled with a double spectacle: the arrest of Councilman Hernandez on cocaine possession and a Wachs campaign to put an arena initiative on the ballot. The developers and blue bloods held their tongues on the Hernandez bust while they offered Wachs new concessions. Soon after, a *Times* story citing anonymous sources reported that the developers had agreed to repay the city's bond debt of about $6.8 million annually for the next twenty-five years even if they failed to obtain state subsidies. The *Times* claimed that these concessions made "City Council approval of the project a virtual slam-dunk."[68] *Times* columnist Bill Boyarsky, who in his columns had pushed the council to require the developers to disclose their lease agreements with their teams, wrote that the developers had deflated the arena opposition's objections before declaring his support for the project.[69] He appeared to be right. Despite their conciliatory gestures, the developers said that they had no intention of using their own money to repay the city's subsidy. Instead, they hoped the courts would allow them to shift the debt burden from the taxpayers to sports fans in the form of higher ticket prices. Councilman Ridley-Thomas, who had previously voted to keep the developer and team agreement under wraps, also criticized Wachs's initiative drive as "myopic."[70] Ridley-Thomas insisted that "elected officials, not voters, should have control of economic development projects in the city because they are more likely to see the wisdom of investing in depressed neighborhoods," a sentiment reportedly echoed by the Federation of Labor's Contreras.[71] In opposing the initiative, Ridley-Thomas had contradicted his progressive image. He now expressed disdain for opening up economic planning to public vote, although such planning had historically excluded constituents in his district. The initiative unveiled on August 26 would, if passed, require a majority of voters to approve the use of city funds or bonds for development, construction, remodeling, or operation of "any professional sports facility." Its supporters had until December 24, 1997, to collect 61,170 valid signatures to qualify the measure for the June 2, 1998, ballot.[72]

The initiative, the *Los Angeles Times* responded, contained a "poison pill," a "retroactive clause" that would override any City Council decision to approve the arena project. The *Times* also said the measure blazed "with provocative language" and provisions that would "kill" the project.[73] Tim Leiweke, president of the Anschutz and Roski–owned Kings, raised the rhetoric a notch when he said that the Wachs initiative campaign "now potentially makes it impossible to do business with the city of Los Angeles." "Simply filing the initiative," the *Times* seconded, "threatened the city's ability to sell the project's bonds." The paper quoted a blue-blood attorney to back its claim. "If the bonds are to be secured by revenues from the arena, then an initiative, I would think, would prevent the issuance of bonds," said attorney Richard Jones, a municipal bond specialist with the Los Angeles law firm of O'Melveny & Myers.[74]

The idea that the city might wait until June before obtaining project bond financing struck at the very core of blue-blood power. Since the redevelopment projects of the late 1940s, L.A. elites had used the euphemism of "public and private partnership" to disguise their appropriations of local government's planning and policy-making apparatus. But now, in 1997, they confronted an opponent insolent enough to demand an active role in making urban economic policy. In essence, the *Times* said, policy-making equality would trigger an economic catastrophe. Efforts to democratize urban economic planning would hamper the city's ability to meet its development commitments because they would encourage "dissident" politicians to put all public-private partnerships to a popular vote. Passage of the initiative could threaten "major industrial and commercial projects, such as the Alameda Corridor, on which the government and railroads are cooperating in financing a high-speed freight line from the harbor to downtown." The paper punctuated this point by quoting the arena's "leading" advocate, Parks and Recreation Commission president Steven Soboroff: "It's a downhill bulldozer toward the end of public-private partnerships in the city."[75]

Wachs appeared to hold his ground under the onslaught. Two days later, however, the pressure produced its desired effect. Wachs struck a conciliatory note: he would stop the initiative if the developers could personally guarantee repayment of the city's $70 million subsidy without resorting to any add-on taxes. A week later, the city agreed to pay $12 million in land acquisition and site preparation costs. The developers promised to guarantee the project's $70.5 million financing package without charging add-on taxes. The City Council green-lighted the deal in late October.[76] Despite last-minute waffling, Wachs had bolstered his standing among his constituents. He could now say that he had done more than anyone else to defend taxpayer pocketbooks. His bargaining had cut the city's arena debt obligations by more than $58 million. He had stood up for the Valley and made the developers and blue bloods blink. Yet Wachs's fiscal arguments against downtown development revealed political limitations. They lost their oppositional standing as soon as the developers conceded on the debt issue and promised to reveal their agreements with the teams. Without their arguments for fiscal accountability and open government, the Wachs-led arena opponents could no longer pursue the corporate welfare issue at the moment when it had begun to resonate with middle-class voters.

LAANE, after months of behind-the-scenes bargaining, walked away from the arena battle with mixed results. It lost a valuable opportunity to build bridges to the suburbs and to inner-city communities of color when it failed to advance the issues of corporate welfare and downtown overdevelopment. The progressives could not yet play a role in fashioning a political agenda that would give Latinos, and other marginalized groups, a bigger voice in the city's economic planning and policy-making process. Moreover, the final arena deal stipulated that the developers would make every effort to hire and train workers living within a three-mile radius of the project. But the agreement did not establish specific employment or training targets, only that the developers would document their efforts for the city.

Janis-Aparicio acknowledges that LAANE will have to keep the heat on the developers and the city to ensure that the agreement's hiring and training provisions produce meaningful results.[77] Given its profitability, Wachs aide Greg Nelson has said that the final deal represented "a golden opportunity for arena developers to give back to the community. And they could have done it early on, and not have driven us to take up the initiative. The Latino community could have come up with a $20 million project, let's say, and been far better off."[78] The conviction of Councilman Hernandez, a vocal LAANE supporter, proved another setback. "He was substantially weakened by his personal problems," according to Janis-Aparicio. "There was a point where he just changed." That change came in the midst of the arena debate, which compromised his ability to serve LAANE and the Living Wage Coalition. "Since his recovery," she adds, "he is making the arguments for equity and justice issues again."[79]

LAANE's discoveries, however, do not erase the images of the meltdown of Latino political leadership. At the crucial moment when he could have joined Wachs to secure promises of long-term development for his district, Hernandez had taken refuge in a drug rehab program.[80] Eastside Councilman Richard Alatorre had also slipped out of the public negotiating picture when he became the target of an ethics probe investigating allegations that he had used his influence to secure favorable treatment for his wife's nonprofit fund-raising corporation. His credibility would suffer again. In an unrelated child custody case, Alatorre admitted overcoming a cocaine and alcohol addiction and then was caught in an apparent lie when a surprise court-ordered drug test revealed that he had recently ingested cocaine.[81] Although no Latinos publicly condoned Alatorre's and Hernandez's behavior, many asked in private why, over the years, the *Times* had not reported on its friends and allies with the same investigative zeal.

Still, LAANE and the Living Wage Coalition scored important successes that may pay off big in the long run. The arena development agreement guaranteed union access to the job site and a living wage for the arena's permanent jobs, a stipulation that could benefit as many as twelve hundred full-time arena service jobs.[82] The Living Wage Coalition's sensitivity to the class and ethnic composition of the low-wage workforce also inspired Latino participation without promoting an ethnic or racialized politics. And rather than continue to play a junior partner role to the developers or continue slow-growth opposition to development, LAANE forged a third option. It used its understanding of post-Fordist landscapes to intervene in local stealth government: those aspects of the political-economic planning process traditionally dominated by big business. The agreement LAANE hammered out with TrizecHahn, which is rebuilding Hollywood's Mann's Chinese Theatre into a huge multiscreened movie, hotel, and dining complex, illustrates the coalition's new thinking. LAANE discovered in the months after the arena deal's signing that the CRA, another stealth agency, could use its power to advance the living wage agenda. LAANE persuaded redevelopers to invest the $12.5 million economic development fee required by the CRA to build a hiring hall and pay living wages and health benefits to the seven to eight hundred workers the complex will hire, a dramatic departure from past practices.[83] Mayor Bradley's administration had pressured the CRA to finance low-cost housing in South-Central as a condition for continued downtown development. For the most part, the city's African American elected leadership supported these policies, a political-economic arrangement that produced short-term benefits and long-term weaknesses. The housing projects failed to rebuild South-Central's economic infrastructure, provide long-term employment, or come close to balancing decades of corporate welfare for downtown development. These failures, when combined with economic restructuring and Latino population growth, precipitated the exodus of African Americans from South-Central that has undercut the electability of African Americans in formerly safe districts. LAANE and the Living Wage Coalition, counting on disciplined union support and Councilwoman Jackie Goldberg's power to decide zoning matters in her district, struck out in a new policy direction. Goldberg insisted that LAANE search for creative ways to fund its agenda. "'Here's $12.5 million,'" Janis-Aparicio recalls Goldberg's instructions. "'What can we do with it?' Let's train one hundred organizers, let's cover health benefits, let's do this, let's do that. We brainstormed on other social uses of CRA funds as long as they were linked to our goals."[84]

Since bringing Mann's Chinese Theatre and Staples Center employees under the living wage umbrella, the Living Wage Coalition has gradually increased the number of airport security screeners, food concession workers, and other minimum wagers covered by the living wage at Los Angeles International Airport (LAX). Although this fortress of stealth government once seemed impenetrable, 750 employees at the federally regulated facility have received living wage increases. The airline subcontractors gave two reasons the remainder, as many as 3,000 other workers, did not qualify for living wage pay hikes: their wages were not solely subsidized by city-funded contracts, and federal regulations prohibit interference with airline rates, routes, and services.[85] The Living Wage Coalition next worked to close the loopholes. It built upon existing council support and favorable Spanish-language media coverage by attempting to dominate the language and imagery of the ensuing debate.[86] In August 1998, for example, living wage organizers brought agitprop into the City Council chambers. Their short play, *LAX Confidential: A Story of Greed, Abuse of Power and Injustice,* dramatized the life-and-death responsibilities of baggage checkers who earn the $5.75-an-hour minimum searching for concealed weapons. A wheelchair attendant said that she could not afford child care for her youngest son. A single Latina mother testified to the hardships of feeding, clothing, housing, and educating a family on the minimum wage. As winter approached, a handful of *Los Angeles Times* reporters and columnists responded with coverage that was either balanced or favorable when it focused upon compelling individual narratives.[87]

In November, a veto-proof council majority voted to amend the ordinance, after which the mayor indicated he would not block its implementation. The mayor's decision was expected to precipitate a showdown with LAX contractors, who had threatened to sue if forced into compliance.[88] The coalition responded with its own threat—it would not support a proposed $12 billion expansion of LAX if developers did not enforce the law. "We're going to the new developers . . . and saying, 'If you're going to go to the public table and ask for subsidies . . . then you have to guarantee a "living wage" and guarantee that workers have the right to organize,'" said Miguel Contreras, executive secretary of the Los Angeles Federation of Labor and Riordan appointee to the airport commission.[89] The coalition also secured a commitment from the city's Department of Water and Power to enforce the ordinance with its subcontractors and helped to pass living wage ordinances in West Hollywood and Pasadena. But even if the coalition prevails in every case, it will improve wages for about fourteen thousand employees, which is just a fraction of the roughly eight hundred thousand workers in the county who earn less than $8 an hour.[90] The campaign must thus be seen as an organizing tool in which the unions demonstrate what they can do for L.A.'s low-wage, mostly Latino workers and its endangered middle class.

At first, it seemed that no group made out like the arena developers. To begin with, the sponsorship deal showed that the $400 million project had never needed a penny of public subsidies. In December 1997, Roski and Anschutz closed a $100 million sponsorship deal in which Staples, Inc., the Massachusetts-based office products chain, bought the right to put its name all over the twenty thousand–seat facility. When the other sponsorship deals were tallied up, the *Los Angeles Business Journal* calculated that the arena project would generate from $404 million to $444 million, or enough to cover its construction costs and perhaps make some profit before the arena opened its doors.[91] Even the $58.5 million subsidy the developers lost thanks to Wachs will be made up later. Steven Soboroff, a real estate consultant appointed by Mayor Riordan to negotiate the arena deal, has stated that the $12 million paid by the CRA to buy and prepare the construction site will, after inflation and interest are factored in, equal the value of $70 million distributed over thirty years.[92]

The arena fits into a larger economic and discursive framework. In just a few years, in addition to its new landlord (Rupert Murdoch) for Dodger Stadium, downtown will get its first Catholic cathedral and a new concert hall. The construction and acquisitions represent new investments in downtown's symbolic economy that will disseminate, via Murdoch's networks, *Times* concert reviews, and papal photo ops, highly marketable images of the Los Angeles landscape. After the new cultural venues open, Anschutz, the fifth-richest American in 1999 with a fortune estimated at $16.5 billion, may enjoy a windfall from his newly merged South Pacific/Union Pacific Railroad thanks to the $2.4 billion in federal, state, and local subsidies paid to complete the twenty-mile-long Alameda Corridor.[93] By 2002, rail traffic between the rail yards north of Long Beach and east of downtown and the nation's two busiest ports at San Pedro and Long Beach is expected to at least triple when cash-strapped Pacific Rim nations increase the amount of merchandise they currently load onto Anschutz's trains.

For a while, no publicity seemed too difficult for the blue bloods to rewrite or evade. After all, the local media, led by the *Times*, had generally lacked the curiosity to question the "facts" that blue-blood and developer public relations operatives affixed to their names. For example, the press that covered the arena debate leading up to the City Council's final approval typically identified Roski as a "real-estate mogul," a "super-rich developer," a "casino magnate," Majestic Realty's president, a Toluca Lake resident, a Los Angeles Kings co-owner, a USC graduate, "loyal," "steady," married father of three, and a fun-loving, bike-riding, world-traveling, adventure-seeking outdoorsman. These adjectives were not completely untrue. Roski indeed emerged as California's biggest developer—at last count, more than 31 million square feet of industrial and commercial construction from San Leandro to Yorba Linda, and 23 million square feet in Los Angeles and Orange Counties.[94] But these assertions constructed absences that hid even more. The local media ignored information that put the developer's personality and development record in a negative light. The *Times*, despite its superior resources, showed the least curiosity of all the local press. It failed to explain how Roski had subsidized the growth of his development empire with public redevelopment dollars. It did not revisit the past or recent controversies ignited by his development projects or investigate his business relationships with four convicted felons. Two of these continue in the city where Roski has had his biggest development success: the City of Industry. Recent property records show that wholly or partially Roski-owned enterprises in the east San Gabriel Valley suburb total more than $18 million in assessed property value, the largest of the family's California holdings. But property records tell little about how Roski amassed his $320 million fortune.[95]

Founded in 1957, Industry, as the locals prefer to understate it, represented the latest in a network of single-use "commercial incorporations" designed as political and economic gerrymanders scattered throughout the once-vacant expanses of eastern and southeastern Los Angeles County.[96] The key to the city's creation was James Marty Stafford, a wealthy rancher, grain dealer, and real estate investor who, federal prosecutors said, ran Industry "as his personal fiefdom."[97] Industry, its critics said, operated more like a business, one that bent the powers of municipal government to satisfy the private needs of industrial developers. These powers enabled Industry's founders—backed by the Union Pacific and Southern Pacific Railroads—to capture arterial rail lines, interstate freeways, and oil and groundwater reserves within its boundaries. Today its fourteen square miles of strategic encirclement, which on a map resembles a griffin with ornate gothic wings, is home to about two thousand mostly manufacturing businesses and a daytime commuter workforce of seventy thousand, but only 580 residents.[98] It is a refuge for high-tech Asian manufacturers and food processing plants where Mexican workers lose limbs to hamburger grinders; the home of the Big Mac, where, inside an ultramodern studio, McDonald's films its TV burger ads; and the county's new Latino heartland.[99] Undocumented Salvadorans living in La Puente garages, two-income Mexican American couples with homes in middle-class West Covina, and college-educated Latino and Asian professionals living in north Whittier and Hacienda Heights live minutes away from their jobs in Industry, but not close enough to vote in the city. In Industry, most voters are linked to business owners and city officials by blood, friendship, and employment ties.[100] Industry thus embodies our post-Fordist present and future. Today, new and existing Sunbelt cities are modeled upon its privatization of public resources and encumbrance of massive public debt, which fuel competition among cities, counties, and states to entice businesses with corporate welfare.

Roski played a key, but low-profile, role in the making of Industry by cultivating his relationship with Stafford and exploiting redevelopment laws. But in September 1983, Stafford dropped Roski's name in a context the developer would probably like to forget—Stafford was in the act of making a bribe to a bank teller who had helped him launder money skimmed from an Industry construction project. Stafford and Roski had cofounded the bank where Stafford had laundered the money. The teller, unbeknownst to Stafford, had tape-recorded this and other conversations. The transcripts of those conversations, and other evidence obtained by the FBI, persuaded Stafford to plead guilty to eighteen criminal charges, including fraud, obstruction of justice, and conspiracy. Although Roski was not accused of participating in Stafford's criminal conspiracy, prosecutors and critics said the developer nevertheless benefited handsomely from his friendship with Stafford and the power it gave him.

In April 1989, the Roskis moved against the city that had favored them for years. Citing an earlier agreement, they informed the city that they were ready to exercise an option to add another three hundred rooms to their hotel atop the Industry Hills Exhibit and Conference Center. In April 1991, the Roskis and their partner, John Curci, sued for breach of contract in Los Angeles Superior Court when, the Roskis claimed, the city refused to honor its earlier development agreement.[101] In an apparent effort to exert more legal leverage, the Roskis attacked on a second legal front. They filed a second lawsuit against the city in Pomona Superior Court, echoing allegations leveled at the Roskis a decade earlier. Among other things, the suit claimed that the late Mayor John Ferrero's practice of grazing cattle on twenty-six hundred acres of city-owned land at a minimal fee amounted to a public subsidy of the mayor's business—an issue Paltrow had also raised. The suit further alleged that the city bought the land for $12.1 million with no other objective than to provide the mayor with cheap grazing land.[102] Although the Roskis portrayed themselves as Industry's victims, city officials and high-ranking visitor center employees claimed the lawsuits represented their customary way of doing business. The Roskis settled both suits in 1992 after the city agreed to buy the hotel for $29 million, or $14 million more than it reportedly cost to build.[103]

Roski's past, however, did not figure in the debate leading up to the L.A. City Council's approval of the arena project. The local media deserve most of the blame for the council members' lack of curiosity. In a computer-assisted document search, we found that only 2 of the 178 articles published by the major print media in the western states between April 1996, when the project was first disclosed to Los Angeles readers, and August 21, 1998, mention Ed Roski's Industry history.[104] None of the articles collected in our sample explained how Roski became wealthy enough to join Anschutz

## Bank Job
### Stafford called on Roski in bid to control local lender

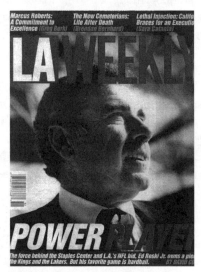

Ed Roski Jr. Photograph courtesy
of L.A. Weekly; reprinted with
permission.

In many ways, City of Industry founder James Stafford's problems began and ended with the Bank of Industry. The wealthy rancher organized the bank's formation in the early 1980s, enlisting Ed Roski Jr. and other Industry insiders to serve on the bank's board of directors. Stafford had already established his practice of laundering checks kicked back from Industry redevelopment projects; soon after the new bank opened for business, Stafford moved his check-laundering operation there from Industry's Bank of America branch.

Lucilla Rowlett was a common denominator in his laundering scheme. She handled many of Stafford's kickback checks while employed as a Bank of America teller. She did the same after she went to work at the Bank of Industry, cashing checks Stafford had drawn on bogus accounts brimming with money skimmed from Industry construction contracts: more than $1.3 million that should have gone toward the construction of a $65 million exhibit and conference center.

Then, in the midst of a deepening FBI corruption probe, Rowlett skipped town. Stafford finally tracked down his favorite teller in her home state. He persuaded her to meet him for dinner at the Holiday Inn in Leesville, Louisiana. Stafford wanted to pay for more than dinner. He wanted to buy Rowlett's silence. Before the meal of steaks and Heinekens had ended, records show Stafford had uttered Roski's name three separate times to reassure Rowlett that he could protect her from prosecution.

The FBI, betting that Stafford would try to cover his tracks, had already persuaded Rowlett to wear a wire that night. Transcripts from this and other tape-recorded conversations not only helped convict Stafford, but federal prosecutors would also cite them as evidence of Stafford's inordinate influence over the city and his closest associates, including Ed Roski Sr. and Jr.

In 1984, after obtaining Stafford's conviction, Assistant U.S. Attorney Gary Feess submitted a sentencing memorandum in which he asked the court to mete out the stiffest sentence possible. Feess argued that the wealthy rancher had "betrayed the trust and confidence" of the city and its agencies, and "abused his position as a preferred customer of the local banks," including the Bank of Industry.

Feess' memorandum, court and bank records, and interviews with former bank officers show that Stafford, without owning a share in the bank or serving as a director, virtually handpicked its first board of directors, breached bank confidentiality by pumping its members for information, and used the bank to launder $123,000 in kickback checks. When the bank's president called a halt to Stafford's check cashing and meddling in bank business, Stafford sought the help of Roski Jr. and other board members to have the bank president fired, these sources show. Feess' allegations weren't entirely new. Reporter Scot Paltrow explored Stafford's ties to the Roskis in a 1980 investigative series in the now-defunct *Los Angeles Herald Examiner.*

Despite repeated attempts to interview them, Paltrow reported that Roski Sr. and Jr. had declined to return his calls or answer his questions about their relationship to Stafford. Recently, however, Roski Jr. maintained that the allegations made against him in Paltrow's articles were untrue.

Separately, Roski has claimed in court papers that in Industry, he was an innocent victim caught up in other people's wrongdoing. But five years after the publication of Paltrow's series, and a year after sending Stafford to prison, Assistant U.S. Attorney Feess concluded in a sentencing memorandum, that the "fundamental allegations contained" in Paltrow's series had "been borne out." Stafford's crimes "were not isolated; they were part of a pattern of conduct extending back to the formation of the City of Industry."

Feess never filed charges against Roski Sr. or Roski Jr. But he made a point of describing the Roskis, and other Industry insiders, as "close friends of Stafford," before concluding in his memorandum that "Through these relationships . . . Stafford has been able to exert his influence at all levels of government in the City of Industry. There is no door in the city that is closed to James Stafford, and few decisions on which his counsel is not sought." Stafford's ties to the Bank of Industry, Feess wrote, illustrated that influence.

Stafford hatched his idea for a bank over lunch at the California Country Club, then the town's unofficial City Hall and the favored watering hole for Stafford and his confidants.

In the mid-1970s, about a dozen of Stafford's closest associates were summoned to a series of meetings at the country club to discuss the bank's formation. Ten of the original 12 bank directors, including Roski Jr., attended these meetings at Stafford's invitation, said former bank officers and Stafford's son in interviews given in the mid-1980s.

Roski Jr. recruited a respected Bay Area banker, Dale E. Walter, to serve as the bank's first president, former bank officers said. With Walter at the helm, the bank's associates and board of directors, including Roski Jr., invested nearly all of the $5.5 million needed to open the bank, bank records show. Stafford bought about $275,000 worth of stock (about 3.2 percent of the bank's total shares) for his grandson, stocks that were held in trust by his former daughter-in-law, according to former bank officers.

Initially, although he held no official position with the bank, Stafford attended the bank's meetings, said Walter and former bank director and chairman Robert K. King. After one bank organizer complained of his presence, Walter said he barred Stafford from the bank's organizational meetings.

Stafford easily bypassed the restriction by pumping friendly bank directors for information, said King, and Donald R. Wheeler, the bank's first chairman, in separate interviews. Sometimes Stafford did not wait for meetings to end, but would telephone directors for in-progress briefings, King said. But Walter's efforts to exclude Stafford failed to reduce his meddling or derail his check-laundering scheme.

Federal-court records show that soon after the bank received its state charter in April 1981, Stafford began laundering money through a series of bogus accounts established solely for that purpose at the bank. From May to September 1981, Stafford cashed about $123,000 in kickback money, court records show.

Eventually, the frequency of Stafford's check cashing aroused Walter's suspicions. That, said Walter, is when he called King into his office, one morning in September 1981, to show him a desk drawer containing several uncashed kickback checks. King, who later pleaded guilty to mail-fraud charges in connection with the kickback scheme, said he was shocked when he saw the checks; he knew he would collect a third of the money himself. King said he told Walter, "Dale, don't cash them. You're gonna wind up like me. I can't get away."

Walter said he immediately ordered the bank's tellers to stop cashing Stafford's checks. The order incensed Stafford, who determined to reduce Walter's influence. That meant a move against Wheeler, who was never party to the kickback scheme.

King said that during a fishing trip in Mexico in late 1981, Stafford and Roski Jr. told him they wanted him to succeed Wheeler as bank chairman. "Eddie [Roski Jr.] says to me, 'We're gonna make you, Bob King, chairman of the board.'

"And I says, 'I'm not interested in being chairman of the board . . .'

"Eddie says, 'What Jim wants, we're gonna give it to him,'" King said in one of several tape-recorded interviews he granted in 1985. In a recent interview, Roski Jr. said that he does not remember King ever being on the bank's board of directors. Nor does he recall Wheeler, whom he described as "a close friend," ever being forced out of the chairmanship. Bank documents list Wheeler as the bank's first chairman of the board, and King as a founding director.

A few months later, bank records show, Stafford's allies on the bank's board did indeed oust Wheeler and elect King chairman. But King said his election to chairman only made him feel more deeply enmeshed in Stafford's schemes. King, who now knew he was the target of the FBI investigation, said he ignored Stafford's orders to make Walter cash his kickback checks, further infuriating Stafford.

In March 1983, Walter again tried to reduce Stafford's "negative influence" over the bank by putting together a group of directors to buy out three of Stafford's most loyal allies. Walter's refusal to cash Stafford's checks, coupled with the successful buyout, prompted a showdown. King said that Stafford instructed him to schedule a meeting to discuss Walter's dismissal.

During a telephone conversation, King said, Stafford complained that "Dale Walter ain't gonna cash our [his and King's] checks. I think we ought to fire his ass. Why don't you and Eddie [Roski Jr.] and I have a powwow."

King followed Stafford's orders. In a certified letter dated April 6, 1983, King, acting in his capacity as bank chairman, informed the bank's directors that "A special meeting of the board of directors of the Bank of Industry, City of Industry, California, has been called by the chairman of the board for 11 a.m., Wednesday, April 13, 1983, in the Laundry Room at Industry Hills. This meeting is for the sole and express purpose [of deciding] the status of Dale Walter, CEO, Bank of Industry."

But King canceled the meeting after Walter fired back a letter in which he threatened to notify state banking authorities of Stafford's attempts to influence the board. A few days later, King, cracking under the emotional strain, announced his decision to sell his stock in the bank and resign from his position as board chairman.

King's resignation apparently triggered one last attempt by Stafford to take control of the bank's affairs. Walter said that Stafford's allies on the board had voted to make Gary A. Bryce, a bank director and close Stafford business partner, bank chairman, and that Roski Jr. had voted for Bryce. Soon afterward, Walter said, he was approached by the FBI. He agreed to cooperate.

On September 13, 1983, with the FBI closing in, Stafford held his first meeting with Rowlett. Stafford paid the former bank teller the first of two $1,000 bribes to "forget" about cashing his kickback checks, FBI transcripts show. During the meeting, Rowlett told Stafford that she feared Walter would blame her for the check laundering. Stafford tried to reassure her:

"Dale [Walter] isn't going to do that and Dale isn't going to remember anything either."

"Okay," Rowlett answered.

"Don't worry about that," Stafford continued.

"You have that covered," Rowlett said, as if trying to convince herself.

"With Roski," Stafford added, completing her thought.

"Roski will take care of [Walter]," Stafford said moments later, a remark federal prosecutors described as "threatening."

These transcripts, along with other evidence obtained by the FBI, persuaded Stafford to plead guilty to 18 criminal charges, including fraud, obstruction of justice and conspiracy.

Roski Jr., who was not charged with conspiring in Stafford's check-laundering scheme, remained on the Bank of Industry's board until 1992. That year, according to an FDIC official, the bank merged with Comerica Bank, a San Jose-based institution for which Roski Jr. serves as a director. Back in Industry, the vacuum created by Stafford's departure appeared to provoke a power struggle among insiders.

This article, by Victor M. Valle and Rodolfo D. Torres, appeared in the November 13–19, 1998, issue of *L.A. Weekly,* volume 20, no. 51. Copyright Victor M. Valle and Rodolfo D. Torres. All rights reserved. Reprinted by permission. Courtesy of L.A. Weekly Media, Inc.

in acquiring the NHL's Kings.[105] A pair of *L.A. Weekly* articles made vague references to Roski's role in the Industry scandals, but without detailing his business relationships to convicted felons. The *Weekly* did not publish its investigation of the Roski development legacy until November 1998, after the City Council had given the project its final approval and construction was well under way.[106]

The *Times*, in particular, had the resources to construct a critical biography. It had run dozens of articles on the Industry corruption scandals, and many, with a modicum of investigation, would have revealed hard evidence of recent controversies. Other articles in the *Times* morgue repeated allegations that Roski was unduly favored by the city's redevelopment agencies. Moreover, a reporter who had covered the Industry corruption scandals and who had personal knowledge of the developer's controversial history still worked at the *Times*. And a search of news stories from the print media in San Bernardino and Riverside Counties would have revealed recent allegations made by city officials there again accusing Roski of unethical business practices.[107] During the arena debate, however, the *Times* looked the other way, as did the City Council members. "All that was unimportant to them," said Greg Nelson, a deputy to Councilman Joel Wachs. "There was never much of a conversation about . . . [Roski's] past. And we knew the [other council members] didn't care about their backgrounds" either.[108]

The silence over Roski's past persisted even when he appeared to revert to the "insider" practices he had honed in Industry. Roski and his partner had threatened to build the arena elsewhere if the city would not deliver a subsidy, and they tried to keep their contracts with the arena's tenants— the Lakers and Kings—secret. Roski acknowledged to the *Times* in October that the disclosures had taught him a lesson. Next time, "in bringing football to Los Angeles," he said, "this needs to be a very open process."[109] And the partners kept their word. In August 1997, Roski and Anschutz permitted the City Council to divulge their side agreement with the arena's resident teams.[110] But neither the council nor the local media asked why Roski had not learned that lesson long ago in the City of Industry.

And then, after the blue bloods and their new allies had won every contest they had needed to win in the battle for downtown, they suffered a series of setbacks that revealed the limits of their power to redefine reality. First, developers like Roski and elements of the blue-blood elite failed to convince local voters that they should provide $150 million in public subsidies to return an NFL team to the Los Angeles Memorial Coliseum. A statewide survey reported that 80 percent of those polled opposed paying public subsidies to attract an NFL team; an earlier *Los Angeles Times* survey of Los Angeles County residents found that 62 percent opposed the use of public subsidies to entice a team.[111] It appears that voters did not forget developer efforts to hide the details of their lease agreements with the arena teams, the blue-blood and developer lobbying blitz that dominated the City Council, and their campaign to prevent the public from voting on the arena project. Second, the *Los Angeles Times,* key founder of the blue-blood elite, suffered a devastating blow to its discursive credibility.

In October 1999, just as the arena was opening for business, the local press revealed that the *Times* had entered into a profit-sharing deal with the Roski and Anschutz–owned Staples Center while it was reporting on the arena. The seeds of the scandal were planted in December 1998, when the *Times* agreed to become a founding partner of the Staples Center. The agreement stipulated that the *Times* and Staples Center would enter into several profit-generating projects. After additional discussions, the *Times* and Staples Center agreed to share advertising from a special edition of the Sunday *Los Angeles Times Magazine* dedicated exclusively to Staples Center. With the help of Staples staff, who solicited ads from the arena's corporate friends, the special edition earned more than $2 million in advertising revenues. Although the reporters who wrote the articles that appeared in the special edition did not know that their paper had entered into a profit-sharing agreement with the arena owners, their stories about the venue were mostly favorable, and only mildly critical. For the most part, these were the same sportswriters who had covered the arena debate prior to its construction. None asked about Roski's past, his controversial development projects, or the social and economic impacts of his development projects.

Although a handful of editors voiced objections to the profit-sharing agreement and Metro reporters refused to write puff pieces for the Staples edition, none had the courage to expose the profit-sharing agreement. As veteran reporter Henry Weinstein tactfully explained, his paper "is not terribly conducive to people raising troubling questions to their bosses, especially not about an endeavor of this magnitude."[112] Afterward, media critics concluded that one of journalism's most important ethical standards had been violated because the paper's publisher, Kathryn M. Downing, and editor, Michael Parks, had implemented the directives of Mark Willes. Loyal corporate soldiers that they were, Downing and Parks helped demolish the wall that protected editorial from the advertisers. But most of the paper's critics failed to see how the paper's corporate politics had intruded upon its editorial agenda, even when the paper's high-ranking editors all but boasted of their role in promoting downtown development. The day after the

164-page Staples issue appeared, *Times* editor Michael Parks congratulated the paper's editorial staff: "The Magazine and Sports staffs combined to put out a great magazine Sunday on the new Staples Center and what it will mean not only for fans but for the resurgence of downtown L.A. Very nice work indeed!"[113] As *Times* media critic David Shaw later discovered, Parks knew of the profit-sharing agreement when he sent his congratulatory note, yet failed to inform the staff of this in his memo. What he wrote was as important as what he had withheld. Parks, in effect, congratulated the staff for becoming partisans of downtown development. By this point in the contest, the history of downtown over development had already been drained of its embarrassing controversies, which made it easy for the corporate culture to resort to booster rhetoric to fend off critics.

In explaining why the *Times* had entered into the profit-sharing deal, Times Mirror spokeswoman Martha Goldstein asked readers to see the Staples edition from the advertisers' perspective. They "were interested" in it, she said, "because the Staples Center is very important to the rebuilding of downtown."[114] The comments of Goldstein and Parks offer insights into their corporate culture. To the *Times*, the only public that really mattered was advertisers, a public that voted with dollars to promote the Staples Center. And because the consensus of advertisers echoed Willes's pro-downtown development agenda, the paper's top managers and editors convinced themselves that corporate interests were the same as the public's interests, a conflation that one of the *Times*'s most talented reporters found inexcusable, yet symptomatic. "It [the *Times*] has done a shameful job covering development and redevelopment in our own backyard for more than half a century," said the veteran reporter, who asked not to be identified. "It is just nowhere to be found. What makes it more shameful, L.A. is the kingdom of sprawl. So to fall down on this story in a city like L.A. is to miss the biggest story in the community."[115]

Parks and Willes faced new pressures when the profit-sharing deal was exposed. Former *Times* publisher Otis Chandler roused himself from retirement to dictate a memo to *Times* staffers, lamenting the scandal as the "most serious single threat to the future survival and growth of this great newspaper during my more than fifty years of being associated with The Times." Chandler also criticized Willes for "the downsizing, downgrading and changing of the company's character back into what it was in 1958," but with an unstated difference.[116] The new boosterism, in contrast to the days when family ideology dominated the paper, now championed *Times* corporate ideology.

While Parks and Willes made apologies, journalists inside and outside the *Times* dissected their actions and professionalism.[117] A handful of journalists, including a few *Times* editors, even intimated that the Staples edition revealed more than just a simple appetite for money. The *New York Times* noted that *Los Angeles Times* editorials had previously presented Staples Center as "the centerpiece of a downtown renewal movement." The *L.A. Weekly* noted that the Staples edition's profile of Edward P. Roski Jr. failed to mention the "millions Roski has made from controversial redevelopment deals he cut with public funds in the City of Industry."[118] Yet none of the paper's critics put all the puzzle pieces together.

Meanwhile, the pressure on Parks mounted. After facing a rebellion in the newsroom from staffers demanding an independent investigation, and then discovering from that investigation that the Staples deal represented one of several ethically compromising ventures, he appeared to capitulate. Parks promised to reverse the "corporatization" that had taken hold of his, the editor's, office. And the *Times* pulled the plug on its other questionable cross-promotional schemes. Yet, despite the resounding calls for their resignations, neither Parks nor Downing offered to resign.[119]

The Staples scandal did not appear to worry *Times Mirror*'s board of directors either. After all, Willes and his team of managers and editors had presided over a tripling of *Times Mirror*'s stock price since he had taken charge in 1995. But as news of the scandal spread, *Times Mirror* stock slid 35% from the $72 a share peak it hit in the fall of 1999, when the scandal broke. *Times* reporters and other media critics blamed the scandal for the decline. Although they said nothing in public, the Chandler family apparently agreed with that conclusion in private. The decline in stock price triggered by the scandal, coupled with Willes's failure to position the company to exploit the new information technology, confirmed their growing disappointment in his leadership and their willingness to consider selling *Times Mirror*. After all, Willes had himself acknowledged in a 1998 annual report that failure to implement his growth plan "would mean dismantling the company and returning capital to the shareholds."[120] Events now persuaded the Chandler family to pursue that option. Merging with an internet-savvy partner seemed the only profitable exit left to the more than century-old media dynasty. The Chandler family members sitting on the *Times Mirror* board went ahead with plans made in 1998 to sell the franchise. On March 11, 2000, more than four months after the Staples scandal came to light, the board announced that they had agreed to sell *Times Mirror* for more than $6 billion to the Tribune Co. After calling the shots in Southern California for most of the twentieth century, the historically conservative

*Times* merged with another conservative and powerful media conglomerate, one which happens to be based in Chicago.[121]

Meanwhile, as one chapter of the elite city making ends, another continues. As of this writing, the developers of the Staples Center have proposed the construction of a multimillion dollar entertainment and hotel complex next to the arena. Their promises of continuing the revitalization of downtown will require millions more in new public subsidies, money that could instead be invested in the historic, yet neglected, portions of downtown radiating from Broadway that still function as places where citizens, many of them Latinos, still may meet. While funding the construction of another generic corporate playground will not stop downtown from reverting into a ghost town after the office workers go home, it does threaten to delay the rebirth of the center Los Angeles does not yet have.

# 5

# Significant Space

## Public Areas in the Greater Eastside

Place-making is a way of constructing history itself, of inventing
it, of fashioning novel versions of "what happened." For every
developed place-world manifests itself as a possible state of
affairs, and whenever these constructions are accepted by other
people as credible and convincing . . . they enrich the common
stock on which everyone can draw to muse on past events,
interpret their significance, and imagine them anew.

**Keith H. Basso, *Wisdom Sits in Places: Landscape and Language
among the Western Apache*, 1996**

The San Gabriel Valley was the rat's ass of Los Angeles County—
a 30-mile stretch of contiguous hick towns due east of L.A. proper.

**James Ellroy, *My Dark Places: An L.A. Crime Memoir*, 1997**

The social and political construction of landscape becomes observable in
the act of mapmaking. The manner in which a landscape is represented, the
manner in which names and boundaries are affixed to that map, reveals how
a particular society is organized, what significance that society attaches to
the particular features of a landscape, and what it expects of those features. Said simply, geographic representations are also symbolic acts.[1] Mapmaking, like the military conquests that often precede it, is also an expression of power. A state that attempts to normalize a particular map hopes to
convince its citizens and neighbors that its representation of national borders is natural and immutable. The Mexicans of the Southwest are quite familiar with borders as political constructs. For them, the border is both an
international boundary and a discursive act. It is a barrier to be negotiated,
exploited, and crossed, and a symbolic act to be contested. The immigrant

who illegally crosses the border simultaneously seeks to ensure a community's survival—money earned in the United States will be sent to Mexico or Central America, or spent in constructing a new community on the U.S. side of the border—and contests the dominant state's construction of the landscape.

But the discourses of power also function internally by marking certain landscapes as peripheral spaces whose resources can be sacrificed to enhance the livability of more privileged places. For example, such financial forms of discrimination as redlining often reinforce the marginalized imagery associated with such racialized urban spaces as barrios or ghettos. A critical reading of landscape can help deconstruct the social, political, and economic processes through which a privileged space in an earlier epoch of empire building was later reclassified as a barrio or industrial sacrifice zone by the new economic regime. Even in those cases where the physical remains of a previous regime of landscape construction appear to have been obliterated, the historical process by which a former central place was relegated to a subordinate status can be reconstructed from the dialectic of place representations. Moreover, reading the dialectics of place representations in one locality can help us understand how those processes played out throughout a whole region. The case of the Whittier Narrows area, which is located at the western edge of the San Gabriel Valley, offers such a metaphor of regional landscape construction. Its transformation from a central to a subordinate place offers important clues that can help us understand the Greater Eastside's social and political construction, the possibilities for the Eastside's discursive redefinition, and the resources needed to begin such an undertaking.

In 1771, the Franciscans built the Los Angeles area's first mission, which they named after Saint Gabriel the Archangel, in the middle of a narrow, wooded floodplain created by two rivers. They called the eastern stream the San Gabriel River and named the western one the Rio Hondo, or deep river. These agents for the Spanish crown initially saw the floodplain and its rivers as a perfect place to a build their mission and to establish a settlement large enough to serve as a staging area for colonial operations in Alta California.[2] The redundant names affixed to the floodplain expressed the elevated meaning it momentarily held for the colonial enterprise.

Its representation as a privileged landscape appeared to make sense. The rivers provided a steady supply of water, the woods provided building materials, and the floodplain provided a long swath of rich, tillable soil. During the succeeding phase of capital accumulation, the floodplain was renamed the Whittier Narrows due to its funnel-like topography. Over the eons, the region's complex and violent geology had opened a gap between the hills and mountains that otherwise barricade the large valley, also named after San Gabriel. The rain that falls in the valley, and on the steep San Gabriel Mountains that form the valley's high eastern wall, drain into the Rio Hondo and the San Gabriel River. These streams nearly converge at the narrows, and sometimes, during periods of peak rainfall, indeed merge, thus revealing the powerful hydraulic and geologic forces that carved their banks and formed the floodplain.

The Franciscans discovered this feature of local geology after building their mission. Earthquakes, which were followed or preceded by periods of torrential rains and flooding, rendered the mission uninhabitable. Four years later, while their first mission crumbled and faded into history, the padres rebuilt a second San Gabriel Mission five miles north, in what was later named the City of San Gabriel.[3] The settlement at San Gabriel Mission would be eclipsed by another mission and settlement built several miles to the northwest along the banks of another erratic stream—the Los Angeles River.

More than 180 years later, the narrows witnessed the completion of far larger constructions, but not a commensurate revision of meaning. In 1954, the U.S. Army Corps of Engineers, in cooperation with the Los Angeles County Flood Control District, completed the Whittier Narrows Dam and Reservoir, one of a series designed to protect surrounding suburbs from the fifty- to one hundred-year catastrophic floods that originally formed the narrows. The dam and reservoir became fully operational two years later.[4] Three years later, the corps, together with the county's recreation and flood control departments, completed the Whittier Narrows Recreation Area, a project that eventually reclaimed fifteen hundred acres inside the reservoir for recreational purposes. Clever public relations used the metaphor of diversion—of dangerous floodwaters and human energies—as the rationale for the newly created recreation area.[5] But the social history of the narrows, its geology, its man-made reservoir, and its recreational facilities have failed to qualify it as a bona fide tourist attraction. Tour guides do not place its parks and riverbeds on any must-see lists.[6] The Whittier Narrows Recreation Area, in other words, is no Central Park; it is not even a Griffith Park. To varying degrees, those parks evolved into public spaces that symbolically identify their respective cities, New York and Los Angeles, as cultural metropolises. The narrows do not appear to identify a comparable cultural place.

Nevertheless, this place does have a story to tell. In contrast to La Placita, the founding public space of Mexican Los Angeles, the Whittier Narrows Recreation Area embodies the new central space of the Greater

Eastside's growing Latino suburbs. Its centrality is more than literally spatial. The narrows offers the Greater Eastside social and political construction, but in microcosmic scale. Each stage of the Greater Eastside's economic development, from market agriculture to the extraction of oil resources, to the mass production of residential housing, to the post-Fordist reorganization of industrial production, has been predicated upon infrastructure projects in the narrows. The freeways, rail lines, and flood control projects concentrated there have a cultural impact as well, effectively marking the narrows as a sacrifice zone for regional development and thus disappearing its public spaces from the region's symbolic economy.

The narrows, however, remains an unfinished text, a landscape upon which new meanings may yet be inscribed. The infrastructure projects that transformed the shape and meaning of the narrows represent one side of a dialectic. Successive generations of local residents have not only contested developments in the narrows, but reinterpreted the same public spaces modified by development. Our reading of landscape formation in the narrows thus completes a cycle by returning to the thematic arc we traced at this book's outset. Understanding the story of what people have destroyed and built in the narrows, how they have represented what they have destroyed and built, and how others have subsequently reinterpreted what was built, offers a method of taking stock of the region's political, social, and cultural resources. The new Latino majority must undertake such an inventory of the regional landscape, and discourses that reproduce power relations in that landscape, if it expects to modify or create local institutions that truly respond to its needs.

To the daily commuter driving through the Whittier Narrows on the Pomona Freeway, viewing the crazy quilt of public spaces, factories, and sewage treatment plants visible from a rapidly moving automobile, this fractured space must seem an indecipherable text. Nor does the built landscape easily betray the clues to its making. Yet the narrows does provide its own Rosetta stone: the Whittier Narrows Visitor Center. Three bureaucracies— the U.S. Army Corps of Engineers and the Los Angeles County Department of Parks and Recreation in cooperation with the Los Angeles County Flood Control District—built this modest facility in 1977 as part of their shared mission to educate the public about the continuing need for flood control in the narrows.[7] If the idea of flood control seems like a relic from another time, a vestigial fear overcome long ago by our ancestors, then it is because the agencies that built the center did that job too well. The dam and reservoir had been built as part of a far larger edifice of environmental engineering designed to control flooding throughout the Rio Hondo and San Gabriel

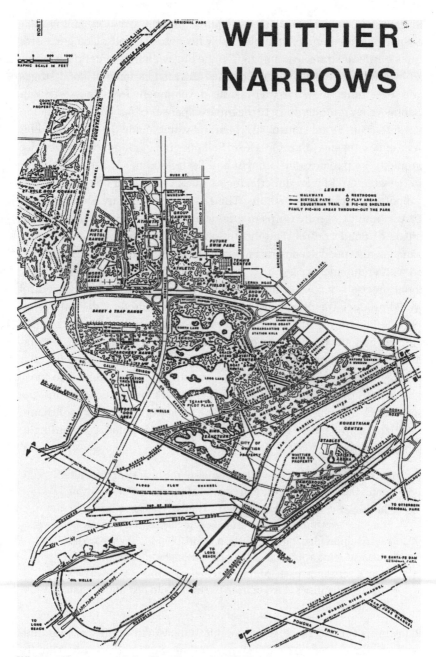

Whittier Narrows and the First Supervisorial District.

River system. Taming these rivers required their reinvention. Lining their channels with concrete, damming their headwaters, and placing massive catch basins at strategic points to trap the huge volumes of debris generated by these streams would reduce their destructive force of flood surges and, over time, allow for wall-to-wall development from the steep San Gabriel Valley foothills down to the broad expanses of flatland ending at the Pacific Ocean. Flood control, like plentiful water, made the suburban lifestyle of Los Angeles County's eastern half possible in a landscape otherwise prone to the paradoxes of drought and flash flooding. Marshaling the resources required by an undertaking as massive as flood control required supporting social constructions. The Los Angeles County Flood Control District and U.S. Army Corps of Engineers would emerge as institutional pillars of flood control. The institutional infrastructure of flood control would in turn need to construct a political consensus that could be entrusted with endorsing its Sisyphean projects. Nothing short of controlling or, more precisely, reconstituting the meanings of floods and flood control would produce the degree of social discipline required by the enterprise.

Runoff from the San Gabriel Valley's watershed indeed passes through, and has periodically flooded, the narrows. Contrary to the valley's reputation as an arid landscape domesticated by suburban sprawl, its peculiar geology and proximity to the ocean have sometimes combined to loose tremendous deluges upon the mountains. Under the right conditions, the storm track that normally slides over the Pacific Northwest veers south into the high, steep barrier raised by the San Gabriel Mountains. According to John McPhee:

> Some of the most concentrated rainfall in the history of the United States has occurred in the San Gabriel Mountains. The oddity of this is about as intense as the rain. Months—seasons—go by in Los Angeles without a fallen drop. Los Angeles is one of the least-rained-upon places in the Western Hemisphere. . . . When certain storm systems approach Los Angeles, though—storms that come in on a very long reach from far out in the Pacific—they will pick up huge quantities of water from the ocean and just pump it into the mountains.[8]

Rainstorms such as these, which are often measured in fifty- or hundred-year cycles, can assume Noah-like proportions. Such a flood visited Southern California in the winter of 1938. McPhee writes that "thirty inches of rain had fallen in six days. Publications of the United States Forest Service later described the event as 'the greatest rainstorm in the recorded history of the San Gabriel Mountains.'"[9] The deluge flooded the narrows and many of the low areas downstream. Today, the county's chief water agency estimates that the flooding caused 113 deaths and $40 million in property damages.[10] Not surprisingly, the Whittier Narrows Visitor Center's exhibits dramatize the loss of life and property with photos of the inundation from numerous floods. The exhibits include photos of farms and the first suburban developments downstream from the narrows in cities such as Downey, Artesia, and Lynwood damaged by flooding, thus reinforcing the county's discursive bottom line. The exhibit's photos, captions, and dam diagrams thus lead its imagined visitor to an inexorable conclusion: the narrows offers a perfect shutoff valve with which to prevent future disasters.

Like early versions of the county's flood myth, the visitor center's exhibits represent flood disasters to justify the need for the Whittier Narrows Dam and Reservoir, yet suppress the political process that created the flood control infrastructure and the role it played in unleashing regional development. Tellingly, the agency completed its first major project in 1921 at the Ports of Long Beach and Los Angeles. Built in partnership with the U.S. Army Corps of Engineers, this flood diversion work set the stage for the development of the nation's busiest commercial ports and Los Angeles's emergence as the Pacific Rim's leading warehousing and distribution center.[11] Beginning in the mid-1920s, the Flood Control District, together with a chorus of county, federal, and local water agencies, set upon its next objective—building a comprehensive flood control system for the entire Los Angeles Basin. In a discursive motif that other local agencies would repeat with great success, flood control began building a consensus for its mission by retelling the story of the great floods—not Noah's, but the nine major floods that had hit the Southern California basin since 1876. In every case, the flood control agency's narratives reminded Angelenos that they could prevent future destruction and loss of life if they supported the agency's projects.

Local elites had their own reasons for supporting flood control's mission. For the *Los Angeles Times*, and the *Times*-dominated Los Angeles Chamber of Commerce, flood control meant fewer weather-spawned distribution foul-ups, more suburbs, and thus more home owners and more subscribers.[12] The flood control agency's water conservation program also gave credence to *Times* claims that Los Angeles could not thrive without securing new sources of water. Harry Chandler's *Times* trumpeted the benefits of flood control and water conservation at the same time the Chandler-controlled Los Angeles water department secretly bought up the remaining Owens Valley irrigation districts.[13] In 1922, despite earlier completion of the

Owens River Aqueduct, a sustained drought in the Owens Valley reduced aqueduct flows in the midst of Los Angeles's biggest development boom. In a series of sophisticated maneuvers, the *Times* swiftly appropriated flood control's water conservation rhetoric to justify its search for new water supplies and pushed for the city's annexation of the San Fernando Valley to bolster its pro-development schemes. The water conservation projects built by flood control thus became one more tool for constructing the image of a thirsty city. By the 1930s, the newspaper's editorial stance helped Chandler, together with investor syndicates he organized, reap huge windfalls from San Fernando Valley real estate development. With Owens Valley water, the Chandler-controlled syndicates could subdivide and sell huge swaths of arid farmland at many times its original value.[14] The *Times* and its blue-blood allies also supported flood control for ideological reasons.

In the early 1900s, proposals had been made to reclaim the Los Angeles River as a nature preserve to satisfy the city's growing need for open public places. In the two decades that followed, writes Mike Davis, no comprehensive plan for a parks and recreation system had been adopted, although population and development continued to grow exponentially:

> Developers had stubbornly ignored official pleas to dedicate parks for their subdivisions, and powerful homeowners' groups had opposed every attempt to pass specific assessments for parks or recreation; thus, as the population soared, per capita recreation space shrank drastically. By 1928 parks comprised a miserable 0.6 percent of the surface of the metropolis. . . . No large city in the United States was so stingy with public space.[15]

In 1930, some of the city's most distinguished citizens drew up a plan to protect Southern California's remaining open spaces from uncontrolled development. Drafted by the Olmsted Brothers urban design firm and endorsed by the 162-member Citizens Committee on Parks, Playgrounds, and Beaches, the plan proposed converting the basin's river channels and floodplains into lush parkways. The 440-mile network of greenbelts would have a treble function: flood control, public recreation, and transportation. Instead of attempting to contain the rivers, the plan would allow them to spill their banks and replenish their fifty-year floodplains. In the long run, preventing development within the floodplains would save taxpayers the monumental expense of encasing rivers in concrete or rebuilding homes damaged by flooding. And because the county's poorest lived in often overcrowded conditions and constituted the majority of the population, the parkways would create a necklace of beautiful commons for those who needed them most. Finally, using the parkways as rights-of-way for road-ways would provide efficient transportation in pleasant surroundings that would spare neighborhoods the disruption of highway construction.[16] Per-ceiving it as a socialistic threat to the city's pro-capitalist, open-shop repu-tation, the blue bloods mobilized and defeated the legislation that would have implemented the Olmsted plan, which would have created a metro-politan park district. The *Los Angeles Times,* in particular, disdained pro-posals to municipalize almost one hundred thousand acres of private land; Davis writes, "Under pressure from the *Times,* 27 prominent members of the Citizen's Committee withdrew their support from the park legislation, thus killing the Olmsted plan."[17]

Despite the plan's defeat, and the growing power of the pro-development forces, the Whittier Narrows Dam and Reservoir project did not proceed unopposed. "Property owners immediately above the struc-ture objected that it would flood 3,700 acres and force abandonment of two thousand homes in addition to farms, dairies, and some small indus-trial plants near El Monte. They also charged that it would obstruct flow of underground drainage."[18] The L.A. County Flood Control District, with the backing of blue bloods and other regional developers, nevertheless imple-mented several administrative procedures to circumvent the various green-belt plans and the opposition of local property owners.

The Flood Control District's formation in 1915 as a semiautonomous agency under the control of the Los Angeles County Board of Supervisors represents an early prototype of stealth government. State law permitted the Flood Control District to hire private contractors to perform construc-tion work. It granted the agency additional contracting freedom by exempt-ing it from enforcing civil service regulations.[19] The agency's authority to exercise the power of eminent domain, which it used to secure rights-of-way for construction projects, and its authority to obtain approval for con-struction bonds with a simple majority vote instead of the two-thirds mar-gin required of other branches of county government, further reduced the Flood Control District's accountability to voters. Meanwhile, the agency took advantage of the push to create a national flood control system, modi-fying its rhetoric to mesh with changes in federal policy. During and after the Depression, the Flood Control District repackaged its projects as a jobs program, demonstrating the discursive flexibility that has, over the years, helped it secure hundreds of millions of dollars in federal funding. The agency's increasing dependence on federal funds after the 1930s also moved the setting in which water policy debates occurred from downtown Los Angeles to Washington, D.C.[20]

Over time, the U.S. Army Corps of Engineers, the Flood Control District, and neighboring cities benefited from their symbiotic relationships. Each could call upon its counterparts to present expert testimony or muster political support for pet projects. Naturally, such an arrangement enhanced each agency's discursive authority in the face of local opposition. When local groups have attempted to modify a project, the Corps of Engineers, county government, and "most cities in the affected area, as well as of private groups with by now vested interests in the project would come to the Corps's defense, and so simulate the appearance of popular support. As a result, Congress generally accepted the testimony of the Board of Supervisors and the Flood Control District as the voice" of the region.[21]

The Flood Control District built this consensus in stages. In 1931, it entered into a strategic alliance with the U.S. Army Corps of Engineers, with the objective of developing a comprehensive flood control plan for the Los Angeles Basin, which included building a reservoir at the narrows. During that decade, Los Angeles political elites threw their support behind the approval of a national flood control program, which was approved in the Flood Control Act of 1941. For differing reasons, both blue bloods and New Dealers calculated that the adoption of a comprehensive national policy would bolster implementation of their preexisting plan to create a countywide flood control system. In 1952, another round of destructive flooding, together with mounting pressure to complete the surburbanization of Lakewood and Long Beach, continuing water agency demands that the county replenish falling aquifer levels, and renewed public demands for the creation of a regional parks system, prevailed against local opposition to the Whittier Narrows Dam project.[22] The dam builders now had the backing to make the public an offer it could not refuse. Suburban sprawl would be allowed to continue spreading in floodplains, water agencies could continue supplying groundwater to ever-growing suburbs, and recreational advocates would finally get miniaturized versions of the Olmsted plan in the Whittier Narrows, Hansen, and Santa Fe Dam reservoirs. Unfortunately, the concessions made to recreational interests were granted only after Southern California's huge citrus orchards had been uprooted. By 1970, Davis notes, 96 percent of the three hundred thousand acres of farmland that had existed south of the San Gabriel Mountains in 1939 had been cleared for development. "One of the nation's most emblematic landscapes—the visual magnet that had attracted hundreds of thousands of immigrants to Southern California—was systematically eradicated."[23]

Not surprisingly, the Whittier Narrows Visitor Center's exhibits do not present greenbelts in flood-prone areas as an alternative to the financial and environmental costs of building a massive flood control system. Instead, the center strives toward drama. The center's 4,680-square-foot building houses an "upward-spiraling mezzanine ramp" that displays a stylized scale map of flood control projects along the San Gabriel River and Rio Hondo as they snake their way down from the mountains. Arriving at the top of the mezzanine's overlook, visitors can look down and take in the exhibit's representations of the flood control system and the recreation area's artificial lakes and park facilities. Downstairs, tucked in a dark corner, a far smaller display gives a nod to the cultural history of Whittier Narrows. Presented as a historical triptych, the exhibit acknowledges that Native Americans and Mexicans had settled in the narrows first. But, after a brave defense, the Mexicans lost in 1847 to General Kearny's U.S. troops at a place several miles southwest of the narrows. This exhibit concludes with still photos shot in the narrows in 1914 during the filming of D. W. Griffith's *Birth of a Nation*. The panel glosses over the Californio mistreatment of Native peoples, the Anglo majority's subordination of the Mexican population, and the white supremacist message of Griffith's film, which portrays the Ku Klux Klan as defenders of Christian civilization.[24] Obviously, the creators of this exhibit did not anticipate how patronizing it would appear today. The cultural exhibit offers a weak apology for manifest destiny, whereas the flood control exhibit shows the Corps of Engineers defending "people and property" from the rampaging Rio Hondo and San Gabriel River. These discourses mesh well. Both are epic narratives of conquest: one of a society, the other of nature. Still, we doubt that the cultural exhibit ever caused anyone's pulse to quicken. Rather, its mediocre execution merely smooths over disturbing colonial memories and the subsequent takeover of water policy and resources by corporate developers and local water agencies.

Like most projects in California involving water, Los Angeles County's extensive flood control, water conservation, and reclamation projects have, from the start, sparked confrontations and controversy. These projects have required the seizure of private property and water rights, the destruction of riparian habitats, and the implementation of policies that have sustained Southern California's land development industry. Although it is rarely acknowledged, flood control complemented the massive water projects that fueled Southern California's suburbanization. The building of upscale homes in the Altadena and Azusa foothills could not have proceeded without the construction of enormous basins to catch debris flows of rocks, mud, and trees that roar down the canyons after fires have denuded the mountains. And the construction of vast housing tracts in low-lying areas would have proved to be uninsurable investments if one of the world's largest flood control systems had not also been built to control the region's erratic storm runoff. As McPhee observes, "People of Gardena, Inglewood, and Watts no less than Azusa and Altadena pay for the defense of the mountain front, the rationale being that debris trapped near its source will not move down and choke channels of the inner city, causing urban floods."[25]

The sheer scale of flood control in Los Angeles County is astounding. Building "a more than 2,000 mile system of underground conduits and concrete-lined open stream channels—a web of engineering that does not so much reinforce as replace the natural river systems," required billions in tax dollars and an unprecedented level of cooperation among government bureaucracies.[26] Paving over river channels and building more than fifty thousand catch basins, more than sixteen thousand maintenance holes, and more than two thousand drainage areas also resulted in a far less noble accomplishment: the destruction or endangerment of the county's fragile riverine habitats.[27] By the 1930s, the dams and flood control projects completed along the San Gabriel River had finished off its run of steelhead trout.

The L.A. County Flood Control District and the Army Corps of Engineers responded to environmental concerns by stressing the project's benefit to "property and people." In the Whittier Narrows, both agencies deployed the threat of flooding and debris flows against farmers and ranchers, who refused to give up their pastures and orchards, and against taxpayers, who objected to subsidizing uncontrolled real estate development. The agencies divided and isolated their adversaries by pitting them against nervous property owners, developers, and local governments downstream, who, responding to the Corps of Engineer's reports of flood danger, clamored for protection.[28] Even one of flood control's apologists acknowledged its uneven benefits: "There is no doubt," writes Bigger, "that some persons in the metropolitan area profit more from the project than others, in terms of monetary and similar benefits."[29] In 1959, more than two million people and more than $4 billion in property enjoyed some benefit from the system. "Certainly, the closer a person is to the channels and the more property he owns," Bigger wrote at that time, "the more returns he receives, and nearby protective works bring 'unearned' increases in property value."[30] The discourse of control had achieved closure with the completion of the last river-lining projects in the 1960s.

By 1978, however, a year after the completion of the Whittier Narrows Visitor Center, the political ground under the narrows shifted. The passage of Proposition 13 required the county's Department of Parks and Recreation to cut back on extraneous services and facilities.[31] It is easy to see why the visitor center was an early victim of these cutbacks. By then the local water agencies had put the finishing touches on the county's flood control system, thereby reducing their need to invest in continued public relations. After all, the local water agencies and developers had already won the economic and political battle of building the infrastructure of suburbanization.

Meanwhile, the visitor center failed to win a following from the recreation area's growing Latino constituency. The records of the Whittier Narrows Advisory Council, a local citizens' group formed to support the recreational and educational uses of the narrows, show that it never expanded beyond its constituency of hobby clubs, such as the San Gabriel Valley Bow Hunters, the Sporting Dog Council, and various equestrian groups. Except for complaints regarding excessive drinking and littering by Latino soccer clubs using the recreation area's playing fields, club minutes and Advisory Council records show no participation from local Latino communities. About the only official acknowledgment of Mexican history in the Whittier Narrows Recreation area was the bicentennial year commemoration of the 1775–76 De Anza expedition. But the Anglo horse club members, San Gabriel Mission docents, and L.A. County Supervisor Peter Schabarum turned the event into a celebration of the Hispanic fantasy myth.[32] The Advisory Council's chairman, moreover, fits perfectly the description of a San Gabriel Valley good old boy. Fred Coleman's résumé includes his having served as president of the California Brittany Club and the Sporting Dog Council of Southern California, as well as memberships in the Redondo Beach Masonic Lodge and the Azusa Chapter of the Royal Arch Masons—not the social circles where he could expect to rub elbows with working-class Latinos.[33]

The recreation area also lost political support. As the effects of Proposition 13 deepened, Schabarum, whose First District included the Whittier Narrows Recreation Area, failed to secure county or federal funds to match those committed by the U.S. Army Corps of Engineers for park improvements.[34] And the visitor center did very little to endear itself to the Latino community, which, not surprisingly, ignored the center's financial difficulties. As a result the facility was abandoned, and its doors were closed for twenty years. Overshadowed by a grove of tall trees, the center's exhibits today show signs of that neglect. Dated photos and explanatory subtexts have slipped from their mountings—a visitor center without visitors is a de-centered space.

Standing at midmorning in the middle of the Greater Eastside's largest recreation area produces similar sensations of marginality. The crackling power lines and popping sounds rising from the trap and skeet range across Rosemead Boulevard cannot be ignored, nor can the roar of the two major freeways that divide the narrows in two places. The Pomona Freeway bisects the fourteen hundred–acre recreation area's northern lobe, and the San Gabriel River Freeway, along with a rail line that follows the course of the San Gabriel River, forms a barrier along the area's eastern flank. The narrows offered the path of least resistance to the dam, reservoir, and other infrastructure projects, a fact acknowledged by a photo taken during dam construction and on display at the visitor center: the Edison Company strung its power lines right through the heart of the recreation area. The reservoir's concrete and boulder rim, low on the western horizon, is barely visible through the smog. Nearby, but not visible, derricks scattered throughout the reservoir continue pumping oil up from deep underneath. Two sewage treatment plants in the narrows reclaim water from the San Gabriel Valley's vast network of residential sewers and release a year-round water supply into those stretches of the San Gabriel River and Rio Hondo that pass through the narrows. Ironically, the reclaimed water has given these riverbeds a degree of semitropical lushness. Prior to flood control and water reclamation, the San Gabriel and Rio Hondo's riverbeds remained mostly dry and cracked. The county launched a conservation program in 1959 in which the Metropolitan Water District diverted about one hundred thousand acre-feet of water each year, via the San Gabriel River and Rio Hondo, to settling grounds downstream from the narrows. Later, sewage treatment plants began releasing reclaimed water into the streambeds. Both methods of water conservation used the river to transport water to spreading grounds as a means of recharging local aquifers. Since then, local water districts have pumped this water up and sold it to ratepayers. In 1969, passage of the National Environmental Policy Act gave the Corps of Engineers the added responsibility of protecting riparian habitats, including those revived by artificial means. Over the county's periodic objections, the corps has since presided over the return of duckweed, tules, sedges, mule fat, and trees to the narrows. The lush foliage, which is plainly visible from the Pomona and San Gabriel River Freeways, has proved a continuing irritant to the Flood Control District. "There's a lot of resistance to doing anything like this," according to Rick Harlacher, an ecologist with the Army Corps of Engineers. "The engineers [in flood control] have been trained to clear channels, that flood control and habitat protection are mutually exclusive."[35] The Flood Control District would prefer to see these revived streambeds stripped of plant life, which it claims may undermine bridges downstream in flood time.[36]

To the northwest on the Montebello Hills, barely visible through the trees, power lines, and smog, one can make out the newest industry to reshape the narrows. The Montebello Town Center, a successful Southern California retail complex that caters to a Latino and Asian clientele, has recently covered up the north-facing talons ravaged by oil drilling.[37] Looking southeast across the narrows, one can see a plume of steam rising from atop the taller Puente Hills; at night, an infernal red glow suffuses the steam. Both glow and steam are by-products of an energy conversion system that burns methane collected from the nearby county-run landfill. For decades, the growing agglomeration of suburbs and towns east of downtown L.A. have crammed their garbage into these hills. A police training academy, a community college, and the Rose Hills Cemetery complete the visible panorama that helped transform quiet farmlands, orchards, and isolated barrios into wall-to-wall residential and industrial suburbs.

In dramatic contrast to its surroundings, the Whittier Narrows Recreation Area strives toward an English estate's landscape of green pastures, woods, and ponds, but not at all convincingly. The decline in funding for county parks means that the grounds receive minimal attention. Moreover, the park's panorama is disturbingly fragmented, offering up a contradictory mix of industrial and pastoral images. That contradiction should have repulsed park users, but the opposite occurred. The public spaces created in the narrows have become increasingly central to the Greater Eastside. People do recreate there—more than 1.87 million a year, according to most recent estimates. Most people who frequent the area live in the communities that ring the narrows and know their way around the area's facilities.[38]

These communities share more than their proximity. According to recent census data, more than 86 percent of their residents are Latino. Other sources estimate the Latino population in the five-mile area near the recreation area at more than 63 percent.[39] Recreation area patrons reflect the ethnic diversity of the surrounding cities. A survey conducted by the L.A. County Department of Parks and Recreation found that more than 65 percent of those using the area's facilities are Latino. The next-most-frequent park patrons are classified as white, at 13.6 percent, followed by Asian Americans at 4.9 percent, African Americans at 1.2 percent, and Native Americans at 2.5 percent. More than 12 percent of visitors did not respond to the survey.[40] By far, soccer was the most frequently reported of the area's athletic activities.[41]

A stroll through the public spaces in the narrows confirms the Latinization of park culture suggested by the survey. On most weekends, people from all along the Greater Eastside's social and ethnic spectrum can

Sunday afternoon *fútbol*, Whittier Narrows, 1999. Photograph by Elliott Johnson.

be found enjoying their respective niches. Immigrant Latino families give the park's three artificial fishing ponds, named after Herbert Legg, a county supervisor who earned a reputation for corruption, a working-class atmosphere.[42] Large clusters of people show the persistence of extended families, especially during holidays and birthdays, which call for piñata bashings. Strummed guitars and beer-mellowed voices come out in the early evening. Merengues, *cumbias,* and *banda* riffs blare from boom boxes during the heat of day. The air wafts aromas of scorched corn tortillas and carne asada. Chicano car club members and girls in tank tops gather around tricked-out low riders, some with hoods lifted, others bouncing or tilting in the parking lots. During the day, from the left lane of the Pomona Freeway, commuters can see the northernmost reaches of the recreation area, where small crowds gather around soccer matches. On other days, dog shows and model airplane flying take center stage. Still further out, on the network of bike trails built by the county along the banks of the San Gabriel River and Rio Hondo, middle-class Latinos from nearby Montebello, Hacienda Heights, and Pico Rivera, but also more removed cities such as Glendora and Santa Fe Springs, speed by on expensive mountain and road bikes. Below the bike trails, in the riverbeds, Latino and Southeast Asian families picnic, play in the water, fish for carp and catfish, or forage in waist-deep water for crayfish. The scene is distinctly pastoral (if one ignores the concrete riverbanks, shopping carts rusting in mossy water, the previous night's homeless encampment hidden by dense stands of bamboo, and delinquents who have been known to use the cover of freeway overpasses to ambush bike riders and joggers). Today, the Latino immigrants who go there say the riverbeds remind them of the rural landscapes left behind, which explains their attraction. Whether they have visited them since childhood or only last summer, the habitats created by rivers that flow through the arid landscapes of the Southwest or Northern Mexico remain familiar. Previous generations of Latino residents have thus claimed these places as theirs. Author Luis Rodriguez recalls with fondness summers spent at Marrano Beach (literally Hog Beach), a bend in the Rio Hondo named with self-deprecating Chicano humor:

> Vatos locos pulled their pant legs up and waded in the water. Children howled with laughter as they jumped in to play, surrounded by bamboo. . . . There were concrete bridges, covered with scrawl, beneath which teenagers drank, got loaded, fought, and often times made love. At night, people in various states of undress could be seen splashing around in the dark. And sometimes, a body would be found wedged [between] stones near the swamps or floating face down. The place stunk, which was why we called it what we did. But it belonged to the Chicanos and Mexicanos. It was the barrio beach. Ours.[43]

The Edenic and profane meanings coexisting in Rodriguez's recollections betray the contours of an oppositional model of cultural space. In naming it Marrano Beach, local residents stressed their class orientation, especially their lack of public recreational and transportation resources, but also their resourcefulness in the face of poverty. If they could not afford to live in homes with swimming pools or transportation to a real beach, then they could at least enjoy their imagined beach during the hottest summer months. Through the recovery of memory, his ownership of place and joy of barrio camaraderie, Rodriguez becomes an active and critical participant in place making on at least two levels. On the one hand, his place making expresses an implicit criticism of power relations in his community,

Marrano Beach, looking north on the Rio Hondo, 1999. Photograph by Elliott Johnson.

particularly its marginalization from public spaces. Unrestrained suburban sprawl had left few open recreational spaces in the San Gabriel Valley, or throughout Los Angeles County, for that matter. On the other hand, Rodriguez's place making attempts to regain the former coherence of such Mexican spatial conceptions as the plaza, which concentrates the sacred and the profane, the public and the private, and even the natural and human realms in one space. That model, argues William Estrada, curator of El Pueblo de Los Angeles Historic Monument, will continue to energize a cultural dialectic in places like the narrows as long as Latinos see it as a place to actualize their memories of ancient public spaces. These memories embedded in Latino uses of the narrows, he concludes, "represent challenges to the imposed urban models that have separated our communities

Marrano Beach, looking south on the Rio Hondo, 1999. Photograph by Elliott Johnson.

along racial and class lines with the coming of the railroads and the new Anglo elites. This conflict is played out in urban geography, in the way we use space."[44]

Latinos now stake their cultural claims more forcefully, when, for example, as many as a hundred thousand gather in the area's park to celebrate the independence of six Latin American countries with pop concerts featuring singing stars such as Marco Antonio Solis.[45] The Pico Rivera Sports Arena represents another place where Latinos have inscribed new cultural meanings in the narrows. Less than a mile downstream from the Pomona Freeway overpass, above the east bank of the San Gabriel River, the arena stands as one of the newer alterations of the narrows landscape. In distinct contrast to almost all the other recreational facilities in the narrows, the arena is dedicated to celebrating Latino culture. Mexican *charros* on both sides of the border test their skills in competition here (set to raucous *conjunto* renditions of *banda* tunes played from the stands). Sometimes *rock en Español* bands and Latino religious evangelists perform in the evenings; flea markets featuring Latino foods and merchandise spring up around the arena during the day. The *charros* stable their horses near the arena, and, when not competing, ride them on bridle paths wending through the narrows. The food, produce, and flower vendors who set up shop at the rim of the dam, where Rosemead Boulevard bisects the narrows from the north, also contribute to the area's cultural mosaic. Depending on the season, produce vendors sell New Mexican green and red chiles, white corn, sugar cane, or watermelons from their truck beds. Latino flower and fruit vendors work the intersection of Rosemead and San Gabriel Boulevards on foot. Near the intersection's northeast corner, the Los Angeles River Conservancy, in cooperation with the county agencies that oversee the narrows, recently built a rest stop named Bosque del Rio Hondo, with a shaded pathway, natural history display, rest rooms, drinking fountain, parking area, footbridge, and pathway to Marrano Beach. The Plexiglas-encased natural history display gives equal time to English-language and Spanish-language translations and images describing the primeval woodland environment that flourished there before European conquest. The display also briefly summarizes the Gabrieleno, Spanish, and Mexican presence in the narrows, yet ignores the Mexican community's long-standing cultural uses of Marrano Beach. Still, even the *bosque*'s attempt to address its culturally appropriated Latino patrons signifies an incremental improvement over previous representations of the narrows landscapes.

The recreation area's recently appointed superintendent, Velia Rosales, would like to go a step further; she just hasn't decided what that direction is: "My plans keep changing. First it was educational, then artistic, then cultural. I simply haven't had enough time to get my ideas down on paper."[46] But the South El Monte native said in interviews conducted in 1998 that she has rediscovered the centrality of the narrows since her appointment in April 1997. She noted that Los Angeles-area gangs, including the Crips and Bloods, view the narrows as neutral, and thus a safe place, because no gang claims it as turf. Rosales said that Los Angeles County Supervisor Gloria Molina, in whose district the recreation area is located, shares her enthusiasm for developing its unrealized potential. Rosales said her decision to reopen the visitor center in December 1997 represents one of her first steps toward making better use of the facility. Still, she said, she is dissatisfied with the center's exhibits, which she plans to modify using recreation area

Bosque del Rio Hondo, 1999. Photograph by Elliott Johnson.

revenues. But except for proposing truly interactive exhibits (the present ones simply require patrons to push buttons that light up bulbs marking recreation facilities on a large map), Rosales could not describe what their content or purpose might be.[47]

Whatever plan she devises, she will need to consider basic financial realities. Relying on park revenues to finance improvements in the visitor center will prove limiting. However, after years of struggle owing to the fiscal austerities of the recession years, Los Angeles County budgets have begun to enjoy the benefits of an improving economy. For example, the Los Angeles County Parks and Recreation Department was budgeted $30.9 million for fiscal year 1997–98, whereas in fiscal year 1999–2000, the department's budget was $40.6 million—a 77 percent increase over two years. Moreover, because the Parks and Recreation Department budget costs are categorized as discretionary, effective lobbying efforts may increase future outlays.[48] Rosales also said that she will solicit advice from academics and community members. We hope that they will advise her to cultivate community involvement while seeking additional funding to carry out a creative reinterpretation of the center's interior and exterior spaces. For example, the center's upward-spiraling exhibit is perfectly suited to a display that would mimic a pre-Columbian serpent motif celebrating the creative/destructive duality of rivers and narrates the environmental destruction caused by flood control. Asian motifs or local historical anecdotes could also be woven into a current display that glorifies the technological conquest of nature. Redesigning the center's exhibits in a way that invites visitors to see the surrounding landscape through the eyes of local Latinos and environmentalists can raise new questions about the purposes of flood control in particular, as well as create a common ground for community and coalition building to occur. On a grander scale, new features could be built to mitigate the barriers that divide the area's spaces. Perhaps pedestrian overpasses could be used to connect the area's parts into a new whole. But when asked whether one of the center's modifications would recognize the working-class cultural history of Marrano Beach, Rosales did not respond. We believe her silence marks an important juncture in the evolution of the Los Angeles area's Latino leadership. Her peers in government, labor, and the private sector now find themselves weighing and devising strategies with which to exploit new leadership opportunities, which sometimes appear in unexpected places. For example, in formerly gentrified, white, middle-class Catholic churches such as St. Mary's in uptown Whittier, largely immigrant Latinos now fill the pews and dominate the congregations' social and cultural agendas. Collecting food for United Farm Worker families striking in the strawberry fields of Salinas and organizing the Festival De las Americas, an annual event that promotes pan-Latino identity, are now routine pastoral functions.

A few miles east, in the Montebello School District, Margie Rodriguez, principal of Winter Gardens Elementary School, used her institutional space to circumvent Proposition 227, the anti–bilingual education initiative. Responding to the curricular changes mandated by the initiative, Rodriguez stimulated a series of parent meetings that focused on offering parents three instructional choices, one of them being bilingual education. Stressing the progress that Spanish-speaking students had already made under the school's bilingual curriculum, Rodriguez persuaded many parents to exercise their option to waive the initiative's English-only requirement and continue with the bilingual curriculum. More than 97 percent of the school's 538 Spanish-speaking students, or English-language learners, remained enrolled in the school's bilingual program.[49]

Later, the fatal drive-by shooting of a two-year-old girl on the Winter Gardens school grounds prompted the parents who had preserved bilingual education to form a Neighborhood Watch chapter. First, the parents pestered local service and law enforcement agencies to address the gang problem. Next, they tackled another pressing issue: Los Angeles County's street sweepers. For years, the East Los Angeles residents on North Clela Street had either risked being ticketed for parking in front of their homes or were forced to park blocks away because the street sweepers swept both sides of their street on the same day. The Winter Gardens Neighborhood Watch took up the matter with First District Supervisor Molina. She promised action. Now the street sweepers offer the Clela Street residents the basic courtesy of sweeping one side of the street at a time. Rodriguez believes the unexpected synergies of civic involvement cultivated at Winter Gardens Elementary are being quietly rediscovered in and beyond the greater district.[50]

# 6

# Class and Culture Wars
# in the New Latino Politics

Although events in the Whittier Narrows and other public spaces of the Greater Eastside may tempt some to imagine scenarios of Latino hegemony in the twenty-first century, the social, economic, and cultural complexities of Los Angeles will prevent the attainment of any simple notions of outright dominance. Population trends suggest that Latinos may have to wait until past the midcentury mark before their numerical dominance becomes irresistible. When and if that moment arises, increasing social differentiation and class divisions within the Latino community, complicated by globalism's unforeseen permutations, will make simple notions of ethnic cohesion problematic.

Rather, if Latino power is to have any real constructive and lasting meaning, it should be seen as both the catalyst for and the foundation of a new conception of the multicultural metropolis. Up to this point, we have suggested through our criticism that the only multiculturalism worth striving for should not disguise and obscure social inequalities with brotherly platitudes or allow the processes of racialization to continue reproducing themselves behind the benign facade of tolerance. Now we would like to be more explicit and focus our attention upon the immediate future. The Latino community, due to its current social composition, historical experience, and size, has the potential to play a crucial role in the construction of a new cosmopolitanism. Recent events suggest that such a building process is already under way in the political arena.

Spurred on by record levels of Latino voter registration and participation in California, twenty-four Latino and Latina candidates, or one in five members of the state legislature, were elected during the 1998 election cycle, an increase of eighteen over the 1996 election cycle.[1] More important for our study, most of the newly acquired seats were won in Los Angeles County. Yet several factors have distracted many analysts within and outside of the Latino community from grasping simultaneously the political *and* cultural significance of these electoral gains.

For one, dramatic increases in Latino political representation are recent. Not since the nineteenth century has Southern California's Latino community enjoyed such levels of political representation.[2] Still, there is something rather presumptuous about asking whether increased political representation should somehow translate into increased cultural influence. Latinos have viewed themselves as being in the minority for so long that the possibility of becoming the majority seems disorienting. The same goes for Latino leadership. Few Latino scholars have studied politics as an arena for cultural representation because, until relatively recently, it was assumed that, as a politically marginalized group, Latinos enacted their cultural lives in private, or at least in their neighborhoods. Now, however, Latino-elected leaders and their constituents have an opportunity to imagine and enact their cultural lives in public. We intend to show that the opportunities for increased cultural influence offered by enhanced public participation go beyond the simple administrative and legislative remedies available to Latino leadership. The political arena also offers a kind of stage upon which Latinos can construct new public identities. We intend to show that that transition has already been prefigured, and in many ways enabled, by the increasing reach and power of the various forms of Latino media, especially the Spanish-language media. When artists like Los Lobos create music that expresses a profound self-acceptance of their working-class and mestizo roots, when Spanish-language television broadcasters present illegal Latino border crossers as heroic survivors, when Mexican fans fill the Los Angeles Memorial Coliseum to capacity to root for the home team—La Selección Nacional—in a match against the U.S. national team, and when clubs like La Conga Room create a space where Latinos of all national origins can gather to enjoy the best in Afro-Cuban music, via Havana, one can already see the variety of cultural forms from which new public behaviors are being constructed.

As the presidential impeachment scandal of 1999 reminds us, politics is a kind of social practice where subjective, or cultural, forms are produced and circulated for public consumption. It is indeed a cliché of contemporary politics that elections and legislative battles are won or lost in the media. At both the national and the local levels, politicians increasingly debate questions once considered issues of private morality—gay marriage, abortion, adultery, school prayer—in the nation's virtual electronic town squares. And as the country has drifted further to the right, and the national political culture has fallen still more deeply under the sway of the corporate media and corporate dollars, political life, to the degree it is concerned with the production and consumption of moral discourse, is now dominated by the subjective. So it would seem that the same forces that have converted politics into cultural warfare would have further marginalized minority forms of counterrepresentation. Until recently, that judgment would have seemed especially applicable to Latinos, at least at the level of national discourse. Even though African Americans have lost discursive ground in recent decades, they, of all minorities, continue to play the lead role in the national political and cultural dialogue, especially as it concerns urban "race relations." By contrast, and with such notable exceptions as United Farm Workers labor and environmental struggles, Latino contributions to the national political discourse are usually obscured or absorbed by stronger voices. And but for the individual exceptions, it has been more common to conceive of Latino political leaders simply as creatures of their local political environments and not as shapers of the greater political culture.

Not surprisingly—and this is especially true of the practitioners of cultural studies—cultural and social historians have tended to privilege the analysis of marginal spaces and texts to understand how Latinos have contested hegemonic culture or constructed ethnic identities. Hence the recent studies that seek to understand, or read, how Latinos construct their lived cultures, and hence the emphasis on the texts of lived culture, from cookbooks to graffiti to low riders. But recent developments in cities such as Miami and Los Angeles now require a reconceptualization of the way Latinos negotiate the transition from political and cultural minority to political and cultural majority. In Los Angeles, the work of reconceptualization becomes especially urgent as Latino political leadership increases its policy-making role in the transition to an economy based upon cultural production, as evidenced by the explosion of such entertainment projects as the Staples Center, the proposed DreamWorks studio, and the city's first Catholic cathedral. Increased Latino political representation will mean greater access to the levers of government and, as a result, a larger niche in the state's ecology of representation. Now, for the first time since the city's founding, Latinos have the opportunity to acquire the institutional standing to open up what has been a closed dialogue on the matter of race and class.

In a strictly quantitative sense, then, the future already looks promising when considered in the light of recent political history. In the 1970s and 1980s, organizations such as the National Organization of Latino Elected and Appointed Officials measured success by counting electoral victories.

Consistent with such thinking, most Latino officeholders replicated mainstream political thinking, making a religion of narrow political pragmatism. As in the major parties, raising money, winning elections, and holding onto political office were their method, objective, and reward. As apathy in the electorate broadened and deepened, ideas and issues played second fiddle to the art of deal making, fund-raising, polling, and media campaigning. Some of this narrowness was understandable. Increases in Latino voter participation had not kept pace with the quickened rate of Latino population growth during the 1970s and 1980s. As a result, Latino candidates remained dependent upon corporate donors, party bosses, and the demands of media campaigning. The dearth of Latino political ideas, however, also reflected weak leadership. The running rivalry between Councilman Richard Alatorre's and Supervisor Gloria Molina's political machines, the decision of Latino elected officials to soften their opposition to Proposition 187 to avoid alienating white voters, and the recent drug scandals engulfing Alatorre and Councilman Mike Hernandez illustrate some of the worst of the past generation of Latino political leadership.[3] By the late 1980s, and continuing until the mid-1990s, Latino population growth, coupled with the consequences of immigration legislation and California's attempt at ethnic cleansing, dramatically altered both the quantity and quality of Latino voter participation in state politics, and, as a consequence, the possibilities for new leadership.

The first tremors of the political earthquake were registered in Orange County when Democrat Loretta Sanchez defeated ultraconservative incumbent Republican Robert Dornan for a seat in the U.S. House of Representatives by a 984-vote margin in 1996. Although Dornan's defeat in the Forty-Sixth Congressional District rocked conservatives where it hurt most, in a seat long considered safe by Republicans, a growing Latino presence in Santa Ana made the upset foreseeable. Groups like La Hermandad Mexicana Nacional, a cross between an old-fashioned Mexican mutual-aid society and a labor and immigrant rights organization, helped translate that presence into votes, an achievement that quickly drew a reactionary response. In the already hostile climate created by the passage of Proposition 187 two years earlier, Dornan played up anti-Latino, anti-immigrant hysteria, accusing La Hermandad of a sinister conspiracy. Meanwhile, the *Los Angeles Times,* according to the *O.C. Weekly,* "manufactured incriminating evidence; declared *Hermandad* guilty months before a grand jury had even convened; and effectively sided with Dornan's laughable accusations that nuns, military men, residents of entire apartment buildings and 'thousands' of noncitizens quietly conspired to unseat him."[4] Local and federal authorities launched investigations, but two years later an Orange County grand jury, citing a lack of evidence, refused to hand down any indictments. In the end, all that could be established with any certainty was that "noncitizens who had passed all immigration tests and who were awaiting formal swearing-in ceremonies" had jumped the gun. They had improperly registered to vote and then exercised their franchise prematurely.[5] The most sinister charge that could be leveled against La Hermandad was that a pair of its voter registration volunteers may have been overzealous in their efforts to increase Latino political participation.

Ironically, the Dornan-manufactured media panic fueled new efforts mobilize Latino voters. To protect their families, jobs, and civil liberties from continued Republican-led scapegoating, California's Latino immigrants took advantage of a period of immigration amnesty, became citizens, and then voted in record numbers. Although Latinos remain underrepresented at the polls, the 1996 election results show that newly enfranchised Latino immigrants voted "at a rate exceeding that of the state's voters as a whole." These new voters participated at rates that effectively surpassed the overall voter turnout, with "a little less than two-thirds" of them going to the polls.[6] Los Angeles County, where the 1996 turnout among both new and veteran Latino voters jumped from 11 percent to 18 percent, registered the biggest bounce. In Orange County, the setting for the Dornan-Sanchez race, the Latino vote rose from 6 percent to 9 percent.[7] The 1996 elections marked two other historic firsts: Latino voter participation in the Los Angeles mayoral race hit 15 percent, which surpassed African American participation and matched the Westside Jewish turnout.[8] Not surprisingly, several recent studies show that Governor Pete Wilson, the most powerful and aggressive spokesman for the anti-immigrant backlash, did long-term damage to the Republican Party's credibility among new immigrant voters. But the Latino turnout, which rose at a time when Jewish political representation in Los Angeles County's top one hundred political offices had declined by 30 percent since 1986, also gave the Westside's Democratic establishment much to ponder.[9]

Nativo Lopez, executive director of La Hermandad's Orange County branch, sees the emergence of the "postamnesty" Latino voter as a turning point in Southern California politics. The state's 1.7 million immigration applicants all became eligible to apply for amnesty at the end of 1995.[10] After January, February, and March 1996, these applicants became citizens in increasing numbers, and a growing cohort of high school–aged U.S.-born Latinos began voting thanks to the passage of President Clinton's "motor-voter" law. Equally important, groups such as the Southwest Voter Registration Education Project, La Hermandad, and the Los Angeles County

Federation of Labor laid the organizational groundwork that translated legal opportunities into electoral gains. In 1996, their combined efforts succeeded in bringing as many as 1.3 million new potential Latino voters to the California polls.

"Certainly," Lopez said in an interview, "organization was a part of it, not just La Hermandad, but many others spurring people on to obtain their citizenship, and then registering them to vote." La Hermandad takes credit for qualifying anywhere from 175,000 to 180,000 people to enter the amnesty pipeline. "Many are still in the pipeline," Lopez added. "Locally, we have more than 10,000 applicants who have been waiting for twelve months to twenty-four months to get their final citizenship interview." And this trend will continue. "In the Los Angeles INS district," Lopez said, "there are more than a half a million people waiting for citizenship. By the year 2000 that backlog will be eliminated," which will produce another surge in Southern California's Latino vote just in time for the presidential election.[11]

During the 1998 election cycle, eleven Southern California Latino Democrats, most of whom can be classified as pro-labor progressives, rode this confluence of demographic and political forces into the California State Legislature. These victories helped Democrats regain a slim Assembly majority in Sacramento and lifted Antonio Villaraigosa from Assembly majority leader to the powerful position of Assembly speaker. In yet another portent of Latino political power, Los Angeles City Councilman Richard Alarcon handily won his San Fernando Valley State Senate seat after narrowly defeating former Assemblyman Richard Katz, a Westside political power broker, in a bitter Democratic primary. Other Latino candidates who lost close races in the last election cycle will be back for the next round, Lopez said: "There is no reason why in the year 2000, we shouldn't be close to 30 percent of the state assembly," or in other words, "close to parity with our numbers in the state's population."[12] Even Lopez, despite the onslaught of hostile media coverage, benefited from the postamnesty surge when he was elected president of the Santa Ana Unified School District Board of Education in 1996.

The city of Los Angeles—where Latinos are projected to constitute more than 49 percent of the population by 2001—promises future political opportunities, even though the charter reform movement, various City Council expansion schemes, and the San Fernando Valley secession movement have temporarily clouded that picture.[13] Latinos should continue to gain strength in the Valley, whichever way it goes, and in South-Central Los Angeles, where Latinos already made up 44 percent of the population in 1990.[14] There, Latinos will soon constitute as much as 60 percent of some districts. For the moment, few Latino or African American political leaders will publicly discuss that eventuality. But soon, Lopez said in another interview, "you are going to see Latinos running for those seats that have always been held by African Americans," competition that will increase tensions between Latino and African American political leaders.[15] Some analysts have already predicted that African American council member Rita Walters will be the first to be challenged by a Latino contender.[16] African American political leaders in Los Angeles must negotiate not only changing political demography but the growing fault line that divides a small but thriving African American middle class from the black urban poor. However, Latino office seekers and their supporters should resist the temptation to use ethnic loyalties to exploit the tenuous position of African American political leaders. Although such ploys may yield short-term gains, ethnically targeted appeals reinforce the city's divided political geography while leaving the Latino victors vulnerable to those who would exploit emerging class divisions among their own constituencies. Instead, African American and Latino elected officials representing inner-city districts need to develop strategies that address racialized class inequalities. By acknowledging, rather than obscuring, the class divisions in the Latino and African American communities, a new generation of leaders can build a movement based upon commonalities of class.

The anticipated growth of Latino populations in the suburbs and the unexpected consequences of legislative term limits will mean that "termed-out" Latino legislators will return from Sacramento or Washington to run in city districts both within and outside of the safe barrios now dominated by Latinos. Assembly Speaker Villaraigosa, State Senator Richard Polanco, Assemblyman Gil Cedillo, and Congressman Xavier Becerra, among others, may carpetbag into the seats vacated by Alatorre and Hernandez or run in the South-Central or Hollywood district, potentially doubling the number of Latinos on the City Council from three to six. Even a Villaraigosa mayoral challenge is conceivable if liberals and progressives can construct a viable post-Bradley-era coalition. The next census will also provide the numbers to translate a decade of Latino population growth into district reapportionment that increases Southern California's Latino congressional representation.

For the moment, however, many analysts appear preoccupied with calculating the new political math made possible by increased Latino participation while downplaying the content of the new postamnesty Latino leadership. Conventional political analyses still focus on identifying safe districts, reinforcing the conventional wisdom that the most important divisions in Los Angeles politics are racial or ethnic. Although these analytic prejudices are understandable, given the empiricist bias of professional political science and the racialized representation of the city's social divisions, both tendencies promote the Eastside-versus-Westside turf mentality that reinforces a fragmented status quo. But a closer examination of the postamnesty voter's role in the local and global economy offers important ways of reinterpreting the meaning of Latino voting patterns for the city and county as a whole.

In Nativo Lopez's view, "The most important demographic statistic left out of these discussions is that, in Los Angeles County, Latinos constitute more than 65 to 70 percent of the economically active workforce."[17] When Asian immigrant workers are factored into the equation, the emergence of new Latino and Asian leadership in the local labor movement seems logical. Already, Latino and Asian immigrant workers have begun to revive and expand decaying service sector unions into a new force in Los Angeles politics. The historic victories of the Service Employees International Union bear remembering in this context. An organizing practice that discovers the class interests of Latina, Asian American, and African American female home health-care workers shows how political alliances can be built across seemingly insurmountable local racialized boundaries.

Such victories, as well as union gains made earlier in the 1990s, have been felt far beyond the county line, providing the kinds of tactical and strategic knowledge that is transforming the AFL-CIO's national policies. At another level, the transformation of Los Angeles unionism bears comparison to the Irish immigrant takeover of New York's labor unions at the beginning of the twentieth century, except that now, Latino and Asian immigrants work under profoundly different economic and cultural circumstances.

Interpreting late capitalism remains tricky, however. The true believers in market solutions still promise that the emerging knowledge-based economy will eventually lift a sufficient number of boats, Latino vessels included, by providing a steady supply of new jobs. But increasing poverty in the midst of so-called full employment has, for the moment, disarmed their glib predictions and fueled postmillennial pessimism. Under the most noirish scenarios, the unequal development fostered by postindustrial society, with its concomitant transition to an information-based, post-Fordist industrial regime, will continue to produce massive economic and social dislocations. At the same time, the complex dialectics of capital, markets, and resources in the developing world will continue to make cities such as Los Angeles the destinations of choice for Latin American, Asian, Near

Eastern, and African immigrants, thus creating a future theater of racial-ized conflict. Worse, during the next economic downturn, the opportunists will attempt to revive the anti-immigrant hysteria of the mid-1990s. Mean-while, technological innovation will continue to demassify the media and facilitate the emergence of a knowledge elite whose job it will be to create and service the hardware and cultural software of an information/culture-based society. The new knowledge elites, we are told, will emerge as a domi-nant class of an economic regime based upon post-Fordist production, leaving behind those cultural and social sectors still dependent upon less efficient Fordist modes of production. Under post-Fordism, where infor-mation and culture industries emerge as the dominant productive force, the winners will either own or control the production of culture and infor-mation in all its economic and political applications. Everyone not owning or participating in these new knowledge-based industries stands to lose social prestige, not to mention financial and political viability. How the Latino community will fare in the ensuing transition to a society organized around digitized information and cultural production is hard to predict. But Latinos—either as members of a working and an incipient owning class—cannot expect to participate in, let alone influence, the knowledge-based industries except as consumers if they remain tied to inefficient Fordist in-dustries. The emergent knowledge elites who serve at the pleasure of post-Fordist capital reserve the best roles for themselves.

Some may take heart in knowing that the *maquiladoras* concentrated along the northern Mexican border and scattered throughout Southern California's old and new suburbs will at least employ huge numbers of Latinos in the region's post-Fordist industries. The increased earning power of some Latinos has already tempted a few to mistake middle income for middle-class social position. But many middle-income Latinos, the pes-simists say, have taken longer to acquire the social privileges and status that come with university-trained professions and upper-management corpo-rate positions. Moreover, the Latinos who have joined the skilled, profes-sional, and university-trained workforce remain in the minority. Most of the highly decentralized industries that employ Latinos do so at the lowest skill levels, offering them the lowest pay, benefits, and opportunities for educa-tional advancement. For example, many of the low-skilled industries that employ Latinos in the Greater Eastside do not appear to have benefited from the globalization that has been so profitable for the knowledge indus-tries, increasing their vulnerability to technological displacement and ex-cess industrial capacity worldwide. The post-NAFTA international trade that has brought new investment and high-salary jobs into places like

Santa Monica, Westlake Village, and Beverly Hills has not, according to one study, reached such Greater Eastside cities as Huntington Park, Cudahy, and Maywood, where minimum-wage jobs are plentiful.[18] Nor do the job niches Latinos currently hold in post-Fordist production promise greater access to the means of cultural representation; up to now, Latinos with a few strategic exceptions, have been excluded from the means of mental production. The retrenchment of anti–affirmative action policies in higher education will act as a further drag on Latino integration in the knowledge-based economy.

Meanwhile, technological innovation will continue to facilitate the breakup of mass-media audiences into smaller, more socially isolated segments, while at the same time promoting the emergence of an information elite whose job it will be to create the information and cultural commodities that service a growing cybereconomy. The information elite will emerge as a dominant economic class of a social regime based upon post-Fordist production, leaving behind those cultural and social sectors still affiliated with Fordist modes of production. Under post-Fordism, where information and culture industries emerge as the dominant productive force, the winners will either own or create the production of knowledge. Everyone else, as Michael Rustin writes, stands to lose social prestige: "Insofar as mental labor does become more central to the production process, it is not surprising that those who live by it gain in social power, just as the depopulation of the countryside earlier had its consequences for class relations."[19]

According to some analysts, the noir scenarios are already visible in the inner city and in Greater L.A.'s aging near-in suburbs. The triple threat of a growing poverty-wage job sector, the steady evaporation of middle-income jobs, and meteoric salary increases for a select few knowledge workers at the top of the employment pyramid has already eroded the tax bases of Los Angeles and the older suburbs that Latinos have recently inherited. The crude inequalities of the new economy deliver the coup de grâce to a post–Proposition 13 history of disinvestment and physical decay in the recently Latinized suburbs. As Mike Davis notes in his latest book, *Ecology of Fear*:

> In addition to the dramatic hemorrhage of jobs and capital over
> the last decade, aging suburbia also suffers from premature physi-
> cal obsolescence. Much of what was built in the postwar period
> (and continues to be built today) is throwaway architecture, with
> a functional life span of 30 years or less. . . . At best, this stucco
> junk was designed to be promptly recycled in perennially dynamic

housing markets, but such markets have stagnated or died in
much of the old suburban fringe.[20]

And as these suburbs decay, white flight—at least for those with the skills to
land higher-paying jobs in the knowledge-based and trade-based jobs of
the edge suburbs—hastens the loss of tax revenues in the older suburbs.

The noir scenarios may underestimate the role Los Angeles will play
in the regional, national, and global economy as well as the Latino community's resolve to salvage places written off as unredeemable, for Latinos will
continue to seek social progress wherever they can obtain it. But compared
to California's shameless boosters, the noir critique provides a sober correc-
tive to unfounded optimism. For example, some analysts point with pride
to increasing Latino household incomes as evidence of a growing Latino
middle class. Gregory Rodriguez shows that in 1990 slightly more than 25
percent of Latino households in five Southern California counties earned
incomes that exceeded $35,000, which was then the national median in-
come. According to this income standard, slightly more than 25 percent of
Latino households in Southern California's five counties were earning 1990
incomes that could be classified as middle-class. Recent immigrants, contrary to the underclass stereotype, constituted a significant portion (34 percent) of the Latino households earning at or above the median income
level, registering some of the fastest income increases among Latinos.
Latinos, both foreign-born and U.S.-born, showed rates of home ownership
second only to Anglos and on par with Asians. Finally, Latino households
earning at or above the middle-income level grew faster than the growth of
Latino households living in poverty.[21]

Although impressive and important, studies that equate income with
social status are nevertheless misleading. Latinos are indeed becoming
more socially mobile, but the income numbers also show that 75 percent of
Latino households earn below the national median, a proportion that is
just as significant if one is interested in understanding the size of a low-
wage, low-skilled Latino working class. And even for those Latinos categorized as middle-class, the high number of Latino households with three or
more wage earners (more than 52 percent among the foreign-born and more
than 25 percent among the U.S.-born, compared to 13.5 percent for U.S.-
born whites and 19.4 percent for African Americans) suggests the pooling
of several working-class salaries under what would appear to be a single
middle-class roof.[22] To be contextualized accurately, studies of Latino social class need to look at per capita earning to understand how middle-
income wealth is transmitted between generations. It is also important that

researchers account for educational levels of wage earners when attempting to describe Latino social mobility. For example, as Rodriguez correctly notes, only 8.9 percent of foreign-born Latinos classified as middle-class had earned bachelor's degrees. Among U.S.-born Latinos categorized as middle-class, only 15.7 percent had earned bachelor's degrees, compared to more than 40 percent for both U.S.- and foreign-born whites.[23] When per capita income, education levels, and the working-class character of Latino labor force participation are taken into account, Latino movement into the middle class is more ambiguous than the household income figures would suggest. Although one can acknowledge that social mobility is occurring, one can also conclude that that progress is recent and still subject to the reversals produced by the transition to a knowledge-based, post-Fordist economy.

Still other analysts point with optimism to the growing number of Latino entrepreneurs as indicators of social mobility, for what better denotes middle-class social position than business ownership? Again, at first glance, the numbers appear impressive. The number of Latino-owned businesses in the Los Angeles area has grown three times faster than the population in recent years. In 1992, California led the nation in Latino-owned business, and Los Angeles County led the state with 109,104 Latino-owned firms employing 65,000 workers, earning $7.8 billion in revenues. Manufacturers of traditional Mexican and Latin American cheeses, such as Industry-based Cacique, Inc., and Paramount-based Ariza Cheese Co., represent a few of the county's multimillion-dollar successes, employing several hundred employees. The average Latino business owner, however, employed about three-fifths of an employee per business, underscoring the ambiguities of Latino entrepreneurship.[24] According to sociologists Ivan Light and Elizabeth Roach, many of the new Latino businesses were created as a defense against underunemployment, especially among new immigrant arrivals. As employment opportunities for Latinos dropped during the 1990 recession, the number of marginal, unincorporated businesses owned by Latinos tripled to 54,768 from 18,480 in 1980.[25] Most of the unincorporated businesses were started by foreign-born Latinos, many of whom earned slightly below the national median income. In 1990, self-employed Latino entrepreneurs earned an annual mean of $29,599. By contrast, owners of incorporated businesses, most of whom were native-born Latinos, earned a mean of $44,981 a year. Likewise, the foreign-born Latinos realized a $4,737 average adjusted benefit for self-employment; native-born Latinos realized a $9,067 average adjusted annual benefit.[26] And although Latino entrepreneurship increased in Los Angeles, as a group Latinos ranked near the bottom, slightly below whites and slightly above African Americans. Self-employment rates among native- and foreign-born Latino males averaged 8 percent, and between 4.5 percent and 6.1 percent for native- and foreign-born Latinas.[27] For Latinos at least, entrepreneurship is not a panacea that will deliver the American Dream, but neither has it failed to produce any rewards. Rather, the truth lies somewhere between these extremes. Light and Roach write that the

> growth of Hispanic entrepreneurs certainly drove down the rewards of business ownership among this group to a greater extent than any other. In a way, however, the Hispanic situation was superior to what the whites faced. They were developing new economic niches in garment manufacturing, gardening, and hotel and restaurant work as whites were losing their comfortable niches. Admittedly, the Hispanics were poorly paid, but getting a bad job may be easier to endure than losing a good one.[28]

Despite notable successes, which the media use to illustrate their model-minority narratives, most Latino businesses manage to employ only their entrepreneurs. Moreover, only a fraction of these entrepreneurs, available data show, have obtained the capital to invest in the knowledge-based businesses of the new economy. As a result, the Latino community cannot afford to put all its faith in market forces, when doing so would risk abandoning those with the least technical skills to combat poverty and despair. In other words, although the benefits of the market economy offer promise for a small but growing minority, the working-class Latino majority must preserve worker-oriented social and political action as a short- and long-term option if it hopes to address present and future structural inequalities. But the meaning of worker-oriented social and political action, as we have attempted to show, must be expanded and reconceptualized to incorporate new forms of struggle.

## Toward a Class-Oriented Political Culture

To the degree that immigrant Latino and Asian workers continue taking control of local labor institutions, they will create a power base with the autonomy and human and financial resources to influence the electoral process and further diminish the clout of entrenched party machines. The Los Angeles County Federation of Labor, led by Miguel Contreras, together with immigrant rights groups, demonstrated this fact during Gil Cedillo's 1997 primary bid for the Forty-Sixth Assembly District. The federation, which had identified and canvassed nine thousand newly registered voters in the downtown district, brought an unprecedented 45 percent of these voters to the polls by emphasizing Cedillo's labor-organizing credentials and eagerness to fight Governor Wilson's political agenda.[29] Under Contreras's leadership, the 738,000-member federation also helped the Democrats recapture the State Assembly, enact school bond measures, and pass the living wage ordinance.[30]

Enlightened pragmatism, not leftist idealism, requires that present and future Latino leaders fashion an industrial and urban policy that transcends the worn-out discourses of race relations and identity politics. To achieve this, Latino elected leaders need to broaden and deepen their notions of representation to encompass the class interests of their constituents in the context of the new realities of globalized post-Fordist production. The foregoing may sound too theoretical for some, but the post-NAFTA economic realities that permit Mexican capital to invest in Southern California provide the concrete experiences that underlie these abstractions. Latino immigrant workers, Nativo Lopez explains, are "being employed more and more by other immigrants, other Latinos, and Asian immigrant entrepreneurs who are developing small and medium manufacturing or service plants." As these experiences become commonplace, immigrant workers will see through the mystification of ethnic or racial unity to discover that their "fundamental interests are class interests, not racial interests." At that moment of realization, Lopez argues,

> the possibility of developing multinational, multicultural coalitions will become easier. As a result of NAFTA, the owners of the plants will be Mexicans, and the workers in those plants will be Mexicans. The class lines will be more clearly established for our community. I think that's a very good development for fighting racism, and for fighting economic disadvantage.[31]

And as Latinos begin to make the transition from acting as a class in itself to thinking as a class for itself, they can begin to construct a political culture that represents and advances their interests. Lopez believes this sorting-out process has already begun. Cedillo, for example, received his political training while organizing students against Proposition 187 and leading the Los Angeles County Employees Union. Villaraigosa organized for the United Teachers of Los Angeles and served as president of the ACLU.[32] Becerra, leader of the Congressional Hispanic Caucus, demonstrated political courage by visiting Havana, without making apologies to the Cuban American members of the Congressional Hispanic Caucus, and by voting against moving Israel's capital from Tel Aviv to Jerusalem, without making apologies to Westside Democrats.[33] "This new crop of leaders is better educated, both academically, formally, and in their practical organizing experiences," Lopez said in an interview. "I think that we will have better-quality leadership and a greater ability to mobilize more broadly. I think it's possible, absolutely possible."[34]

Reorienting Latino political discourse toward a deeper appreciation of class issues will require Latino leaders, elected or not, to engage in the culture wars. As the Republicans recently demonstrated with their Contract with America and family values rhetoric, it is possible for one side to so dominate the political discourse that opponents are forced to speak that faction's language. Likewise, Latino elected leaders must be prepared to reframe the context of political dialogue in ways that are advantageous to their constituents. Whether at Whittier Narrows, in the heartland of the Greater Eastside, or in the newly won jurisdictions of the San Fernando Valley, reframing the political culture of Los Angeles demands a coherent long-term discursive strategy. The conventional functions of representation, such as lawmaking and issue-oriented debate, must be expanded to accommodate new tasks. The bully pulpit, in other words, must be reconceptualized as both political and cultural space. Timid Latino political leaders who cannot capture the cultural space to articulate a transnational human rights agenda, who fail to attack racialized media representations of immigrant workers and to advance an industrial policy that addresses the needs of their predominantly immigrant and working-class constituents, and who fail to utilize Latino-oriented media in a proactive manner risk reinforcing the existing hegemonic order.

Admittedly, the unequal power relations that define the Los Angeles political landscape, particularly the overconcentration of media in the hands of local and transnational corporate elites, present formidable obstacles to Latino representation. But recent history also shows that the pre-amnesty generation of Latino elected leaders often failed to create a discursive umbrella under which coalition building among progressives and Latino-led grassroots organizations could occur. Although they had attained the bully pulpit, this generation of Latino political leaders rarely published or broadcast their ideas outside their districts or legislative chambers. Worse, their poor to mediocre Spanish-speaking skills hindered their ability to utilize the Spanish-language media effectively, which represents a serious failing.

These Latino leaders, particularly those second- and third-generation Mexican Americans with rudimentary Spanish-speaking skills, have been slow to acknowledge the fact that the local and national Spanish-language media, especially radio and television, have permanently changed the political and cultural landscape of Los Angeles. For better or for worse, Spanish-language media, particularly broadcast forms, increasingly function as the space where Latino panethnicity is modified and constructed. And although advertising and marketing decisions play a large role in how the broadcast media construct Latino ethnicity, the narrow marketing focus of these media also creates significant spaces for other forms of political and cultural dialogue to occur. The anecdotal evidence suggests that increases in local and network Spanish-language television news coverage have helped increase Latino political awareness and participation, especially among urban immigrant audiences. In turn, modest increases in news and public affairs coverage have aided urban Latino politicization in at least two ways.

First, although they lack the financial resources of their counterparts in the English-language media, Spanish-language journalists reporting for Spanish speakers in the United States feel a stronger obligation to inform their audiences. Latino journalists' more developed sense of social responsibility stems from pragmatic acknowledgment that their immigrant audiences rely upon their news reports to survive in a new society. But these journalists and their audiences also, even when using empiricized American news formats, expect to be addressed in different discursive forms. Media researcher Virginia Escalante, a former *Los Angeles Times* reporter who is writing a history of Spanish-language newspapers in the United States, argues that Latino-owned newspapers tend to address their readers as citizens, whereas the major English-language newspapers first view their readers as consumers.[35] Whatever factor predominates, economics or culture, recent content studies show a marked discursive difference between English-language and Spanish-language news styles. For example, Spanish-language television news appears to place a greater emphasis upon reporting the social context surrounding crime, which stands in dramatic contrast to the sensational, decontextualized crime-by-crime water torture practiced by English-language television news.[36]

Second, the Spanish-language news media continue to assume an advocacy role on behalf of their audience, but usually within a narrow range of immigration-related and urban issues. In a lucrative, immigrant-supported media market such as Los Angeles, the Spanish-language broadcast media have acquired the economic independence to take bold stances on certain issues, at least compared to their English-language counterparts. Language and narrow marketing focus, in other words, offer Spanish-language news media a degree of discursive freedom not enjoyed by English-language media. Future studies should determine whether this discursive freedom has produced measurable political results. For example, it would not be unreasonable to hypothesize that the Spanish-language broadcast media's coverage of the Proposition 187 policy debates and the televised beating of a truckload of undocumented Latinos by two Riverside police officers helped to mobilize a large Latino voter turnout.[37] The coverage of the Proposition 187 campaign thus represented a kind of discursive victory, one in which the Spanish-language media succeeded in framing the debate from a pro-immigrant perspective. The coverage became so intensely pro-immigrant that Governor Pete Wilson felt compelled at times to complain that he was being "vilified" by the Spanish-language media. By the time the governor had finished his campaigns for Proposition 187 and the anti–affirmative action initiative, the Spanish-language media had effectively transformed Wilson into the Latino community's number-one enemy, which made sense, especially in marketing terms.

Although some Spanish-language media owners contributed funds for and against the Proposition 187 campaign, the news and public affairs coverage rarely forgot which master the owners served: the immigrant audiences that bought the products advertised on their networks. Even the historically conservative Spanish-language newspaper *La Opinión* took a strong stand against the proposition, "running stories of how different segments of the community might be impacted and on the fear 187 was generating." Publisher Monica Lozano also "put a personal stamp on her opposition, reducing ad rates to solicit money for anti–Prop. 187 groups, helping host a fund-raiser for Taxpayers Against 187, and donating $5,000 of her own money."[38] The boost in voter turnout triggered by Proposition 187 pushed Latinos back into the Democratic camp at a time when a shrinking Republican Party most needed new immigrant blood. Latino leaders and pundits, for their part, treated the strong Latino rejection of Wilson's policies as a blessing. The governor and his Republican allies, they argued, had succeeded in mobilizing Latino voters where others had failed. Yet few pundits or scholars credited the role the Spanish-language media played in mobilizing the Latino vote, or in fixing Wilson's racist and anti-immigrant image in the minds of Latino voters.

Still, Spanish-language media, like other media, have maintained a reactive posture to events that limits their discursive independence. The event-oriented focus of daily news coverage is obviously a structuring influence independent of language, as are the symbiotic relations between the media and the state. Another inhibiting factor is the absence of a dynamic Spanish-language print media. *La Opinión,* still the dominant Spanish-language newspaper in Southern California, remains the weakest link in the city's Latino media ecology. Although the paper continues its historic mission as an important forum for Latin American policy and cultural debates and sports coverage, it has not developed an investigative or political reporting tradition that breaks the major stories that shape policy or precipitate government action. Ideally, a paper like *La Opinión* should have the resources to do the more complicated stories on local politics, economics, and culture that would influence the news budgets of other local Spanish-language media. Moreover, sustained, aggressive, in-depth print reporting could better prepare Latino readers to increase their levels of civic participation and lay the groundwork for more enterprising Spanish-language broadcast reporting. Many had hoped that *La Opinión*'s impressive circulation gains and the infusion of new capital following Times Mirror Corporation's purchase of a half interest in the paper would have resulted in greater editorial independence and a more pronounced improvement in editorial quality. Recently, however, its growth has stalled. The paper's circulation gains have not been able to go beyond the hundred thousand level. And despite the new energy brought to the paper by Associate Publisher Lozano, the conservative family-run paper has yet to make a significantly larger investment in its editorial product. *La Opinión*'s news staff remains small, low paid, and, some say, demoralized, and the paper's imitation of English-language news formats remains uncritical. Others point to an excessively timid management style hamstrung by corporate interference from Times Mirror.[39] Whatever the reasons, *La Opinión* remains an underachiever when it comes to local news. And as we saw in the arena policy debate, the local English-language broadcast or print media cannot be relied upon to provide critical coverage for their own target audiences, let alone underserved Latino, African American, or Asian American audiences.

A comparable disconnect also characterizes the Spanish-language broadcast media's weak ties to the more assimilated Latino intellectuals and political leadership. For the latter groups, success in the university, the publishing world, and legislative politics rests on the ability to communicate in English, not in Spanish. Success in one realm has not directly facilitated the Latino intelligentsia's ability to cultivate support in the other. But given the Spanish-language news media's pro-immigrant stance, and its special access to the country's largest Latino community in Los Angeles, Latino leaders and intellectuals must make a systematic effort to bridge this gap. Latino academics can constructively engage the industry by investing more resources in the study and development of Latino-targeted media; by organizing conferences where academics, journalists, and progressives can discuss ways to improve news coverage; and by conducting workshops where community members can acquire media skills. Starting at the most elementary level, such dialogues could help the professional journalists expand their sourcing contacts in the academic community while providing journalists working in Latino-oriented media a chance to impress upon the academics and intellectuals the informational, rhetorical, and linguistic needs of their media. The Latino intelligentsia could also support the efforts of Spanish-language journalists to improve salaries and working conditions. All too often, journalists in the Spanish-language media are treated like second-class professionals; aside from its demoralizing effects, such treatment hinders the development of a Latino critical infrastructure. Addressing the concerns of Latino news editors who say that Spanish-language journalists lack the knowledge, skills, and contacts to cover local government effectively, Latino academics can use their institutional affiliations to organize special workshops on investigating City Hall and development politics. Better ongoing political and economic reporting could help shift the Spanish-language media from a relatively reactive to a more proactive discursive stance. Better coverage of the political economy could help immigrant audiences expand their levels of political participation beyond the immediate survival issues of immigration, health care, and gang violence.

Despite recent political gains, Latino elected officials in Greater Los Angeles represent another weak discursive link, especially when one contrasts them with the creative, vital, and varied Latino union leaders, community arts organizations, individual artists and intellectuals, church and environmental groups, and postamnesty political leaders who have begun to coalesce with non-Latino progressives on a range of issues. Coalitions such as the Los Angeles Alliance for a New Economy (LAANE) and the Bus Riders Union have reached across ethnic, gender, occupational, and neighborhood divisions to build social movements. As previously mentioned, LAANE and organizations like it continue to challenge the social relations of production within the region's largest cultural industry: the combined amusement, sporting, shopping, and multiscreen movie theater complexes packaged as megacultural destinations.[40] In another context, artists have joined forces with workers to engage important cultural empowerment. *Oficios Ocultos/Hidden Labor,* created by Common Threads Artists, stands out as one of the most interesting and creative of these collaborations.

Inside department store windows, where displays formerly showed off women's high fashion, a collective of women artists, academics, and garment workers narrated the history of female garment workers in Los Angeles. The display, or rather counterdisplay, illustrated how workers and progressives can expand the arena of contestation by occupying, reinterpreting, and denaturalizing one of the spaces the garment and retail clothing industry has used for fetishizing women's bodies.

Fortunately, some of the discursive preconditions for building a progressive coalition in Los Angeles already exist. Buoyed by the emergence of a Latino and Asian working class in the nation's largest industrial area, the postamnesty Latino leaders are already promoting varying degrees of multiethnic, multigendered, and class-sensitive social justice agendas. This new cadre of leaders will need to develop strategies that reject the racializing identity politics of the present and previous decades and find ways to address Los Angeles residents who believe that their city is fatally fractured, especially for suburban home owners who assume reactionary postures when negotiating their demands for equality with other groups. Obviously, leadership that fails to address the increasing disparity between rich and poor, between racialized inner-city residents and multiethnic suburban home owners, between the landscapes of elite leisure and degraded places of industrial production, cannot expect much success. At the same time, these leaders will have to find ways to deconstruct the elite discourses that promote lopsided, top-down notions of corporate development under the aegis of multicultural tourism and economic empowerment. Moreover, the Latino and Latina leadership of the twenty-first century should begin preparing answers to the divisive, racializing initiatives the next recession is sure to spawn.[41] As LAANE and other groups have begun to demonstrate, an effective progressive agenda can advance simultaneously on political, economic, and cultural fronts because these seemingly distinct spheres are in fact mutually constitutive. So far, these movements have combined an updated class analysis of low-wage immigrant labor and the discourse of multicultural diversity to build tolerance and unity amid ethnic differences. The challenge of integrating class and cultural discourses is more than theoretical.

Latinos, who constitute the majority of industrial workers and residents in both the city of Los Angeles and Los Angeles County, currently endure a symbolic economy that devalues their labor, creativity, and political participation. Patterns of representation have material effects to the degree that they reinforce existing power arrangements. Conventional labor and political organizing alone cannot challenge the cultural discourses that keep immigrant workers isolated and alienated. Moreover, in the first decade of

Assemblywoman Hilda Solis. Photograph courtesy of David Bacon, Northern California Coalition for Immigrant Rights.

the twenty-first century, Latinos will gain only slim majority margins. And given the still-lagging rates of Latino voter participation and the prevailing class and ethnic divisions that fragment the regional political landscape, no one elite or social sector can attain dominance without building coalitions. The process of weaving a coalition along class lines will help, but it will not overcome the years of socially constructed distrust that divide potential allies along the fault lines of class, ethnicity, gender, and sexual orientation.

## Desconstructing "Race Relations"

Constructing the Latino metropolis must also demystify the culture industries that construct and reinforce the discourses of race itself. This task requires an understanding of the new linkages between culture industries and the new urban political economy, an understanding of the changing social relations within and between cultural sectors, and a deeper appreciation of the vitality of lived popular culture in the Latino metropolis.

Although Latinos engage the city's culture wars without moral advantages, are clearly susceptible to petty tribalism, and are capable of racializing themselves and others, they nevertheless possess a historic and cultural legacy that can, in the long term, help overturn two particularly divisive aspects of urban "race relations." First, Latinos must elaborate a critical discourse of cultural *mestizaje,* one shorn of essentializing romanticism, to disarm racialized discourses that disguise the economic causes of urban conflict and social inequality. If there is anything the lesson of *mestizaje* teaches, it is that pseudoscientific racial categories are crisscrossed by the actualities of Latino genetic diversity and cultural hybridity. Second, a critical discourse of *mestizaje* grounded in the realities of the global city can be turned against those discourses of cultural production that treat ethnicity and race as commodities of "multicultural" tourism. As the vitality of popular culture continually reminds us, the freeways of cultural appropriation run in two directions. Edward W. Said emphasizes this point when he writes, "Cultural experience or indeed every cultural form is radically, quintessentially hybrid, and if it has been the practice of the West since Immanuel Kant to isolate cultural and aesthetic realms from the worldly domain, it is now time to rejoin them."[42]

What has not become sufficiently evident to Said and other cultural studies scholars, however, are the groundbreaking contributions of Latino intellectuals on the meanings and forms of mestizo hybridity, particularly when the discourse is expressed as one of the earliest critiques of Western colonialism.[43] In fact, Chicana feminist scholars have done some of the most ambitious work on this subject by resituating *mestizaje* in and along the borderlands.[44] The result has been to expand the meanings of *mestizaje* from a cultural to a political metaphor and, in the process, reconceptualize the meaning of culture itself.

Contrary to the construction of the southwestern borderlands and their Latinized cities as a zone of degradations, the Latinos who reside there, argues Renato Rosaldo, occupy one of the world's richest zones of "creative cultural production," which the dominant discourse renders as transitional and empty.

> Similarly, the borders between nations, classes, and cultures were endowed with a curious kind of hybrid invisibility. They seemed to be a little of this and a little of that, and not quite one or the other. Movements between such seemingly fixed entities as nations or social classes were relegated to the analytical dustbin of cultural invisibility. Immigrants and socially mobile individuals appeared culturally invisible because they were no longer what they once were, and not yet what they could become.[45]

In many ways, journalists' nonresponsiveness to multiple Latino identities resembles the academy's attitude toward border regions. Academic institutions maintain "fields" of social science the way the media inscribe the "race relations" discourse—by creating and maintaining boundaries that mutually validate their discursive authority. Under such marginalizing circumstances, political *mestizaje* survives as an outlaw discourse, acknowledged by Latino intellectuals and lived by the Latino community, but ignored by the nation's dominant institutions. Marginalization, however, does not imply the absence of a documented history or discourses. Since the end of the nineteenth century, Latin American writers and intellectuals such as José Martí have translated lived *mestizaje* into written discourse.

Although Latino *mestizaje* in the United States has its antecedents in Mexican and Latin American history, its "lived" experience in the United States has produced discursive innovations. On the U.S. side of the border, immigration accelerates the process through which Latinos simultaneously encounter the First World and other immigrants from the developing world whom they would have been less likely to meet had they stayed at home. On the U.S. side, the meaning and experience of *mestizaje* have also evolved beyond the bounds of official ideology, such as Mexico's ruling PRI, which has historically constructed its meanings so as to maintain a one-party state. Whereas in Mexico the term *mestizaje* have been co-opted to legitimate and integrate the nation's mestizo middle class and regional cultures, in the United States its lived experience occurs beyond official sanction and outside of institutionalized urban "race relations."

In its most mundane form, *mestizaje* on the U.S. side of the border expresses itself as a refusal to prefer one language, one genome, one national or cultural heritage at the expense of others. Culturally speaking, then, *mestizaje* is radically inclusive, a stubborn refusal to make the Sophie's choice between cultural identities and races. At times, its inclusions take the form of a literal transgression of political borders. These transgressions can be, especially when expressed by artists and intellectuals, overtly ideological. Thus, in the manner of Caliban, who uses Prospero's language to blaspheme his colonial enterprise, mestizo hybridity makes a virtue of appropriating elite culture for popular ends. Publishing ethnographies of elite power, for example, represents one way of turning the methods of neocolonialism against the neoliberal global city, in a practice Guillermo Gómez-Peña aptly calls "reverse anthropology."

The day-to-day expressions of *mestizaje*, however, are adaptive. Stated in economic terms, the globalization of capital, with its power to penetrate and dominate regional markets and undermine native economies, obliges the Mexican peasant or Guatemalan worker to ignore certain rules and boundaries in order to survive. Sentimental loyalty to a particular nation-state and, by extension, that state's idealized "traditional" culture becomes an impoverishing, even life-threatening luxury. To this extent, then, the lived transcultural experience of *mestizaje* must also be considered transnational and potentially postnational. And policies such as granting voting status to immigrants in school board elections, for example, represent important ways of granting institutional recognition to Latino political *mestizaje*.

To again borrow Gómez-Peña's phrasing, the border crosser thus operates as a kind of cultural "cross-dresser" who willfully blurs political, racial, or cultural borders in order to survive in an unjustly constructed world. The lived experience of cultural *mestizaje* is not schizoid, nor does it lack the boundedness to produce identity. Instead, Latinos have evolved a countertradition, or anti-aesthetic, of juggling languages, music, clothing styles, foods, gender, anything with which to fashion a more meaningful social and cultural coherence. And it is this aspect of cultural *mestizaje* that allows Latinos to participate in and express the most contemporary manifestations of modernity.

Whatever the terminology, the "styles" of mestizo cultural construction evolve dialectically, generating adaptive responses to changing material conditions and forms of cultural representation. Contrary to the musings of some European postmodernists, who see the multicultural Americas as an orgy of limitless conjunctions, heterodoxy in this hemisphere occurs within materially and culturally defined combinatory systems. Some combinatories are identified with specific cultural spaces—Nuevo Laredo or New Orleans—whereas others, like thousands of migrant Mexican workers, float or migrate, as it were, from place to place, physical or virtual, as individual or communal stylistic expressions. Whether rooted or moving, mestizo border culture coheres, acquires integrity and patterning from its mode of construction, which, depending on the circumstances, may be pragmatic, strategic, or ideological in its orientation to the world. Over time, these strategies take on the appearance of what some would call tradition but could more properly resemble the dialectic between genetics and environment. Like an individual's DNA, cultural *mestizaje* obeys its own rules of inclusion and exclusion, conjunction and disjunction. Whatever internal consistency it achieves is derived over time from the culture's repertoire of responses to a specific landscape, its material conditions and social relations. Latinos may have evolved a particular style of border crossing, but they are not unique in this practice. "All of us," Rosaldo writes, "inhabit an interdependent late-twentieth century world marked by borrowing and lending across porous national and cultural boundaries that are saturated with inequality, power, and domination."[46] Chicanos who live in the border-

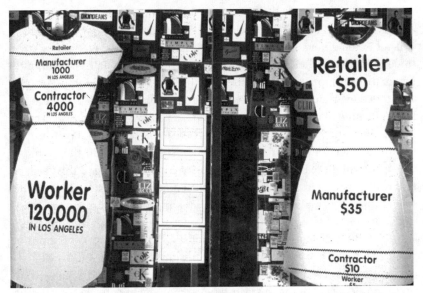

"The Shape of Low Wages and High Profits," Seventh Street and Grand. From the exhibit *Hidden Labor/Oficios Ocultos: Uncovering LA's Garment Industry.* Photograph courtesy of Common Threads Artists.

lands know this instinctively when they acknowledge their cultural differences and similarities to Mexicans or other Latinos.

However, *mestizaje* is one of many strategic responses to the decline of the imperial West, and is thus symptomatic of a world in flux. The lived cultural experience of more and more people occurs outside the cultural norms idealized by the state and its enabling institutional apparatus. Cultural *mestizaje*'s aggressive disregard for boundaries and unexpected inclusions should therefore be appreciated for its political possibilities in a context of global transformations.

Giving political expression to the praxis of mestizo border culture also offers a pragmatic alternative to representations that thwart coalition building in a multicultural city. The news media's reiteration of the "race relations" discourse has framed inner-city life as a competition in which contestants are defined by means of racial taxonomy. For Latinos, whose lived cultural experience spills beyond racialized boundaries, bending to or cooperating with the urban politics framed by the "race relations" discourse only delays the birth of a new political culture. Representations that encapsulate Latinos in essentialized racial or ethnic identities discourage use of the very tool—knowledge of their profound hybridity—with which they can unmask the lie of "race" and build an urban politics based upon common-alities of culture and class. Coalition builders in Los Angeles, Latino or not, will fail in imagining, let alone constructing, a new hegemony if they continue to represent their potential allies and friends in racialized terms and ignore the common interests created by the post-Fordist economy. The fail-ure to deconstruct the discourse of "race relations" may make the attain-ment of Latino majority status, even when backed by political power, a cruel disappointment. Latino leaders who continue to perpetuate minority think-ing by advancing their narrow ethnic interest in fact put off the moment when they might reap the fruits of majority power. Coming to this realiza-tion will mark the first step toward political maturity for Latino leadership. Acting upon this realization, by developing appropriate strategy and tac-tics, represents the second challenge.

Finally, a dialogue between journalists and intellectuals on cultural *mestizaje* could help reinforce certain healthy discursive tendencies al-ready present in Latino journalism. Latino academics should acknowledge those moments when the Spanish-language media effectively counter the mainstream media's racializing representations of Latinos and criticize the Spanish-language media when they reaffirm "race" as an objective reality. Latino intellectuals should encourage the Spanish-language media's efforts to construct a pan-Latino political culture based upon a critical analysis of Latino multiethnicity and criticize those media when they commodify *mestizaje* as a means to mercenary marketing ends.

Constructing a political dialogue that mitigates the weaknesses and exploits the strengths of Latino media becomes all the more crucial if we remember that the discourses of dominance will continue to face crises of signification. Some crises will be triggered by social upheavals caused by the growing disparities of late postindustrial capitalism, whereas others will result from the "multicultural" conflict powered by migration, demograph-ic change, and the continuing communication revolution. The blurring dis-tinction between media programming and computer software will also con-tinue to produce periods of discourse disequilibrium, as will the continuing decline of Fordist mass media and emerging post-Fordist demassified infor-mation industries. The atomization of media markets into ever smaller units will provide temporary tactical opportunities for Latino cultural workers to develop innovative progressive programming for economically viable eth-nic audiences, but only if they can obtain needed technical assistance. The recent upsurge in computer purchases among Latinos suggests that some of the cultural benefits of Internet access may become more widely avail-able to middle- and working-class Latinos than initially anticipated. In

"They Took Our Jobs and Sent Them Overseas," Seventh Street and Grand. From the exhibit *Hidden Labor/Oficios Ocultos: Uncovering LA's Garment Industry.* Photograph courtesy of Common Threads Artists.

this way, members of the emerging ethnic pluralities in the nation's image-making cities, both as consumers and workers, may acquire the tools with which to mobilize discursive responses when social and cultural upheavals recur. Each moral panic constructed by the state and the media also presents an opportunity for critical analysis and community action when anticipated in the Latino metropolis. The Latino community's success at advancing a political as well as cultural discourse of *mestizaje* can thus acquire strategic significance, both for the community itself and for other communities disappeared by dominant media discourses. Counterdiscourse based upon inclusion, that renders hybridity, ambiguity, and border experience meaningful and empowering, and that makes racialized categories uninhabitable will provide a nation as heterodox as the United States the acid with which to deconstruct its prisons of race and gender. To the degree a discourse of cultural *mestizaje* is not touted as a new orthodoxy, we believe it represents the greatest contribution Latinos will yet make to the United States. And Los Angeles, the nation's multicultural metropolis, will be the place where that contribution will first become evident.

# Notes

## Foreword

1. Saskia Sassen, *The Global City: New York, London, Tokyo*, rev. ed. (Princeton, N.J.: Princeton University Press, 2000).

2. See Frank Bonilla, Edwin Meléndez, Rebecca Morales, and María de los Angeles Torres, eds., *Borderless Borders: U.S. Latinos, Latin Americans, and the Paradox of Interdependence* (Philadelphia: Temple University Press, 1998).

3. See Alejandro Portes, ed., *The Economic Sociology of Immigration: Essays on Networks, Ethnicity, and Entrepreneurship* (New York: Russell Sage Foundation, 1995).

## Introduction

1. Selected portions of this introduction are taken from a research proposal written by David Theo Goldberg and Rodolfo D. Torres, "After 'Race' in the Metropolis: Racialized Relations in 'Postindustrial' Los Angeles," submitted to the Scholars and Seminars Program, Getty Center for the History of Art and the Humanities, 1996, and from Antonia Darder and Rodolfo D. Torres, " Latinos and Society: Culture, Politics, and Class," in *The Latino Studies Reader: Culture, Economy and Society*, Antonia Darder and Rodolfo D. Torres (Oxford: Blackwell, 1998).

2. As Jeremy Rifkin observes, white-collar jobs also are being eliminated at a rapid rate—more than three million during the past ten years, with more to follow. Although Rifkin does not specifically address the issue, the continuing displacement of jobs through technological innovation will only serve to heighten hostility toward Asian and Latino immigrants at all levels within the economy. See Jeremy Rifkin, *The End of Work: The Decline of the Global Labor Force and the Dawn of the Post-Market Era* (New York: Tarcher/Putnam, 1995).

3. In the summer of 1995, a garment subcontractor in El Monte, California, was discovered to have been holding seventy-two Thai immigrants—mostly female—in virtual bondage. See George White, "Workers Held in Near-Slavery, Officials Say," *Los Angeles Times*, August 3, 1995, A1, A20. Despite having one of the more robust economies in Southeast Asia, Thailand has developed a thriving trade in illegal immigration to the United States and other advanced capitalist societies. See

John-Thor Dahlburg, "Smuggling People to U.S. Is Big Business in Thailand," *Los Angeles Times,* September 5, 1995, A1, A8–A9.

4. County of Los Angeles, 1998, Urban Research Division, Chief Administrative Office, unpublished report released October 5, 1998. In the Los Angeles Unified School District, as of 1998, Latinos made up 69 percent of the total enrollment of 655,889. See Los Angeles Unified School District, Information Technology Division, "Ethnic Survey Report: Fall 1998," Publication 131 (Los Angeles, December 1998). During the 1997–98 school year, more than half of the students in L.A. County public schools were Latino (57 percent of the total enrollment of more than 1.5 million). See United Way of Greater Los Angeles, *State of the County Report: Los Angeles, 1998–99* (Los Angeles, March 1999). New census estimates show that Latino populations are increasing in other Southern California counties. Orange County is estimated to have 760,000 Latinos, making up 28 percent of the total county population, the fifth highest in the nation. See Megan Garvey, "Power in Numbers," *Los Angeles Times,* September 14, 1999, B1. The number of Latinos is expected to increase to 1.9 million, or 48 percent of the population of Orange County, according to projections released December 17, 1998, by the California Finance Department. See David Haldane, "O.C. in 2040: Near Majority of Latinos, Far Fewer Whites," *Los Angeles Times,* December 18, 1998, B1.

5. J. Scott and A. S. Paul, "Industrial Development in Southern California, 1970–1987," in *Our Changing Cities,* ed. John Fraser Hart (Baltimore: Johns Hopkins University Press, 1991). Although economic changes lie at its core, "post-Fordism" represents, according to several leading theorists, a wide range of social, political, and cultural forms. We recognize that there is considerable theoretical debate over how best to describe the changing nature and direction of the modern capitalist economy. For example, see Ash Amin, ed., *Post-Fordism: A Reader* (Oxford: Blackwell, 1994); Ellen Meiksins Wood, "Modernity, Postmodernity or Capitalism?" *Monthly Review* 48 (July/August 1996); Michel Aglietta, "Capitalism at the Turn of the Century: Regulation Theory and the Challenge of Social Change," *New Left Review* 232 (November/December 1998). There are competing opinions about the extent and meaning of these changes and whether they represent a new kind of epochal shift in the basic logic of capitalist accumulation. In the age of "postmodern" excess, where critiques of capitalism seem to be out of fashion, we maintain that class and capital still matter. For a perceptive and critical reading of the postmodern project, see Ellen Meiksins Wood, *Democracy against Capitalism: Renewing Historical Materialism* (Cambridge: Cambridge University Press, 1995). We find much to admire and learn from Wood's timely and much-needed critique of postmodernism and its failure to treat capitalism with analytic specificity. Nevertheless, our use of a critical "post-Fordist" framework to theorize about Latino Los Angeles is firmly rooted in Marx's critique of political economy.

6. Jack Kyser, *Manufacturing in Los Angeles* (Los Angeles: Los Angeles County Economic Development Corporation, 1999), 2. In 1998, L.A. County, with its 667,800 workers, was able to remain the nation's largest manufacturing area for the second year in the row.

7. Saskia Sassen, *The Global City: New York, London, Tokyo* (Princeton, N.J.: Princeton University Press, 1991). A new, updated edition of this volume was published in 2000.

8. James P. Allen and Eugene Turner, *The Ethnic Quilt : Population Diversity in*

*Southern California* (Northridge: California State Unversity, Center for Geographical Studies, 1997).

9. California Assembly, Select Committee on the California Middle Class, *The Distribution of Income in California and Los Angeles: A Look at Recent Current Population Survey and State Taxpayer Data* (Sacramento, May 16, 1998).

10. Don Lee, "L.A. County Jobs Surge since '93, but Not Wages," *Los Angeles Times,* July 26, 1999, A1.

11. Quoted in ibid.

12. Saskia Sassen, "New Employment Regimes in Cities: The Impact on Immigrant Workers," *New Community* 22 (October 1996): 590.

13. Richard B. Freeman, *The New Inequality: Creating Solutions for Poor America* (Boston: Beacon, 1999). For an excellent discussion of increasing class inequality and the need for a progressive movement to combat it, see William Julius Wilson, *The Bridge over the Racial Divide: Rising Inequality and Coalition Politics* (Berkeley: University of California Press, 1999). See also Jared Bernstein, Elizabeth C. McNichol, Lawrence Mishel, and Robert Zahradnik, *Pulling Apart: A State-by-State Analysis of Income Trends* (Washington D.C.: Center on Budget and Policy Priorities/Economic Policy Institute, 2000).

14. Stuart Hall, "The Local and the Global: Globalization and Ethnicity," in *Culture, Globalization, and the World-System,* ed. Anthony D. King (Minneapolis: University of Minnesota Press, 1997), 27.

15. David Harvey, *The Condition of Postmodernity* (Oxford: Blackwell, 1989).

16. Mike Davis, *City of Quartz: Excavating the Future in Los Angeles* (New York: Verso, 1990); Edward W. Soja, *Thirdspace: Journeys to Los Angeles and Other Real-and-Imagined Places* (Cambridge, Mass.: Blackwell, 1996); Roger Keil, *Los Angeles: Globalization, Urbanization and Social Struggles* (New York: John Wiley, 1998); Louis F. Miron, "Corporate Ideology and the Politics of Entrepreneurism in New Orleans," *Antipode* 24 (October 1992).

17. David Harvey, *Justice, Nature, and the Geography of Difference* (Cambridge, Mass.: Blackwell, 1996), 359.

18. Quoted in Kuan-Hsing Chen, "Cultural Studies and the Politics of Internationalization: An Interview with Stuart Hall," in *Stuart Hall: Critical Dialogues in Cultural Studies,* David Morley and Kuan-Hsing Chen (London: Routledge, 1996), 400.

19. For an impressive study of the Watts uprising and an informative epilogue on the 1992 civil unrest, see Gerald Horne, *Fire This Time: The Watts Uprising and the 1960s* (Charlottesville: University Press of Virginia, 1995).

20. For an excellent analysis of the forces that produce the internal shape of cities, see Ronald Van Kemper and Peter Marcuse, "A New Spatial Order in Cities," *American Behavioral Scientist* 41 (November/December 1997): 205–90.

21. See Robert Miles, *Racism* (London: Routledge, 1989); Robert Miles, *Racism after Race Relations* (London: Routledge, 1993); Michel Wieviorka, *The Arena of Racism* (London: Sage, 1995); Colette Guillaumin, *Racism, Sexism, Power and Ideology* (London: Routledge, 1995); David Theo Goldberg, *Racist Culture: Philosophy and the Politics of Meaning* (Cambridge, Mass.: Blackwell, 1993); Steve Small, "The Contours of Racialization: Structures, Representations, and Resistance in the United States," in *Race, Identity, and Citizenship: A Reader,* ed. Rodolfo D. Torres, Louis F. Miron, and Jonathan Xavier Inda (Malden, Mass.: Blackwell, 1999); Rodolfo D. Torres

and Chor Swang Ngin, "Racialized Boundaries, Class Relations, and Cultural Politics: The Asian American and Latino Experience," in *Culture and Difference: Critical Perspectives on the Bicultural Experience in the United States,* ed. Antonia Darder (Westport, Conn: Bergin and Garvey, 1995); Victor M. Valle and Rodolfo D. Torres, "The Idea of Mestizaje and the 'Race' Problematic: Racialized Media Discourse in a Post-Fordist Landscape," in *Culture and Difference: Critical Perspectives on the Bicultural Experience in the United States,* ed. Antonia Darder (Westport, Conn.: Bergin and Garvey, 1995); Antonia Darder and Rodolfo D. Torres, "Latinos and Society: Culture, Politics, and Class, " in *The Latino Studies Reader: Culture, Economy and Society,* ed. Antonia Darder and Rodolfo D. Torres (Oxford: Blackwell, 1998); Peter McLaren and Rodolfo D. Torres, "Racism and Multicultural Education: Rethinking 'Race' and 'Whiteness' in Late Capitalism," in *Critical Multiculturalism: Rethinking Multicultural and Antiracist Education,* ed. Steven May (London: Falmer, 1999); K. Anthony Appiah, "Race, Culture, Identity: Misunderstood Connections," in *Color Conscious: The Political Morality of Race,* ed. K. Anthony Appiah and Amy Gutmann (Princeton, N.J.: Princeton University Press, 1996); Barbara Fields, "Slavery, Race, and Ideology in the United States of America," *New Left Review,* 181 (May/June 1990): 95–118.

22. Miles, *Racism,* 75.

23. As Stuart Hall has pointed out, a critical notion of ethnicity is required to "position" the discourse of racialized relations within particular histories related to the structure of class formation and regional and cultural traditions. Stuart Hall, "Ethnicity: Identities and Difference," *Radical America* 23, no. 4 (1989): 9–20.

## 1. Economic Geography of Latino Los Angeles

1. David Freed, "Few Safeguards Protect Workers from Poisons," *Los Angeles Times,* September 6, 1993, A1.

2. Ibid.

3. These data were gathered and analyzed by Geotz Wolff, "County Business Patterns, Change in Number of Small Manufacturing Establishments, Los Angeles County (1979–1990)," in U.S. Department of Commerce, *Resources for Employment and Economic Development* (Washington, D.C., May 1994).

4. Tom Larson and Miles Finney, *Rebuilding South Central Los Angeles: Myths, Realities and Opportunities,* final report (Los Angeles: California State University, School of Business and Economics, 1996), 152.

5. See J. Scott and A. S. Paul, "Industrial Development in Southern California, 1970–1987," in *Our Changing Cities,* ed. John Fraser Hart (Baltimore: Johns Hopkins University Press, 1991), 190–91.

6. Ibid., 209.

7. See Sharon Zukin, *Landscapes of Power: From Detroit to Disney World* (Berkeley: University of California Press, 1991).

8. Ibid., 16.

9. Ibid., 5.

10. See Joel Garreau, *Edge City: Life on the New Frontier* (New York: Doubleday, 1991).

11. Rodolfo F. Acuña, *Community under Siege: A Chronicle of Chicanos East of the Los Angeles River, 1945–1975,* Monograph 11 (Los Angeles: University of California, Chicano Studies Research Center, 1984), 7–10.

12. Ibid., 10–11.

13. Ibid., 10–13.

14. George J. Sanchez, *Becoming Mexican-American: Ethnicity, Culture and Identity in Chicano Los Angeles, 1900–1945* (New York: Oxford University Press, 1993), 65–70.

15. Mike Davis, "The Empty Quarter," in *Sex, Death, and God in L.A.,* ed. David Reid (New York: Pantheon, 1992), 56–58.

16. Scott and Paul, "Industrial Development," 198.

17. Ibid.

18. Bill Boyarsky and Nancy Boyarsky, *Backroom Politics: How Your Local Politicians Work, Why Your Government Doesn't, and What You Can Do about It* (Los Angeles: J. P. Tarcher, 1974), 52.

19. Victor Valle and Rodolfo D. Torres, "The Economic Landscape of the Greater Eastside: Latino Politics in 'Post-industrial' Los Angeles," *Prism* 1 (fall 1993): 15.

20. Boyarsky and Boyarsky, *Backroom Politics,* 62–70.

21. Mike Davis, *City of Quartz: Excavating the Future in Los Angeles* (New York: Verso, 1990), 165–69.

22. Dan Morain and Victor Valle, "City of Industry: It Has Clout Where It Counts—in the State Capitol," *Los Angeles Times,* April 15, 1984, A3.

23. The following analysis of SIC categories in the First District was based on the database compiled in Los Angeles Area Chamber of Commerce, *Southern California Business Directory and Buyers Guide* (Los Angeles: Los Angeles Area Chamber of Commerce, 1992), which lists the number of employees, year established, payroll information, type of business, plant size, annual revenue, and description of each business, as well as primary and secondary SIC codes. Chamber of Commerce officials claim that the database includes a 60 percent sampling of manufacturing businesses in California. These data, however, must be placed in proper context, because the twenty-one-city group for which SIC codes were analyzed accounts for only 53 percent of the district's total population. Further analysis of districtwide data is needed; however, other studies provide some partial answers. Scott and Paul, for example, estimate that more than 96,000 workers are employed by apparel and other textile manufacturers, almost all of which are located within the First District's boundaries ("Industrial Development," 197, Table 11.4; 199, Figure 11.3). By contrast, only 2.95 percent of, or 3,714, jobs fell under SIC 23 (apparel and other textile products) in the First District's twenty-one-city group, a figure that suggests a lack of sampling redundancy.

24. The Rebuild L.A. organization used Dun & Bradstreet direct-access software to identify firms located in "economically neglected" areas of Los Angeles County according to SIC code, company size, number of employees, zip code, and other variables. It defined as economically neglected communities where more than 20 percent of the population lives below the poverty level and included the Greater Eastside, the downtown area, South-Central, and Compton, among others. Results of the RLA survey are presented in Linda Wong, "The Role of Immigrant Entrepreneurs in Urban Economic Development," *Stanford Law and Policy Review* 7 (summer 1996).

25. Joel Kotkin, Los Angeles business economist, interview by Victor Valle, tape recording, Los Angeles, May 1992.

26. Vilma Ortiz, "The Mexican-Origin Population: Permanent Working Class or Emerging Middle Class?" in *Ethnic Los Angeles,* ed. Roger Waldinger and Mehdi Bozorgmehr (New York: Russell Sage Foundation, 1996), 275.

27. Miles Corwin, "Vernon Redevelopment Plan Is Sticky Business," *Los Angeles Times,* November 10, 1991, B1, B3.

28. See Frank Escher and Ravi GuneWardena, eds., *Cruising Industrial Los Angeles* (Los Angeles: Los Angeles Conservancy, 1997), 32; David Ferrel, "Top-Paid City Official in State; Vernon Administrator—a Study in Power, Control," *Los Angeles Times,* May 20, 1989, A1; City of Vernon, "Light and Power Gross & Net Revenue, 1988–1993," statement attached to a letter from city administrator Bruce V. Malkenhorst to attorney Roy Ulrich, November 16, 1993; Corwin, "Vernon Redevelopment Plan," B1, B3.

29. Davis, "The Empty Quarter," 60.

30. Scott and Paul, "Industrial Development," 205.

31. City of Industry, "City of Industry Data, Chamber of Commerce," on-line at http://www.cityofindustry.org/ctycncl.htm, accessed May 6, 1999.

32. We analyzed tax increment diversions by calculating the total number of city- and county-run redevelopment projects within each of the five supervisorial districts. Increment figures were obtained from the Office of the State Controller, *Annual Report 1989–1990 Financial Transactions Concerning Community Redevelopment Agencies of California* (Los Angeles: California State Division of Local Government Fiscal Affairs, 1991), 296–340.

33. Office of the State Controller, *Annual Report 1991–1992 Financial Transactions Concerning Community Redevelopment Agencies of California* (Los Angeles: California State Division of Local Government Fiscal Affairs, 1993), 320–63, Table 6.

34. Office of the State Controller, *Annual Report 1994–1995 Financial Transactions Concerning Community Redevelopment Agencies of California* (Los Angeles: California State Division of Local Government Fiscal Affairs, 1996), 341–89, Table 6.

35. The Second District's largest tax increment recipient—the Carson Redevelopment Agency—represents the exception to the rule. In the 1994–95 fiscal year, the agency received more than $14.3 million in increments, most of which went to developing a corridor of electronics factories and warehouses along the 90 Freeway.

36. Office of the State Controller, *Annual Report 1989–1990 Financial Transactions Concerning Community Redevelopment Agencies of California* (Los Angeles: California State Division of Local Government Fiscal Affairs, 1991), 313, 323.

37. Industry Manufacturers Council, *City of Industry Factbook* (City of Industry, Calif.: Industry Manufacturers Council, 1990), 6.

38. Shawn Hubler, "South L.A.'s Poverty Rate Worse than '65," *Los Angeles Times,* May 11, 1992, A1.

39. Valle and Torres, "The Economic Landscape," 15.

40. Ibid.

41. Magit Mayer, "Politics in the Post-Fordist City," *Socialist Review* 21, no. 1 (1991): 112.

42. Ibid., 113.

43. Myron Orfield, "Salvaging Suburbia: How to Stop Communities from Growing Farther and Farther Apart," *Los Angeles Times,* November 15, 1998, M1. For an excellent book-length study of regional economic trends and policy solutions, see

Myron Orfield's *Metropolitics: A Regional Agenda for Community Stability,* rev. ed. (Washington, D.C.: Brookings Institution Press, 1998).

44. Quoted in Nancy Cleeland, "Home-Care Workers' Vote for Union a Landmark for Labor," *Los Angeles Times,* February 26, 1999, A1.

45. Harold Meyerson, "Caretakers Take Charge: 75,000 Workers (in 75,000 Work Sites!) Form a Union," *L.A. Weekly,* February 26–March 4, 1999, 16.

46. Roger Waldinger and Michael Lichter, "Anglos: Beyond Ethnicity?" in *Ethnic Los Angeles,* ed. Roger Waldinger and Mehdi Bozorgmehr (New York: Russell Sage Foundation, 1996), 453.

## 2. "Policing" Race

1. These poll results were revisited in "Separate Lives: Dealing with Race in L.A.," *Los Angeles Times,* November 16, 1992, special section, "Understanding The Riots—Six Months Later," JJ4.

2. According to a *Times* article, 77 percent of the city's households tuned to local television news by 8 P.M. on the first evening of the riot. See Daniel Cerone, "L.A. Turns on TV Sets as Disturbances Erupt," *Los Angeles Times,* May 1, 1992, F1.

3. Paul Lieberman and Richard O'Reilly, "Most Looters Endured Lives of Crime, Poverty," *Los Angeles Times,* May 2, 1993, A1.

4. Jean Merl, "City Still Viewed as Racially Split;" *Los Angeles Times,* April 29, 1997, A1.

5. See Ted Koppel and Kyle Gibson, *Nightline: History in the Making and the Making of Television* (New York: Times Books, 1996), 364–69.

6. Ibid., 416–19.

7. Paul Lieberman, "51% of Riot Arrests Were Latino, Study Says," *Los Angeles Times,* June 18, 1992, B3. The proportion is noteworthy. The sophisticated intelligence-gathering methods available to police gave them the means to report higher levels of participation, but they did not. And given that the data did not identify gang members by race, it is safe to assume that not all of the one in ten arrested were black, further diluting the media image of rioting black hoodlums.

8. Lieberman and O'Reilly, "Most Looters Endured Lives of Crime," A1.

9. Joel Kotkin, "Los Angeles Riots: Causes, Myths and Solutions," unpublished manuscript, Progressive Policy Institute, Washington, D.C., October 1992, 4.

10. We acknowledge the limitations of our theoretical compensations. Because cultural studies scholars raise qualitative questions of meaning, the application of semiotic or close reading methodologies cannot evade the subjectivity embedded in interpretive analysis. But, as Stuart Hall reminds us, mainstream media studies that try to measure media effects upon behavior neither directly confirm nor disprove the media's role in the formation of cultural blocs, the social construction of identity, or the maintenance of cultural hegemony—each of these an important theme of cultural criticism. As a result, the narrow focus of mainstream media studies has forced scholars who want to validate the claims of cultural criticism empirically to pursue unorthodox cross-disciplinary pairings of theory and methodology.

11. Erna Smith, "Transmitting Race: The Los Angeles Riot in Television News," in *Press Politics, Public Policy,* Research Paper R-11 (Cambridge: Harvard University, John F. Kennedy School of Government, 1994). Smith coded text and images from 903 stories and 2,228 sound bites. Her content analysis includes 621 riot news items and

282 general news stories, totaling 28.5 broadcast hours aired between April 29, 1992, the day the Rodney King verdict was announced, and May 12, two weeks later (see p. 4).

12. Darnell M. Hunt, *Screening the Los Angeles "Riots"* (Cambridge: Cambridge University Press, 1997), 37–38.

13. Smith, "Transmitting Race," 1.

14. Ibid., 2.

15. Ibid., 3.

16. Ibid., 45.

17. Ibid., 7.

18. Hunt, *Screening the Los Angeles "Riots,"* 44.

19. Smith, "Transmitting Race," 7.

20. Ibid., 9.

21. Ibid., 9–10.

22. Ibid., 10.

23. Hunt, *Screening the Los Angeles "Riots,"* 41–42.

24. Smith, "Transmitting Race," 11–12.

25. Ibid., 9.

26. Ibid., 7.

27. Ibid.

28. Hunt, *Screening the Los Angeles "Riots,"* 43–44.

29. Smith, "Transmitting Race," 7.

30. Hunt, *Screening the Los Angeles "Riots,"* 42–48.

31. Ibid., 45–47.

32. Ibid., 45.

33. Smith, "Transmitting Race," 14.

34. Manuel Pastor Jr., *Latinos and the Los Angeles Uprising: The Economic Context* (Claremont, Calif.: Tomas Rivera Center, 1993), 11–12.

35. Ibid., 9–10.

36. Ibid., 9, Table 1 and Figure 1; 10, Table 2 and Figure 2.

37. Ibid.

38. Ibid., 35, 44.

39. Lieberman, "51% of Riot Arrests," B3.

40. Smith, "Transmitting Race," 13.

41. Ibid., 7.

42. Pastor, *Latinos and the Los Angeles Uprising,* 27.

43. Cornel West, *Race Matters* (New York: Vintage, 1993), 12.

44. Smith, "Transmitting Race," 14–16.

45. Melita Marie Garza, "Hola, America! Newsstand 2000," *Media Studies Journal* 8 (summer 1994): 159. See also National Council of La Raza, "Out of the Picture: Hispanics in the Media"; Jorge Quiroga, "Hispanic Voices: Is the Press Listening?"; and Robert S. Lichter and Daniel R. Amundson, "Distorted Reality: Hispanic Characters in TV Entertainment," all in *Latin Looks: Images of Latinas and Latinos in the U.S. Media,* ed. Clara E. Rodriguez (Boulder, Colo.: Westview, 1997).

46. See Marc Cooper and Greg Goldin, "Some People Don't Count" (45), and Tom Carson, "Do You Fear the Coming Darkness?" (117), both in *Inside the L.A. Riots:*

*What Really Happened and Why It Will Happen Again,* ed. Don Hazen (New York: Institute for Alternative Journalism, 1992); *Los Angeles Times,* May 6, 1992, F1; Patrick McDonnell, "Riot Aftermath; Scores of Suspects Arrested in Riots Turned Over to INS," *Los Angeles Times,* May 6, 1992, B3; Eric Bailey, "Rohrbacher Blasts Rioters in U.S. Illegally," *Los Angeles Times,* Orange County ed., May 7, 1992, A1.

47. Neither Hunt nor Smith developed methods of content observation that focused upon the media's representation of Latinos, even though Latino scholars have developed the conceptual tools to approach the subject.

48. Hunt, *Screening the Los Angeles "Riots,"* 169–70.

49. Adriana Olivarez, "Studying Representations of U.S. Latinos," *Journal of Communication Inquiry* 22 (October 1998): 432.

50. See Franklin D. Gilliam Jr., Shanto Iyengar, Adam Simon, and Oliver Wright, "Crime in Black and White: The Violent, Scary World of Local News," *Harvard International Journal of Press/Politics* 1, no. 3 (1996): 6–23; Hemant Shah and Michael C. Thorton, "Racial Ideology in U.S. Mainstream News Magazine Coverage of Black Latino Interaction, 1980–1992," *Critical Studies in Mass Communication* 11 (June 1994): 141–61; Lichter and Amundson, "Distorted Reality," 57–72.

51. Garza, "Hola, America!" 158; Mike Feinsilber, "Editors Set Goals for Diversity," *Associated Press/AP Online,* October 21, 1998, 2.

52. Thomas S. McCoy, *Voices of Difference: Studies in Critical Philosophy and Mass Communication* (Cresskill, N.J.: Hampton, 1993), 141.

53. Hunt, *Screening the Los Angeles "Riots,"* 155, 157; Mike Freeman, "L.A.'s Local News Takes to the Streets," *Broadcasting,* May 4, 1992, 11.

54. Carson, "Do You Fear the Coming Darkness?" 115; Cooper and Goldin, "Some People Don't Count," 45; Howard Rosenberg, "TV's Double Edged Role in Crisis," *Los Angeles Times,* May 1, 1992, F1.

55. McCoy, *Voices of Difference,* 143–44; see also 156.

56. J. Scott and A. S. Paul, "Industrial Development in Southern California, 1970–1987," in *Our Changing Cities,* ed. John Fraser Hart (Baltimore: Johns Hopkins University Press, 1991).

57. Mike Davis, "The Empty Quarter," in *Sex, Death, and God in L.A.,* ed. David Reid (New York: Pantheon, 1992), 57.

58. Miles Corwin, "L.A.'s Loss: 'Black Flight,'" *Los Angeles Times,* August 13, 1992, A1; Jeremy Rifkin, *The End of Work: The Decline of the Global Labor Force and the Dawn of the Post-Market Era* (New York: Tarcher/Putnam, 1995), chap. 5.

59. Davis, "The Empty Quarter," 57.

60. Shawn Hubler, "South L.A.'s Poverty Rate Worse than '65," *Los Angeles Times,* May 11, 1992, A1.

61. "Understanding the Riots, Part 1: The Path to Fury," special section, *Los Angeles Times,* May 11, 1992, T2–T12.

62. Ibid.

63. Teun A. van Dijk, *Elite Discourse and Racism* (Newbury Park, Calif.: Sage, 1993), 7–12.

64. Hunt, *Screening the Los Angeles "Riots,"* 75.

65. Ibid., 75–76.

66. Ibid., 162–63.

67. Ibid., 163.

68. Quoted in Ruben Martinez, "Perspective on the Latino Community: 'This Was about Something to Eat,'" *Los Angeles Times,* May 18, 1992, B5.

69. Quoted in George Ramos and Tracy Wilkinson, "Unrest Widens Rift in Diverse Latino Population," *Los Angeles Times,* May 8, 1992, A1.

70. Eric Popkin, Lourdes Arguelles DeSipio, and Harry Pachon, *Constructing the Los Angeles Area Latino Mosaic: A Demographic Portrait of Guatemalans and Salvadorans in Los Angeles* (Claremont, Calif.: Tomas Rivera Policy Institute, 1997), 1.

## 3. Mexican Cuisine

1. Charles Fletcher Lummis, *The Landmarks Club Cook Book: A California Collection of the Choicest Recipes from Everywhere . . . Including a Chapter of the Most Famous Old Californian and Mexican Dishes by Chas. Fletcher Lummis* (Los Angeles: Out West, 1903), i.

2. Carey McWilliams, *North from Mexico: The Spanish-Speaking People of the United States* (New York: Greenwood, 1948), 35–47.

3. See Charles Ramirez Berg, "Stereotyping in Films in General and of the Hispanic in Particular," in *Latin Looks: Images of Latinas and Latinos in the U.S. Media,* ed. Clara E. Rodriguez (Boulder, Colo.: Westview, 1997), 113–15.

4. Sharon Zukin, *Landscapes of Power: From Detroit to Disney World* (Berkeley: University of California Press, 1991), 206.

5. Ibid., 215.

6. Sharon Zukin, *The Culture of Cities* (Cambridge, Mass.: Blackwell, 1995).

7. Ibid., 155.

8. Ibid., 180.

9. Michael Dear, ed., *Atlas of Southern California, Prepared for the USC Presidential Roundtable* (Los Angeles: University of Southern California, Southern California Studies Center, November 12, 1996), 26.

10. Zukin, *The Culture of Cities,* 156.

11. Ibid., 7.

12. Maria L. LaGanga, "At a Career Crossroads? Try the Kitchen," *Los Angeles Times,* March 2, 1997, A1, A24; George T. Silvestri, "Occupational Employment to 2005," *Monthly Labor Review* 118 (November 1995): 60–84.

13. California Health and Human Services Agency Data Center, "Labor Market Information, Los Angeles County, Occupational Employment Projections, 1995–2002," Module D, Table 6, line 393 (food, beverage preparation and service occupations), on-line at http://www.calmis.co.gov/file/occproj/latb6.htm; Zukin, *The Culture of Cities,* 161; New York City Press Ofiice, "Mayor Giuliani Celebrates *Restaurant Week* in the Restaurant Capital of the World: 118 Restaurants Will Offer Specials during *Restaurant Week* through Saturday, June 27," June 24, 1998, on-line at http://www.ci.nyc.ny.us/html/om/html/98a/pr295–98.html.

14. Dear, *Atlas of Southern California,* 13; John G. Watson, "Busboys' Night Out; Top Latino Restaurant Workers to Be Feted at Ceremony Jan. 17," *Nuestro Tiempo, Los Angeles Times,* November 5, 1992, 2.

15. James Bates, "Hollywood Is Star," *Los Angeles Times,* January 18, 1998, A1.

16. Zukin, *The Culture of Cities,* 2.

17. For example, Times Mirror Corporation is a major property owner, a mem-

ber of the downtown elite, and, as owner of the *Los Angeles Times,* a member of a regional communications elite. Under certain circumstances, the functions of primary definer and secondary definer of the symbolic economy are discharged by different branches of a single corporate culture, an incestuous relationship that the public often finds difficult to unravel.

18. Charles Fletcher Lummis, *Letters from the Southwest, September 20, 1884 to March 14, 1885,* ed. James W. Byrkit (Tucson: University of Arizona Press, 1989), xxxvi.

19. Ibid, xxxvii.

20. Ibid.; Dudley Gordon, *Charles F. Lummis: Crusader in Corduroy* (Los Angeles: Cultural Assets, 1972), 165–68.

21. C.W., "The Old Missions: They Should Be Preserved as Old-Time Relics," *Los Angeles Daily Times,* January 24, 1896, 24; Lummis, *Letters from the Southwest,* xlv.

22. Lummis, *Letters from the Southwest,* xviii–xxvi.

23. Ibid., xxiii.

24. Quoted in George J. Sanchez, *Becoming Mexican-American: Ethnicity, Culture and Identity in Chicano Los Angeles, 1900–1945* (New York: Oxford University Press, 1993), 71.

25. Mike Davis, *City of Quartz: Excavating the Future in Los Angeles* (New York: Verso, 1990), 24–30.

26. Lummis, *Letters from the Southwest,* xxiv.

27. Sanchez, *Becoming Mexican-American,* 70–71, 76–77.

28. See Uma Narayan, "Eating Cultures: Incorporation, Identity and Indian Food," *Social Identities* 1, no. 1 (1995): 63–86.

29. Chon Noriega, "Birth of the Southwest: Social Protest, Tourism and D. W. Griffith's *Ramona,*" in *The Birth of Whiteness: Race and the Emergence of U.S. Cinema,* ed. Daniel Bernardi (New Brunswick, N.J.: Rutgers University Press, 1996), 206.

30. Ibid., 204.

31. Bertha Haffner-Ginger, *California Mexican-Spanish Cook Book* (Los Angeles: Citizen's Print Shop, 1914), n.p.

32. W. W. Robinson, *Los Angeles from the Days of the Pueblo: A Brief History and Guide to the Plaza Area* (San Francisco: California Historical Society, 1981), chaps. 1–5; Sanchez, *Becoming Mexican-American,* 72.

33. "To Save the Plaza: Landmarks Club Will Oppose Any Perversion of It," *Los Angeles Daily Times,* January 29, 1896, Public Service sec., p. 7; "Afternoon Session: City Attorney's Opinion in the Plaza Public-Market Case," *Los Angeles Daily Times,* February 4, 1896, Public Service sec., p. 9.

34. William D. Estrada, "The Los Angeles Plaza: Myth, Memory, Symbol, and the Struggle for Place in a Changing Metropolis, 1781–1990s" (slide/lecture presentation of archival materials from El Pueblo de Los Angeles Historical Monument, California Polytechnic State University, San Luis Obispo, Department of Ethnic Studies, January 9, 1997).

35. Ray Oldenburg, "Food, Drink, Talk, and the Third Place," *Journal of Gastronomy* 6 (summer 1990): 3–16.

36. Sanchez, *Becoming Mexican-American,* 180.

37. Ibid., 171–87.

38. Victor M. Valle, "'Break of Dawn'—Bilingual Experiment," *Los Angeles Times,* July 5, 1987, F22, F30–F31.

39. Vivien Bonzo and her father, Alfredo Antonio, interview by Victor Valle, tape recording, La Golondrina, Olvera Street, Los Angeles, August 1995; Oldenburg, "Food, Drink, Talk."

40. "Un Sencillo Homenaje a la Señorita Fabregas [A simple homage to Miss Fabregas]," *La Opinión,* May 13, 1927, Society sec., p. 4, our translation. This article appeared next to an advertisement for the play *Divorciémonos.*

41. Bonzo, interview; Sanchez, *Becoming Mexican-American,* 123.

42. Sanchez, *Becoming Mexican-American,* 225.

43. In her interview, Vivien Bonzo acknowledged Sterling's intervention on her mother's behalf; a September 16, 1926, advertisement in *La Opinión* lists a 132 South Spring Street address for the cafe.

44. Rodolfo F. Acuña, *Community under Siege: A Chronicle of Chicanos East of the Los Angeles River, 1945–1975,* Monograph 11 (Los Angeles: University of California, Chicano Studies Research Center, 1984), 7–11. Estrada also discusses Chandler's plans for Spring Street in *The Los Angeles Plaza.*

45. Bonzo, interview; Estrada, *The Los Angeles Plaza.*

46. Francisco E. Balderrama and Raymond Rodriguez, *Decade of Betrayal: Mexican Repatriation in the 1930s* (Albuquerque: University of New Mexico Press, 1995), 57, 122.

47. Mario Garcia and Ruben Salazar, *Southern California's Latino Community: A Series of Articles Reprinted from the Los Angeles Times, July 24, 1983 to August 14, 1983* (Los Angeles: *Los Angeles Times,* 1983).

48. Victor M. Valle, *Recipe of Memory: Five Generations of Mexican Cuisine* (New York: New Press, 1995), 171–72.

49. Mark Preston, *California Mission Cookery: A Vanished Cuisine—Rediscovered* (Albuquerque, N.M.: Border, 1994), x.

50. Ruth Reichl, "Restaurants in the Eighties; L.A. Discovers the Exotic in Its Own Back Yard," *Los Angeles Times,* December 29, 1989, F16; "The Tradition of the New," *Los Angeles Times,* November 7, 1991, H11; Charles Perry, "Fusion Food; Birth of a Nation's Cuisine," *Los Angeles Times,* September 16, 1993, H12; Victor M. Valle, "A Curse of Tea and Potatoes: A Discourse Analysis of Encarnación Pinedo's *Cocinero Español,*" *Latino Studies Journal* 8 (fall 1997): 1–18.

51. See Claude Fischler, "The Michelin Galaxy: Nouvelle Cuisine, Three-Star Restaurants, and the Culinary Revolution," *Journal of Gastronomy* 6 (autumn 1990): 85–91.

52. Ibid., 92.

53. Zukin, *The Culture of Cities,* 209.

54. John Rivera Sedlar, *Modern Southwest Cuisine* (New York: Simon & Schuster, 1986), 13, 16. Rivera Sedlar's latest collaboration with Mark Miller, *Tamales* (New York: Macmillan, 1997), continues along a similar nouvelle vein, but at least begins with a serious acknowledgment of Oaxacan cooking technique and aesthetics.

55. Genaro Padilla, "Imprisoned Narrative? Or Lies, Secrets, and Silence in New Mexico Women's Autobiography," in *Criticism in the Borderlands: Studies in Chicano Literature, Culture, and Ideology,* ed. Hector Calderon and José David Saldívar (Durham, N.C.: Duke University Press, 1991), 54.

56. The Los Angeles Culinary Institute's Web site address is http://www.laci.com.

57. David Rieff, *Los Angeles: Capital of the Third World* (New York: Simon & Schuster, 1991), 230.

58. Richard Rodriguez, "Mexican Food: Filling Loneliness of American Life," *Los Angeles Times*, July 24, 1994, M1.

59. Dear, *Atlas of Southern California,* 18–19; Wang Yin, Fu-Tung Cheng, and Isaac Cronin, "Chinese Cuisine," *California Magazine,* February 1982, 88–98.

60. Davis, *City of Quartz,* 72.

61. William Fulton, *The Reluctant Metropolis: The Politics of Urban Growth in Los Angeles* (Point Arena, Calif.: Solano, 1997), 236–37.

62. Davis, *City of Quartz,* 72; Fulton, *The Reluctant Metropolis,* 242–54.

63. Davis, *City of Quartz,* 74–82.

64. Charles Lockwood and Christopher B. Leinberger, "Los Angeles Comes of Age," *Atlantic Monthly,* January 1988, 31–62.

65. Davis, *City of Quartz,* 71.

66. Zukin, *The Culture of Cities,* 154.

67. Ibid., 159.

68. Ibid., 173.

69. Ibid., 148; Bates, "Hollywood Is Star," A1.

70. Neither state nor federal agencies organize their data in ways that allow us to determine the exact size of the Los Angeles area's Latino restaurant workforce. Nor does the Bureau of Labor Statistics provide countywide data on the ethnic composition of California's restaurant workforce. The State Employment Development Department does provide countywide and regional data, but no data on the ethnic composition of the workforce or on restaurant-related jobs.

71. Dear, *Atlas of Southern California,* 13.

72. David E. Lopez, Eric Popkin, and Edward Telles, "Central Americans: At the Bottom, Struggling to Get Ahead," in *Ethnic Los Angeles,* ed. Roger Waldinger and Mehdi Bozorgmehr (New York: Russell Sage Foundation, 1996), 296.

73. Ethnic composition of New Otani Hotel's workforce provided to the authors by Local 10, Hotel Employees and Restaurant Employees International Union, research department, February 2, 1996; Geotz Wolff, "County Business Patterns, Change in the Number of Small Manufacturing Establishments, Los Angeles County (1979–1990)," in U.S. Department of Commerce, *Resources for Employment and Economic Development* (Washington, D.C., May 1994); Geotz Wolff, "Percent Distribution of Race/Latino Groups by Occupation, Los Angeles County, 1990," in U.S. Department of Commerce, *Resources for Employment and Economic Development* (Washington, D.C., September 1994).

74. Vilma Ortiz, "The Mexican-Origin Population: Permanent Working Class or Emerging Middle Class?" in *Ethnic Los Angeles,* ed. Roger Waldinger, and Mehdi Bozorgmehr (New York: Russell Sage Foundation, 1996), 257.

75. Ibid., 251.

76. Quoted in Carolyn Walkup, "Hispanics: Learning the Language of Success," *Nation's Restaurant News,* September 20, 1993, 144.

77. Anonymous source, former freelance journalist specializing in the Los Angeles restaurant industry and current head of public relations for a major Los Angeles research institution, telephone interview by Victor Valle, Los Angeles, September 24, 1997.

78. LaGanga, "At a Career Crossroads?"A1, A24.

79. Shirley Nicolas, registrar of the California Culinary Academy, San Francisco, telephone interview by Victor Valle, September 26, 1997.

80. Anonymous source, interview.

81. Felipe Cabrera, interview by Victor Valle, tape recording, June 5, 1994; Jose Rodriguez, interview by Victor Valle, tape recording, August 15, 1994.

82. Rosaura Sánchez, "Mapping the Spanish Language along a Multiethnic and Multilingual Border," *Aztlan: A Journal of Chicano Studies* 21, nos. 1–2 (1992–96): 79.

83. "Restaurant Program Enrollment by Sex and Ethnicity, Fall 1995," Los Angeles Community College District. The same pattern persisted with students who graduated with vocational degrees in professional baking, culinary arts, and culinary arts apprenticeships: 32.8 percent were categorized as Latino, 32.6 percent as black, and 22 percent as white.

84. Graduation data obtained from the Institutional Research and Planning Department, California State Polytechnic University, Pomona.

85. Felix Gutierrez and Clint C. Wilson II, *Race, Multiculturalism, and the Media*, 2d ed. (Thousand Oaks, Calif.: Sage, 1995), 8, 206; Zita Arocha and Robert Moreno, *Hispanics in the News Media: No Room at the Top* (Washington, D.C.: National Association of Hispanic Journalists, 1993).

86. Josh Meyer, "County Crackdown on Dirty Restaurants OK'd," *Los Angeles Times*, November 26, 1997, B3.

87. Rodriguez, interview.

88. Josephine Ramirez, interview by Victor Valle, tape recording, April 1998.

89. Americans now drop more bottles of salsa and picante sauce in their shopping carts than ketchup. Packaged Facts, Inc., reports in a press release that the turning point came in 1991, when combined salsa-picante sales increased by 24 percent and totaled $640 million, compared to ketchup sales of $600 million. Since then, the New York-based research firm has reported that salsa-picante sales have grown at a rate of 8 percent to 12 percent until 1998, when they reached $940 million. Combined salsa-picante sales were expected to continue at a double-digit clip through 1999, when salsa-picante sales were projected to reach $1.56 billion. Salsa sales mirror a wider trend. Packaged Facts projected retail sales of Mexican food of $3.45 billion in 1999. See also Molly O'Neill, "New Mainstream: Hot Dogs, Apple Pie, and Salsa," *New York Times*, March 11, 1992, sec. 6, p. 1.

## 4. Contesting "Showtime"

1. Angel Rama, *La Ciudad Letrada* (Hanover, N.H.: Ediciones del Norte, 1984), 37–38.

2. William Fulton, *The Reluctant Metropolis: The Politics of Urban Growth in Los Angeles* (Point Arena, Calif.: Solano 1997), 229.

3. "Disposition and Development Agreement by and among the Community Redevelopment Agency of the City of Los Angeles and L.A. Arena Development Company, LLC (Los Angeles Arena Project)," dated October 31, 1997; "Proposed Convention Center Arena Economic Impact Analysis," prepared for Los Angeles Convention Visitors Bureau, June 27, 1996, 2.

4. Robert Kaplan, "Travels into America's Future," *Atlantic Monthly*, August 1998, 38; Miguel Bustillo, "Secession's Impact on Latinos Probed," *Los Angeles Times*,

December 3, 1998, B5; Miguel Bustillo, "Valley Latinos Would Suffer in Secession, Panelists Say," *Los Angeles Times,* December 6, 1998, B1.

5. For a recent study of themed environments, see Mark Gottdiener, *The Theming of America : Dreams, Visions, and Commercial Spaces* (Boulder, Colo.: Westview, 1997).

6. Rodolfo F. Acuña, *Anything but Mexican: Chicanos in Contemporary Los Angeles* (New York: Verso, 1996), 182.

7. Hector Delgado, *New Immigrants, Old Unions: Organizing Undocumented Workers in Los Angeles* (Philadelphia:Temple University Press, 1993), 7–11; Acuña, *Anything but Mexican,* 181.

8. Acuña,. *Anything but Mexican,* 180.

9. Ibid., 180; Harold Meyerson, "Contracting Out of Poverty: Downtown Hotel Pact Sets New Standard for L.A.'s Service Sector," *L.A. Weekly,* January 23–29, 1998, 2,13,21.

10. Acuña, *Anything but Mexican,* 181–82.

11. Madeline Janis-Aparicio, one of Local 11's early collaborators, has told us that she and Durazo were well aware of the strategic "interplay of [hotel] image and worker justice/injustice"; e-mail correspondence with authors, December 6, 1998.

12. Hotel Employees and Restaurant Employees Union, Local 11, *Los Angeles: City on the Edge,* video, 1992; Acuña, *Anything but Mexican,* 183.

13. Stephen Callis, Leslie Ernest, and Ruben Ortiz Torres, *Murder in My Suite: Bienvenidos al Hotel California* (Salem, Ore.: John Brown, 1997), 16, 30.

14. Acuña, *Anything but Mexican,* 184.

15. Madeline Janis-Aparicio, telephone interview by Victor Valle, Los Angeles, August 26, 1998; Janis-Aparicio, e-mail.

16. Acuña, *Anything but Mexican,* 181; Harold Meyerson, "No Justice, No Growth," *L.A. Weekly,* July 17–23, 1998, 16. Janis-Aparicio, in e-mail correspondence, noted that she lived two years and several summers with her parents in Mexico.

17. Madeline Janis-Aparicio, telephone interview by Victor Valle, Los Angeles, August 11, 1998.

18. Meyerson, "No Justice, No Growth," 16; Danny Feingold, "Putting Faith in Labor: In a New Trend, a Motley Coalition of Southland Clergy Is Taking Up the Workers' Cause—and Winning," *Los Angeles Times,* August 28, 1998, E1.

19. Meyerson, "No Justice, No Growth," 4.

20. Ibid., 5; California Assembly, Select Committee on the California Middle Class, *The Distribution of Income in California and Los Angeles: A Look at Recent Current Population Survey and State Taxpayer Data* (Sacramento, May 16, 1998).

21. Michael Dear, ed., *Atlas of Southern California, Prepared for the USC Presidential Roundtable* (Los Angeles: University of Southern California, Southern California Studies Center, November 12, 1996), 47; Larry Gordon, "Blessing or Curse to Be Evicted?" *Los Angeles Times,* August 3, 1997, B5.

22. Manuel Pastor Jr., *Latinos and the Los Angeles Uprising: The Economic Context* (Claremont, Calif.: Tomas Rivera Center, 1993), 17–18.

23. Meyerson, "No Justice, No Growth," 2.

24. Bill Boyarsky, "Old Business-Labor Alliance Reemerges," *Los Angeles Times,* January 16, 1997, A27; Bobbi Murray, "Organize! Living Wage Lives in L.A.," *Shelterforce Online,* January/February 1998, on-line at http://www.nhi.org/online/issues/

97/organize.html; Meyerson, "No Justice, No Growth," 7; Janis-Aparicio, interviews, August 11 and 26, 1998.

25. Murray, "Organize!"; Meyerson, "No Justice, No Growth," 7.

26. Statement made in LAANE, *The Living Wage Campaign,* video, n.d.

27. Janis-Aparicio, interviews, August 11 and 26, 1998.

28. Ibid.

29. Jodi Wilgoren, "Council Takes Key Step in Building Downtown Arena," *Los Angeles Times,* May 24, 1997, A1, A20.

30. Janis-Aparicio, interview, August 11, 1998.

31. We used the key words *living wage* in conducting a computer-assisted search.

32. Jeffrey Leib, "Anschutz Group Bidding for Kings, Owners Confirm," *Denver Post,* May 13, 1995, B-03; Michele Conklin, "Team Meant Millions to Anschutz; Businessman Backed Out of Pepsi Center When He Couldn't Buy 50% of Avalanche," *Rocky Mountain News,* September 29, 1995, sec. F, p. 56A; "Anschutz Takes on Big Debt to Buy L.A. Hockey Team," *Rocky Mountain News,* October 7, 1995, sec. F, p. 66A; Chance Conner, "Anschutz Scores with L.A.," *Denver Post,* October 15, 1995, sec. D, p. G-01. Miguel Contreras, executive secretary of the Los Angeles County Federation of Labor, acknowledged in an interview that Roski's representatives first contacted him in April 1996; interview by Victor Valle, tape recording, Occidental College, Los Angeles, October 3, 1998.

33. Majestic Realty/L.A. Arena Co., "Reported Client Fees, 1996–97," in Los Angeles City Ethics Commission, *Fourth Quarter 1997 Lobbying Report*; Los Angeles City Ethics Commission, *First Quarter 1998 Lobbying Report*; "Lobbying," City News Service, December 10, 1997.

34. Janis-Aparicio, interview, August 11, 1998; Bill Boyarsky, "At This Game, the Real Players Are in the Crowd," *Los Angeles Times,* September 12, 1996, B1.

35. Greg Nelson, telephone interview by Victor Valle, Los Angeles, March 24, 1997.

36. T. J. Simers, "L.A. and Inglewood in Showdown over Arena," *Los Angeles Times,* August 9, 1996, A14.

37. William Fulton, telephone interview by Victor Valle, August 1998.

38. Simers, "L.A. and Inglewood in Showdown," A14.

39. Data concerning contributions to Hernandez and Ridley-Thomas were obtained from the following public records: "Candidate and Controlled Committee Campaign Disclosure Statements" (California 1994 Form 405, and California 1994 Form 490) for the period beginning March 26, 1995, and ending December 31, 1997; "Independent Expenditure Committee and Major Donor Committee Campaign Statements" (California 1994 Form 461) for the period beginning January 1, 1995, and ending December 31, 1997; Majestic Realty/L.A. Arena Co., "Reported Client Fees, 1996–97"; Los Angeles City Ethics Commission, *First Quarter 1998 Lobbying Report.*

40. Jim Newton, "Sports Deals Transforming L.A.'s Politics," *Los Angeles Times,* October 26, 1997, A1; Jean Merl, "Council Endorses Deal to Build Sports Arena," *Los Angeles Times,* January 16, 1997, A27; "Independent Expenditure Committee and Major Donor Committee Campaign Statement" for the period beginning July 1, 1996, and ending December 31, 1996; David Cogan, "Power Player," *L.A. Weekly,* November 13–19, 1998, 14.

41. David Halberstam, *The Powers That Be*, (New York: Dell, 1979), 167.

42. Robert Gottlieb and Irene Wolt, *Thinking Big: The Story of the Los Angeles Times, Its Publishers, and Their Influence on Southern California* (New York: Putnam, 1977), 484–86; Community Redevelopment Agency, City of Los Angeles, *Downtown Los Angeles: 1982*, brochure (Los Angeles, 1982),14, 18, 29; Community Redevelopment Agency, City of Los Angeles, *Bunker Hill Redevelopment Project Biennial Report, 1993* (Los Angeles, 1993), 29.

43. Alicia C. Shepard, "Mark Willes Shakes Up the L.A. Times," *American Journalism Review* (December 1997): 20, 26.

44. Ibid., 24; David Shaw, "Crossing the Line: A *Los Angeles Times* Profit-Sharing Arrangement with Staples Center Fuels a Firestorm of Protest in the Newsroom—and a Debate about Journalistic Ethics" special report, *Los Angeles Times*, December 20, 1999, sec. V.

45. Shepard, "Mark Willes Shakes Up the L.A. Times," 24.

46. *Los Angeles Times* reporters interviewed by Victor Valle, November and December 1999.

47. Ibid.

48. Shepard "Mark Willes Shakes Up the L.A. Times," 24; e-mail message from Otis Chandler to *Los Angeles Times* staff, November 3, 1999.

49. Shepard, "Mark Willes Shakes Up the L.A. Times," 23.

50. The sample consisted of fifty-five *Los Angeles Times* stories and editorials published between April 1996 and October 1997, which covers the period leading up to City Council's vote to approve the arena project. We constructed the sample by means of hand sorting and Lexis-Nexis data searches using the words *arena, Roski,* and *Anschutz* as search terms. Only stories in which the arena appeared as a primary subject were included in the sample.

51. Wilgoren, "Council Takes Key Step," A4, A20.

52. Mark S. Rosentraub, *Major League Losers: The Real Cost of Sports and Who's Paying for It* (New York: Basic Books, 1997), 17.

53. Raymond Keating, "We Wuz Robbed! The Subsidized Stadium Scam," *Policy Review* (March/April 1997): 57.

54. Robert Baade and Alan Sanderson, "Field of Fantasies," *Intellectual Ammunition*, March/April 1996, 3.

55. The few progressives who dared to speak out responded incoherently. For example, mayoral challenger Tom Hayden identified the arena as another example of urban policy for the corporate elite and Riordan as the ultimate corporate insider. But the state senator confused matters by presenting himself as the outsider running against City Hall, which sounded too much like Riordan's anti-big-government rhetoric and exposed Hayden to allegations that he was trying to hide the years he spent legislating in Sacramento. In another play for fiscally conservative home owners, Hayden called for an audit of the arena project, yet overlooked another scandal— namely, that Roski and Anschutz had tried to keep parts of the arena deal secret.

56. Quoted in Merl, "Council Endorses Deal," A27.

57. Randy Harvey, "The Inside Track: The Clock Is Ticking on a Downtown Arena," *Los Angeles Times*, December 4, 1996, C2.

58. "The Issue Is the Arena, Period; City Council Shouldn't See Vote as

Referendum on Broader Matters," *Los Angeles Times,* January 15, 1997, B8. See also Kevin Starr, "Field of Dreams," *Los Angeles Times,* April 20, 1997, M1, M6.

59. Quoted in Diane Haithman, "Disney Hall Hangs Its Pitch on the Future of Downtown," *Los Angeles Times,* March 11, 1997, F2.

60. Ibid.

61. Susan Seager, "Deal of the Century," *L.A. Weekly,* June 2–8, 1995, 26–28; John Schwada, "CRA Girds for Fight to Retrieve Downtown Plan Redevelopment," *Los Angeles Times,* October 19, 1995, B3.

62. Fulton, *The Reluctant Metropolis,* 243–48, 253, 254; Diane Haithman, "$15–Million Gift for Disney Hall Expected," *Los Angeles Times,* April 10, 1997, A1, A30.

63. Nicolai Ouroussoff, "In Search of Material Gain," *Los Angeles Times,* July 31, 1998, F1; Diane Haithman, "7 Years Later, Disney Hall Breaks Ground Once Again," *Los Angeles Times,* December 8, 1999, B1–B2.

64. Bill Plaschke, "Arena Means Downtown Will Party When It's 1999," *Los Angeles Times,* May 24, 1997, C1, C10. See also Michael A. Hiltzik, "Playing by His Own Rules," *Los Angeles Times,* August 25, 1997, A1, A14; Wilgoren, "Council Takes Key Step," A20.

65. Rick Orlov, "Clippers Will Sail to Staples Center; Murdoch to Buy Part of Downtown Arena," *Daily News of Los Angeles,* April 17, 1998, Valley edition, S1.

66. Motion submitted to the Los Angeles City Council by Councilman Joel Wachs, "L.A. Arena: Allowing Democracy to Work," November 19, 1996; Jodi Wilgoren, "Council Orders Parts of Arena Lease Disclosed," *Los Angeles Times,* July 23, 1997, A1; "Hahn Seeks Disclosure of Arena Terms," *Los Angeles Times,* July 30, 1997, B1, B8.

67. Quoted in Wilgoren, "Council Orders," A1.

68. Jodi Wilgoren, "Arena Builders Ready to Offer Debt Guarantee," *Los Angeles Times,* August 22, 1997, A3, A32. See also Rick Orlov, "City Receives Guarantee from Arena Builders," *Daily News of Los Angeles,* August 22, 1997, Valley edition, N4; Greg Krikorian, "Hernandez Is Charged with 1 Drug Felony," *Los Angeles Times,* August 29, 1997, A1.

69. Bill Boyarsky, "Wall of Secrecy Surrounds Key Part of the Arena Deal," *Los Angeles Times,* June 30, 1997, B1; Bill Boyarsky, "City Hall Holds on to Arena Secrets," *Los Angeles Times,* July 14, 1997, B1; Bill Boyarsky, "Wachs' Uphill Fight against Arena Secrecy," *Los Angeles Times,* July 17, 1997, B3.

70. Quoted in Wilgoren, "Council Takes Key Step," A20.

71. Ridley-Thomas quoted in Cogan, "Power Player," 14; see also Meyerson, "No Justice, No Growth," 7, 8.

72. Ted Rohrlich, "Developers Vow to Drop Arena Plan If Initiative Is on Ballot," *Los Angeles Times,* September 18, 1997, B5; Steven Soboroff, Marvin D. Selter, and Frank Moran, "Perspective on the Sports Arena: The Initiative Negates Los Angeles' Welcome Sign," *Los Angeles Times,* September 26, 1997, B9; Lisa Dillman and Nicholas Riccardi, "Wachs Unveils Initiative for Citywide Arena Vote," *Los Angeles Times,* September 27, 1997, A1.

73. Dillman and Riccardi, "Wachs Unveils Initiative," A1.

74. Ibid.

75. Ibid.

76. Ted Rohrlich, "Wachs Softens Stand against Arena Accord," *Los Angeles Times,* August 29, 1997, A1; Rick Orlov, "Arena Backers OK New Plan to Pay Expenses,"

*Daily News of Los Angeles,* October 9, 1997, Valley edition, N4; "Arena Deal Gets Final Council Approval," *Los Angeles Times,* October 29, 1997, B4.

77. Janis-Aparicio, interview, August 11, 1998.

78. Greg Nelson, telephone interview by Victor Valle, January 27, 1998.

79. Janis-Aparicio, interview, August 11, 1998.

80. Greg Krikorian, "Hernandez Is Charged," A1; "Hernandez Case Could Be Dropped by April," *Los Angeles Times,* September 15, 1998, B3; Beth Shuster, "Hernandez Question Splits Angry Council," *Los Angeles Times,* October 25, 1997, A1, A22.

81. Robert J. Lopez and Rich Connell, "AMTA Probes Charities Promoted by Alatorre," *Los Angeles Times,* July 7, 1997, A1; "Alatorre Admits Former Cocaine Abuse," *Los Angeles Times,* August 27, 1998, B1; "Judge Says Test Shows Alatorre Is Using Cocaine," *Los Angeles Times,* September 30, 1998, A1.

82. Janis-Aparicio, interview, August 11, 1998; "Disposition and Development Agreement," 39.

83. Meyerson, "No Justice, No Growth," 16; Janis-Aparicio, interview, August 11, 1998.

84. Rohrlich, "L.A. Unions Step Up Demands on Developers," *Los Angeles Times,* December 2, 1998, B1, B3; Janis-Aparicio, interview, August 26, 1998.

85. Jim Newton, "Mayor Won't Block 'Living Wage' at LAX," *Los Angeles Times,* December 2, 1998, A2.; Beth Shuster, "Living Wage Law Could Get Boost," *Los Angeles Times,* November 11, 1998, B3.

86. Murray, "Organize!"

87. Beth Shuster, "Tighter Rules Proposed for Living Wage Law," *Los Angeles Times,* August 21, 1998, B1; Shuster, "Living Wage Law," B3; Shawn Hubler, "The Hard Facts of Life without a Living Wage," *Los Angeles Times,* November 12, 1998, B1.

88. Newton, "Mayor Won't Block 'Living Wage,'" A1.

89. Quoted in Rohrlich, "L.A. Unions Step Up Demands," B1.

90. Meyerson, "No Justice, No Growth," 1, 3; Ted Rohrlich, "Living Wage Movement Targets County Government," *Los Angeles Times,* November 4, 1998, A1–A2.

91. Howard Fine and Daniel Taub, "L.A. Arena Deal Getting Sweeter for Developers," *Los Angeles Business Journal,* May 4–10, 1998, 47.

92. Cogan, "Power Player," 12.

93. Martyn Williams, "Bill Gates Tops Forbes Billionaire Ranking," *Newbytes,* June 21, 1999, on-line at http://www.newsbytes.com; Bloomberg News, "Gates, Buffet Top List of Working Rich," *Omaha World-Herald,* June 21, 1999, 2.

94. Steve Raabe, "Industrial Developer Has Big Denver Plans," *Denver Post,* November 28, 1995, sec. D, p. C-03; Melinda Fulmer, "Who Owns the Most: REITs Are Now among Top Holders of Industrial and Office Property," *Los Angeles Times,* November 5, 1997, D1.

95. In April 1997, we conducted a computer-assisted search of the state tax assessor's property records to identify Roski holdings. We used a Lexis-Nexis search of state articles of incorporation, a Lexis-Nexis search of Roski-related business stories, and court records to identify the various forms in which Roski and his family own or control property. We determined Roski redevelopment participation by interviewing officials in those cities where property records showed Roski holdings and by reviewing news articles that disclosed Roski participation in local redevelopment projects. See also Rick Orlov, "Anschutz Fails to Show at NFL Owners Meetings: Billionaire Lets

Partner Carry Ball for L.A. Team," *Los Angeles Daily News* story reprinted in *Rocky Mountain News,* May 22, 1997, sec. F p. 16B.

96. Gary J. Miller, *Cities by Contract: The Politics of Municipal Incorporation* (Cambridge: MIT Press,1981), 34–62.

97. "Government's Sentencing Memorandum" (written by Assistant U.S. Attorney Gary Feess), *United States of America v. James Marty Stafford, et al.,* Case CR 84-359-ER and CR 84-794-ER, U.S. District Court for the Central District of California, filed November 27, 1984, 4.

98. Cecilia Rasmussen, "Community Profile: City of Industry," *Los Angeles Times,* November 14, 1995.

99. Vicki Torres, "Hidden High-Tech Hot Spot," *Los Angeles Times,* December 18, 1996, A1.

100. Dan Morain and Victor Valle, "City of Industry: It Has Clout Where It Counts—in the State Capitol," *Los Angeles Times,* April 15, 1984, A3, A36.

101. *Breach of Contract Complaint filed by Industry Hills Visitor Accommodation Center, a California General Partnership, v. City of Industry, Civic-Recreational-Industrial Authority,* Case C 757 925, Superior Court of California, County of Los Angeles, filed April 1991.

102. *Edward Page Roski Sr., et al., John Ferrero, et al., Defendants,* Case KC 000669, Superior Court of California, County of Los Angeles, filed April 24, 1991; "Suit against City Officials Alleges Financial Conflict," *Los Angeles Times,* June 8, 1990, B3; Irene Chang, "Suit Claims Tax Funds Misused," *Los Angeles Times,* June 10, 1990, J2.

103. Judgment pursuant to stipulation, and stipulation for entry of judgment, filed August 21, 1991, in *Industry Hills Visitor Accommodation Center, a California General Partnership, v. City of Industry, Civic-Recreational-Industrial Authority*; Robert Moran, "Mayo Joins Council after Perez Resigns," *Los Angeles Times,* January 20, 1992, J1; Cogan, "Power Player," 15; Scot Paltrow, "The City of Insiders: How One Man Runs His City," *Los Angeles Herald Examiner,* June 25, 1980, A11.

104. On September 23, 1998, we conducted four on-line searches of the Lexis-Nexis General News database. In our first search, we entered Roski's name into the primary subject categories and searched for articles the database identified as "Western Regional Sources" for the past five years. This search yielded 170 articles; the earliest was published in May 13, 1995, and the most recent was published in August 29, 1998. In our second search, we entered the name of Anschutz in the primary subject category and Roski in the secondary subject category. This search yielded 167 articles; the earliest was published on May 13, 1995, and the most recent on August 21, 1998. We also searched "Business" and "Financial Sources" in General News using Roski and Anschutz in our search strings. We created a record of our searches, printing article lists and saving the stories our searches retrieved on floppy disks. We controlled for redundancy by discarding stories that appeared on more than one list. We further defined our sample by counting only stories that were published after April 1996, the moment at which the local Los Angeles area media first introduced the Roski-Anschutz arena project to local readers. This procedure yielded 178 articles. Finally, after translating each article into Word Perfect or ASCII format, we used a word search program to locate Roski's name in the text. We then reviewed the discursive context in which his name appeared in each article, paying particular attention to the titles and adjectives immediately preceding and following his name.

We acknowledge the limitations of on-line media searches. As Philip A. Kaufman, Carol Reese Dykes, and Carole Caldwell note in "Why Going Online for Content Analysis Can Reduce Research Reliability," *Journalism Quarterly* 70 (winter 1993), newspapers do not consistently apply subject categories in coding their stories for data retrieval. Moreover, they show different degrees of diligence in sending wire or late-edition stories to private databases that archive their stories. Kaufman et al. found that on-line searches did not consistently duplicate the thoroughness of hand coding. Of the databases evaluated in their study, Lexis-Nexis did the most thorough job of retrieving articles from such metropolitan dailies as the *Los Angeles Times*. To obtain reasonably good results, we followed Kaufman et al.'s recommendation and used "various search strings" to construct our media sample. We believe this procedure helped minimize gaps in our sampling method. We also believe that because our search strings consisted of proper names, the likelihood of coding discrepancies was significantly reduced.

105. Lisa Dillman, "Opening Victory for Kings,"*Los Angeles Times,* October 8, 1995, C1; "Kings' Sale Cleared by Bankruptcy Judge; Hockey Deal Could Be Final Tuesday," *Los Angeles Times,* October 6, 1995, C2; "NHL's Board Approves Sale of Kings to Anschutz, Roski," *Los Angeles Times,* September 30, 1995, C11; "Owners to Cut Ties with Kings," *Los Angeles Times,* September 23, 1995, C11.

106. David Cogan and Stacie Stukin, "The Man with the Money: The Quiet Mogul from Colorado Is Fast Becoming a Force in L.A.," *L.A. Weekly,* November 7–13, 1997, 20–23; Charles Rappleye, "Blundering Times: Publisher and Editor Still Have Some Answerin' to Do About the Dumb Staples Center Sellout," *L.A. Weekly,* November 5–11, 1999, on-line at http://www.laweekly.com/ink/99/50/news-rappleye.html.

107. Cogan, "Power Player," 8–12.

108. Nelson, interview, March 24, 1997.

109. Quoted in T. J. Simers, "NFL to Be Presented New Coliseum Plan," *Los Angeles Times,* October 13, 1997, A1.

110. Matt Krasnowski, "Developers Step Up Campaign for Arena by Releasing Lease Agreements," Copley News Service, August 27, 1998; Los Angeles Arena "Memorandum of Understanding."

111. Ralph Frammolino, "NFL Coliseum Deal Not Dead Yet, Officials Say," *Los Angeles Times,* August 7, 1999, D1, D3; Simers, "NFL to Be Presented," A1; Cogan, "Power Player," 15.

112. Quoted in Shaw, "Crossing the Line," V9.

113. Quoted in ibid., V8.

114. Quoted in Felicity Barringer, "Newspaper Magazine Shares Profits with a Subject," *New York Times,* October 26, 1999, C11.

115. *Los Angeles Times* reporter, interview, December 1999.

116. Quoted in Tim Rutten, "Otis Chandler Assails Times' Top Executives amid Controversy," *Los Angeles Times,* November 4, 1999, C1, C4.

117. "The Truth According to Otis Chandler," *New York Times,* November 8, 1999, op-ed page; "Times Publisher Apologizes to Staff," *Star,* October 29, 1999, A7; Felicity Barringer, "Ex-Publisher Assails Paper in Los Angeles," *New York Times,* November 4, 1999, C1; Richard Cohen, "No Way to Do News Business," *Washington Post,* November 11, 1999, A43; Joshua Hammer, "Look Out, the Boss Is Back: An Unexpected Voice Blasts the L.A. Times," *Newsweek,* November 15, 1999, 76.

118. Barringer, "Newspaper Magazine Shares Profits," C1; Rappleye, "Blundering Times," 4, 5.

119. Jeff Leeds, "Times Elevates 2 Senior Editors to New Positions," *Los Angeles Times*, January 8, 2000, B1.

120. David Shaw and Sallie Hofmeister, "Times Mirror Agrees to Merger with Tribune Co. Media," *Los Angeles Times*, March 13, 2000, A1; Sallie Hofmeister and Stuart Silverstein, "Tribune Emphasizes Deal's New-Media Play, Merger," *Los Angeles Times*, March 14, 2000, A1; Michael Janeway, *Republic of Denial: Press, Politics, and Public Life* (New Haven: Yale University Press, 1999), 154.

121. Sharon Waxman, "L.A. Times Staff Suffers Seismic Shock: Word of Merger Rattles Family-Owned Newspaper," *Washington Post*, March 14, 2000, Style, C01; Howard Kurtz, "Top Management Out at L.A. Times: Baltimore Sun Editor Named to Scandal-Weary Paper," *Washington Post*, April 15, 2000, Style, C01.

## 5. Significant Space

1. Benjamin J. Cohen, *The Geography of Money* (Ithaca, N.Y.: Cornell University Press, 1998), 8–9.

2. Antonio Rios-Bustamante, *Mexican Los Angeles: A Narrative and Pictorial History* (Ventura, Calif.: Floricanto, 1992), 33–35.

3. Whittier Narrows Visitor Center display; "Whittier Narrows Visitor Center to Serve SG Valley," *Highlander* (community newspaper, Hacienda Heights, Calif.), August 10, 1977 (clipping available in the offices of the Whittier Narrows Visitor Center, 750 S. Santa Anita Avenue, South El Monte, CA 91733-4300).

4. Whittier Narrows Recreation Area, news release, September 22, 1957; Whittier Narrows Recreation Area, brochure n.d. (available in the offices of the Whittier Narrows Visitor Center; see note 3, above, for address).

5. Whittier Narrows Recreation Area, news release; Whittier Narrows Recreation Area, brochure; Whittier Narrows Visitor Center display.

6. See Automobile Club of America, *California Nevada Tour Book: Attractions, Lodgings, Restaurants* (Heathrow, Fla.: AAA Publishing, 1997).

7. "Whittier Narrows Visitor Center to Serve SG Valley."

8. John McPhee, *The Control of Nature* (New York: Farrar, Straus & Giroux, 1989), 214.

9. Ibid., 242.

10. Richard Bigger, who bases his account of the 1938 flood on congressional testimony, writes that fifty-nine lives were lost and estimates property damages at more than $62 million. Richard Bigger, *Flood Control in Metropolitan Los Angeles* (Berkeley: University of California Press, 1959), 3.

11. Ibid., 3, 12, 14.

12. Ibid., 121; John Anson Ford, *Thirty Explosive Years in Los Angeles County* (San Marino, Calif.: Huntington Library, 1961), 96.

13. Robert Gottlieb and Irene Wolt, *Thinking Big: The Story of the Los Angeles Times, Its Publishers and Their Influence on Southern California* (New York: G. P. Putnam's Sons, 1977), 140–43.

14. Ibid.; Bigger, *Flood Control*, 142.

15. Mike Davis, *Ecology of Fear: Los Angeles and the Imagination of Disaster* (New York: Metropolitan, 1998), 65.

16. Ibid., 67–69.

17. Ibid., 68.

18. Bigger, *Flood Control*, 18.

19. Ibid., 24.

20. Ibid., 139–40.

21. Ibid., 141.

22. Ibid., 131–132, 141–142; Davis, *Ecology of Fear,* 77–80.

23. Davis, *Ecology of Fear,* 79.

24. Clyde Taylor, "The Re-birth of the Aesthetic in Cinema," in *The Birth of Whiteness: Race and the Emergence of U.S. Cinema,* ed. Daniel Bernardi (New Brunswick, N.J.: Rutgers University Press, 1996), 20–22.

25. McPhee, *The Control of Nature,* 195.

26. Ibid., 192.

27. Ibid.

28. Bigger, *Flood Control,* 142.

29. Ibid., 110.

30. Ibid., 111.

31. Velia Rosales, regional park superintendent, Whittier Narrows Recreation Area, interview by Victor Valle, October 3, 1998, and telephone interview by Victor Valle, July 13, 1998.

32. We base these observations on a reading of the Whittier Narrows Advisory Club minutes, articles of incorporation, and publicity scrapbook (available in the offices of the Whittier Narrows Visitor Center; see note 3, above, for address).

33. Fred Coleman, résumé, May 23, 1976, submitted to L.A. County Supervisor Peter Schabarum in application for appointment to the county's Fish and Game Commission (copy available in the offices of the Whittier Narrows Visitor Center; see note 3, above, for address).

34. "Schabarum Fails in Fight for $2 Million Park Funds," *San Gabriel Valley Tribune,* October 8, 1975, sec. B, p. 1; "Fenton Seeks $1 Million for Whittier Narrows," *Mid Valley News,* January 28, 1976 (clipping available in the offices of the Whittier Narrows Visitor Center; see note 3, above, for address).

35. Quoted in Victor M. Valle, "Return of Life: 5–Mile-Long Habitat Testifies to Nature's Resiliency," *Los Angeles Times,* July 4, 1985, San Gabriel Valley sec., p. 7.

36. Ibid.

37. An exit survey conducted by Kirtland Consulting on April 17–20, 1997, at the Montebello Town Center found that 71 percent of the five hundred center shoppers interviewed were Hispanic, 19 percent were Non-Hispanic white, 9 percent were Asian American, and 1 percent were African American. Mexican Americans constituted the majority, 89 percent, of Hispanics interviewed. Household incomes among all those interviewed averaged $31,400.

38. Data contained in a Los Angeles County Recreation Department memo written by Phyllis Trabold, outdoor recreation planner; Los Angeles County Department of Parks and Recreation, "Whittier Narrows Park Patron Signage Survey," April 1998.

39. We obtained the first of these figures by calculating ethnic population averages for cities and county areas adjacent to the dam and recreation area. All municipal figures, except for north Whittier, are based on 1990 census data. North Whittier

figures are from George Ramos, "Latino Middle Class Growing in the Suburbs," *Los Angeles Times,* November 30, 1997, B1. The figure of 63 percent reflects the proportion of the population residing in a five-mile area located near the Montebello Town Center determined to be Latino by Trade Area Demographics, based on data compiled by Claritas, 1997.

40. L.A. County Department of Parks and Recreation, "Whittier Narrows Park Patron Signage Survey." The survey did not solicit responses from people who use the area's nonpark public spaces, such as the San Gabriel and Rio Hondo riverbeds. Obtaining more complete responses from area users and sampling of all the public spaces in the narrows may obtain results that better reflect the ethnic composition of surrounding communities.

41. Ibid.

42. According to Bill and Nancy Boyarsky: "During Legg's uneven public career, he was indicted on charges of accepting a $10,000 bribe in a garbage franchise scandal during the fifties. Legg was dramatically cleared by the deathbed affidavit of his campaign treasurer, who said it was he and not Legg who accepted the bribe. The jury chose to believe the affidavit rather than the man who paid the bribe and who testified that Legg himself had thanked him personally for the 'package' in the corridor of the county administration building." Bill Boyarsky and Nancy Boyarsky, *Backroom Politics: How Your Local Politicians Work, Why Your Government Doesn't, and What You Can Do About It* (Los Angeles: J. P. Tarcher; 1974), 58.

43. Luis J. Rodriguez, *Always Running: La Vida Loca: Gang Days in L.A.* (Willimantic, Conn.: Curbstone, 1993), 62.

44. William Estrada, telephone interview by Victor Valle, Los Angeles, October 6, 1998.

45. Ernesto Lechner, "Dancing Crowd Celebrates the Talent and Sound of Solis," *Los Angeles Times,* September 15, 1998, F4.

46. Rosales, interviews, October 3 and July 13, 1998.

47. Ibid.

48. "Los Angeles County FY 1997–98 Final Adopted Budget $12,609.0 Million" and "Los Angeles County FY 1999–2000 Final Adopted Budget $15.222 Billion, Mandated vs. Discretionary Costs," on-line at http://www.co.la.ca.us/adbdgt2000/3bar.html.

49. Margie Rodriguez, interview by Victor Valle, tape recording, June 1, 1999.

50. Ibid.

## 6. Class and Culture Wars in the New Latino Politics

1. George Skelton, "Now Latinos Are Changing the Face of Both Parties," *Los Angeles Times,* November 23, 1998, A1.

2. A recent study by the United Way of Greater Los Angeles found that as of September 1999 there were 240 Latinos holding elective office in L.A. County, most serving in city posts and on school boards. See United Way of Greater Los Angeles, Research Services, *American Dream Makers: Executive Summary* (Los Angeles, January 2000).

3. Gregory Rodriguez, "The Impending Collision of Eastside and Westside," *Los Angeles Times,* August 3, 1997, M1, M3.

4. R. Scott Moxley, "No Hits, One Run, 200 Errors: Hermandad Probes' Central Figure Returns from Mexico," *O.C. Weekly*, August 14–20, 1998, 14.

5. Ibid.

6. Ted Rohrlich, "Latino Voting in State Surged in 1996 Election," *Los Angeles Times*, December 31, 1997, A1.

7. Ibid.

8. Rodriguez, "The Impending Collision," M1, M3.

9. Ibid., B3.

10. Nativo Lopez, interview by Victor Valle, tape recording, Occidental College, Los Angeles, October 14, 1998.

11. Ibid.

12. Ibid.

13. Beth Shuster, "New Latino Political Picture Offers Opportunity," *Los Angeles Times*, October 5, 1998, B12–B13.

14. David M. Grant, Melvin L. Oliver, and Angela D. James, "African Americans: Social and Economic Bifurcation," in *Ethnic Los Angeles*, ed. Roger Waldinger and Mehdi Bozorgmehr (New York: Russell Sage Foundation, 1996), 382.

15. Nativo Lopez, interview by Victor Valle, tape recording, Occidental College, Los Angeles, October 3, 1998.

16. Jim Newton, "Council Size Issue to Be Put to the Voters," *Los Angeles Times*, October 20, 1998, B 2.

17. Lopez interview, October 14, 1998.

18. Manuel Pastor Jr., "Advantaging the Disadvantaged through International Trade" (Merril College, University of California, Santa Cruz, July 1998, photocopy), 11–13.

19. Michael Rustin, "The Politics of Post-Fordism; or, The Trouble with 'New Times,'" *New Left Review* 175 (May/June 1989): 66.

20. Mike Davis, *Ecology of Fear: Los Angeles and the Imagination of Disaster* (New York: Metropolitan, 1998), 404.

21. Gregory Rodriguez, "The Emerging Latino Middle Class," Pepperdine University Institute for Public Policy AT&T paper, October 1996, 7–12.

22. Ibid., 12.

23. Ibid., 12–13.

24. Robert A. Rosenblatt and Vicki Torres, "Number of Latino Firms Up 76 Percent in 5 Years; California Has Most," *Los Angeles Times*, July 11, 1996, D1; Lee Romney, "Hispanic Cheese: Haute Item," *Los Angeles Times*, June 16, 1998, A1, A32.

25. Ivan Light and Elizabeth Roach, "Self-Employment: Mobility Ladder or Economic Lifeboat?" in *Ethnic Los Angeles*, ed. Roger Waldinger and Mehdi Bozorgmehr (New York: Russell Sage Foundation, 1996), 198.

26. Ibid., 200–201, see Table 7.2.

27. Ibid., 205, see Table 7.4.

28. Ibid., 209.

29. Rohrlich, "Latino Voting in State Surged," A1.

30. Sandra Hernandez, "Inside Agitators: The City's Most Effective Activists," *L.A. Weekly*, October 2–8, 1998, 38.

31. Lopez, interview, October 3, 1998.

32. Harold Meyerson, "Activists Turned Elected Officials," *L.A. Weekly,* October 2–8, 1998, 30.

33. Rodriguez, "The Impending Collision," M1, M3.

34. Lopez, interview, October 3, 1998.

35. Escalante cited in Melita Marie Garza, "Hola, America! Newsstand 2000," *Media Studies Journal* 8 (summer 1994): 157.

36. Vivian Chavez and Lori Dorfman, "Spanish-Language Television News Portrayals of Youth and Violence in California," *International Quarterly of Community Health Education* 16, no. 2 (1996): 121–38.

37. Unfortunately, the underdeveloped state of Latino media studies means that cause-and-effect correlations between media coverage and political participation can still only be surmised.

38. Sandra Hernandez, "Stuck in Translation: La Opinión Searches for Readers—and a Mission—in the Times' Shadow," *L.A. Weekly,* June 11–17, 1999, 6.

39. Ibid., 2–9.

40. For example, the Bus Riders Union, led by Eric Mann, the labor veteran who in the 1980s battled GM to stop it from shutting down its Van Nuys plant, organized a cross section of Los Angeles's working-class bus riders to launch a civil rights court battle that stopped the MTA from allocating hundreds of millions in public funds for sorely needed bus service to underground rail projects targeted for a tiny minority of suburban, middle-class commuters.

41. Sharon Zukin, *The Culture of Cities* (Cambridge, Mass.: Blackwell, 1995), 263.

42. Edward W. Said, *Culture and Imperialism* (New York: Alfred A. Knopf, 1993), 58.

43. Roberto Gonzalez Echevarria, "Latin America and Comparative Literature," in *Poetics of the Americas: Race, Founding, and Textuality,* ed. Bainard Cowan and Jefferson Humphries (Baton Rouge: Louisiana State University Press, 1997), 50.

44. See, for example, the incisive work of Sonia Saldívar-Hull, *Feminism on the Border: Chicano Gender Politics and Literature* (Berkeley: University of California Press, 2000).

45. Renato Rosaldo, *Culture and Truth: The Remaking of Social Analysis* (Boston: Beacon, 1989), 209.

46. Ibid., 217.

# Bibliography

Acuña, Rodolfo F. *Community under Siege: A Chronicle of Chicanos East of the Los Angeles River, 1945–1975* (Monograph 11). Los Angeles: University of California, Chicano Studies Research Center, 1984.

——*Anything but Mexican: Chicanos in Contemporary Los Angeles.* New York: Verso, 1996.

"Afternoon Session: City Attorney's Opinion in the Plaza Public-Market Case." *Los Angeles Daily Times,* February 4, 1896, Public Service sec.

Aglietta, Michel. "Capitalism at the Turn of the Century: Regulation Theory and the Challenge of Social Change." *New Left Review* 232 (November/December 1998).

"Alatorre Admits Former Cocaine Abuse." *Los Angeles Times,* August 27, 1998, sec. B.

Allen, James P., and Eugene Turner. *The Ethnic Quilt: Population Diversity in Southern California.* Northridge: California State University, Center for Geographical Studies, 1997.

Amin, Ash, ed. *Post-Fordism: A Reader.* Oxford: Blackwell, 1994.

"Anschutz Takes on Big Debt to Buy L.A. Hockey Team." *Rocky Mountain News,* October 7, 1995, sec. F.

"Arena Deal Gets Final Council Approval." *Los Angeles Times,* October 29, 1997, sec. B.

Arocha, Zita, and Robert Moreno. *Hispanics in the News Media: No Room at the Top.* Washington, D.C.: National Association of Hispanic Journalists, 1993.

Automobile Club of America, *California Nevada Tour Book: Attractions, Lodgings, Restaurants.* Heathrow, Fla.: AAA Publishing, 1997.

Baade, Robert, and Alan Sanderson. "Field of Fantasies." *Intellectual Ammunition,* March/April 1996.

Bailey, Eric. "Rohrbacher Blasts Rioters in U.S. Illegally." *Los Angeles Times,* May 7, 1992, Orange County edition, sec. A.

Balderrama, Francisco E., and Raymond Rodriguez. *Decade of Betrayal: Mexican Repatriation in the 1930s.* Albuquerque: University of New Mexico Press, 1995.

Basso, Keith H. *Wisdom Sits in Places: Landscape and Language among the Western Apache.* Albuquerque: University of New Mexico Press, 1996.

Bates, James. "Hollywood Is Star." *Los Angeles Times*, January 18, 1998, sec. A.

Berg, Charles Ramirez. "Stereotyping in Films in General and of the Hispanic in Particular." In *Latin Looks: Images of Latinas and Latinos in the U.S. Media,* edited by Clara E. Rodriguez. Boulder, Colo.: Westview, 1997.

Bernstein, Jared, Elizabeth C. McNichol, Lawrence Mishel, and Robert Zahradnik. *Pulling Apart: A State-by-State Analysis of Income Trends.* Washington, D.C.: Center on Budget and Policy Priorities/Economic Policy Institute, 2000.

Biely, Andre. *St. Petersburg.* Translated by John Cournos. New York: Grove, 1959.

Bigger, Richard. *Flood Control in Metropolitan Los Angeles.* Berkeley: University of California Press, 1959.

Bonilla, Frank. "Changing the Americas from within the United States." In *Borderless Borders: U.S. Latinos, Latin Americans, and the Paradox of Interdependence,* edited by Frank Bonilla, Edwin Meléndez, Rebecca Morales, and María de los Angeles Torres. Philadelphia: Temple University Press, 1998.

Boyarsky, Bill. "At This Game, the Real Players Are in the Crowd." *Los Angeles Times,* September 12, 1996, sec. B.

———. "Old Business-Labor Alliance Reemerges." *Los Angeles Times,* January 16, 1997, sec. A.

———. "Wall of Secrecy Surrounds Key Part of the Arena Deal." *Los Angeles Times,* June 30, 1997, sec. B.

———. "City Hall Holds on to Arena Secrets." *Los Angeles Times,* July 14, 1997, sec. B.

———. "Wachs' Uphill Fight against Arena Secrecy." *Los Angeles Times,* July 17, 1997, sec. B.

Boyarsky, Bill, and Nancy Boyarsky. *Backroom Politics: How Your Local Politicians Work, Why Your Government Doesn't, and What You Can Do about It.* Los Angeles: J. P. Tarcher, 1974.

Bustillo, Miguel. "Secession's Impact on Latinos Probed." *Los Angeles Times,* December 3, 1998, sec. B.

———. "Valley Latinos Would Suffer in Secession, Panelists Say." *Los Angeles Times,* December 6, 1998, sec. B.

California Assembly. Select Committee on the California Middle Class. *The Distribution of Income in California and Los Angeles: A Look at Recent Current Population Survey and State Taxpayer Data.* Sacramento, May 16, 1998.

California Health and Human Services Agency Data Center. "Labor Market Information, Los Angeles County, Occupational Employment Projections, 1995–2000," Module D, Table 6. On-line at http://www.cahwnet.gov.

Callis, Stephen, Leslie Ernest, and Ruben Ortiz Torres. *Murder in My Suite: Bienvenidos al Hotel California.* Salem, Ore.: John Brown, 1997.

Carson, Tom. "Do You Fear the Coming Darkness?" In *Inside the L.A. Riots: What Really Happened and Why It Will Happen Again,* edited by Don Hazen. New York: Institute for Alternative Journalism, 1992.

Cerone, Daniel. "L.A. Turns on TV Sets as Disturbances Erupt." *Los Angeles Times,* May 1, 1992, sec. F.

Chang, Irene. "Suit Claims Tax Funds Misused." *Los Angeles Times,* June 10, 1990, sec. J.

Chavez, Vivian, and Lori Dorfman. "Spanish-Language Television News Portrayals of Youth and Violence in California." *International Quarterly of Community Health Education* 16, no. 2 (1996): 121–38.

Cleeland, Nancy. "Home-Care Workers' Vote for Union a Landmark for Labor." *Los Angeles Times,* February 26, 1999, sec. A.

Cogan, David. "Power Player." *L.A. Weekly,* November 13–19, 1998.

Cogan, David, and Stacie Stukin. "The Man with the Money: The Quiet Mogul from Colorado Is Fast Becoming a Force in L.A." *L.A. Weekly,* November 7–13, 1997.

Cohen, Benjamin J. *The Geography of Money.* Ithaca, N.Y.: Cornell University Press, 1998.

Conklin, Michele. "Team Meant Millions to Anschutz; Businessman Backed Out of Pepsi Center When He Couldn't Buy 50% of Avalanche." *Rocky Mountain News,* September 29, 1995, sec. F.

Conner, Chance. "Anschutz Scores with L.A." *Denver Post,* October 15, 1995, sec. G.

Cooper, Marc, and Greg Goldin. "Some People Don't Count." In *Inside the L.A. Riots: What Really Happened and Why It Will Happen Again,* edited by Don Hazen. New York: Institute for Alternative Journalism. 1992.

Corwin, Miles. "Vernon Redevelopment Plan Is Sticky Business." *Los Angeles Times,* November 10, 1991, sec. B.

———. "L.A.'s Loss: 'Black Flight.'" *Los Angeles Times,* August 13, 1992, sec. A.

C.W. "The Old Missions: They Should Be Preserved as Old-Time Relics." *Los Angeles Daily Times,* January 24, 1896.

Dahlburg, John-Thor. "Smuggling People to U.S. Is Big Business in Thailand." *Los Angeles Times,* September 5, 1995, sec. A.

Darder, Antonia, and Rodolfo D. Torres. "Latinos and Society: Culture, Politics, and Class." In *The Latino Studies Reader: Culture, Economy and Society,* edited by Antonia Darder and Rodolfo D. Torres. Oxford: Blackwell, 1998.

Davis, Mike. *City of Quartz: Excavating the Future in Los Angeles.* New York: Verso, 1990.

———. "The Empty Quarter." In *Sex, Death, and God in L.A.,* edited by David Reid. New York: Pantheon, 1992.

———. *Ecology of Fear: Los Angeles and the Imagination of Disaster.* New York: Metropolitan, 1998.

———. "Magical Urbanism: Latinos Reinvent the U.S. Big City." *New Left Review* 234 (March/April 1999).

Dear, Michael, ed. *Atlas of Southern California, Prepared for the USC Presidential Roundtable.* Los Angeles: University of Southern California, Southern California Studies Center, November 12, 1996.

Delgado, Hector. *New Immigrants, Old Unions: Organizing Undocumented Workers in Los Angeles.* Philadelphia: Temple University Press, 1993.

Dillman, Lisa. "Opening Victory for Kings." *Los Angeles Times,* October 8, 1995, sec. C.

Dillman, Lisa, and Nicholas Riccardi. "Wachs Unveils Initiative for Citywide Arena Vote." *Los Angeles Times,* September 27, 1997, sec. A.

Ellroy, James. *My Dark Places: An L.A. Crime Memoir.* New York: Vintage, 1997.

Escher, Frank, and Ravi GuneWardena, eds. *Cruising Industrial Los Angeles.* Los Angeles: Los Angeles Conservancy, 1997.

Estrada, William D. "The Los Angeles Plaza: Myth, Memory, Symbol, and the Struggle for Place in a Changing Metropolis, 1781–1990s." Slide/lecture presentation of archival materials from El Pueblo de Los Angeles Historical Monument, California

Polytechnic State University, San Luis Obispo, Department of Ethnic Studies, January 9, 1997.

Echevarria, Roberto Gonzalez. "Latin America and Comparative Literature." In *Poetics of the Americas: Race, Founding, and Textuality,* edited by Bainard Cowan and Jefferson Humphries. Baton Rouge: Louisiana State University Press, 1997.

Feingold, Danny. "Putting Faith in Labor: In a New Trend, a Motley Coalition of Southland Clergy Is Taking Up the Workers' Cause—and Winning." *Los Angeles Times,* August 28, 1998, sec. E.

Feinsilber, Mike. "Editors Set Goals for Diversity." *Associated Press/AP Online,* October 21, 1998.

Ferrel, David. "Top-Paid City Official in State; Vernon Administrator—a Study in Power, Control." *Los Angeles Times,* May 20, 1989, sec. A.

Fine, Howard, and Daniel Taub. "L.A. Arena Deal Getting Sweeter for Developers." *Los Angeles Business Journal,* May 4–10 1998.

Fischler, Claude. "The Michelin Galaxy: Nouvelle Cuisine, Three-Star Restaurants, and the Culinary Revolution." *Journal of Gastronomy* 6 (autumn 1990).

Flanigan, James. "Remaking L.A. into the New City of Big Shoulders." *Los Angeles Times,* November 15, 1995, sec. D.

Ford, John Anson. *Thirty Explosive Years in Los Angeles County.* San Marino, Calif.: Huntington Library, 1961.

Freed, David. "Few Safeguards Protect Workers from Poisons." *Los Angeles Times,* September 6, 1993, sec. A.

Freeman, Mike. "L.A.'s Local News Takes to the Streets." *Broadcasting,* May 4, 1992.

Freeman, Richard B. *The New Inequality: Creating Solutions for Poor America.* Boston: Beacon, 1999.

Fulmer, Melinda. "Who Owns the Most: REITs Are Now among Top Holders of Industrial and Office Property." *Los Angeles Times,* November 5, 1997, sec. D.

Fulton, William. *The Reluctant Metropolis: The Politics of Urban Growth in Los Angeles.* Point Arena, Calif.: Solano, 1997.

Garcia, Mario, and Ruben Salazar. *Southern California's Latino Community: A Series of Articles Reprinted from the Los Angeles Times, July 24, 1983 to August 14, 1983.* Los Angeles: Los Angeles Times, 1983.

Garreau, Joel. *Edge City: Life on the New Frontier.* New York: Doubleday, 1991.

Garvey, Megan. "Power in Numbers," *Los Angeles Times,* September 14, 1999, B1.

Garza, Melita Marie. "Hola, America! Newsstand 2000." *Media Studies Journal* 8 (summer 1994).

Gilliam, Franklin D., Jr., Shanto Iyengar, Adam Simon, and Oliver Wright. "Crime in Black and White: The Violent, Scary World of Local News." *Harvard International Journal of Press/Politics* 1, no. 3 (1996): 6–23.

Goldberg, David Theo. *Racist Culture: Philosophy and the Politics of Meaning.* Cambridge, Mass.: Blackwell, 1993.

Goldberg, David Theo, and Rodolfo D. Torres. "After 'Race' in the Metropolis: Racialized Relations in 'Postindustrial' Los Angeles." Research proposal submitted to the Scholars and Seminars Program, Getty Center for the History of Art and the Humanities, 1996.

Gordon, Dudley. *Charles F. Lummis: Crusader in Corduroy.* Los Angeles: Cultural Assets, 1972.

Gordon, Larry. "Blessing or Curse to Be Evicted?" *Los Angeles Times*, August 3, 1997, sec. B.

Gottdiener, Mark. *The Theming of America: Dreams, Visions, and Commercial Spaces*. Boulder, Colo.: Westview, 1997.

Gottlieb, Robert, and Irene Wolt. *Thinking Big: The Story of the Los Angeles Times, Its Publishers and Their Influence on Southern California*. New York: G. P. Putnam's Sons, 1977.

Grant, David M., Melvin L. Oliver, and Angela D. James. "African Americans: Social and Economic Bifurcation." In *Ethnic Los Angeles*, edited by Roger Waldinger and Mehdi Bozorgmehr. New York: Russell Sage Foundation, 1996.

Gutierrez, Felix, and Clint C. Wilson II. *Race, Multiculturalism and the Media*. 2d ed. Thousand Oaks, Calif.: Sage, 1995.

Haffner-Ginger, Bertha. *California Mexican-Spanish Cook Book*. Los Angeles: Citizen's Print Shop, 1914.

"Hahn Seeks Disclosure of Arena Terms." *Los Angeles Times*, July 30, 1997, sec. B.

Haithman, Diane. "Disney Hall Hangs Its Pitch on the Future of Downtown." *Los Angeles Times*, March 11, 1997, sec. F.

———. "$15-Million Gift for Disney Hall Expected." *Los Angeles Times*, April 10, 1997, sec. A.

Haldane, David. "O.C. in 2040: Near Majority of Latinos, Far Fewer Whites." *Los Angeles Times*, December 18, 1998, B1.

Hall, Stuart. "The Local and the Global: Globalization and Ethnicity." In *Culture, Globalization, and the World-System*, edited by Anthony D. King. Minneapolis: University of Minnesota Press, 1997.

Harvey, David. *The Condition of Postmodernity*. Oxford: Blackwell, 1989.

———. *Justice, Nature, and the Geography of Difference*. Cambridge, Mass.: Blackwell, 1996.

———. "The Geography of Class Power." In *Socialist Register, 1998*, edited by Leo Panitch and Colin Leys. London: Merlin, 1998.

Harvey, Randy. "The Inside Track: The Clock Is Ticking on a Downtown Arena." *Los Angeles Times*, December 4, 1996, sec. C.

"Hernandez Case Could Be Dropped by April." *Los Angeles Times*, September 15, 1998, sec. B.

Hernandez, Sandra. "Inside Agitators: The City's Most Effective Activists." *L.A. Weekly*, October 2–8, 1998.

———. "Stuck in Translation: La Opinión Searches for Readers—and a mission—in the Times' Shadow." *L.A. Weekly*, June 11–17, 1999.

Hiltzik, Michael A. "Playing by His Own Rules." *Los Angeles Times*, August 25, 1997, sec. A.

Hotel Workers and Restaurant Workers Union, Local 11, *Los Angeles: City on the Edge*. Video, 1992.

Hubler, Shawn. "South L.A.'s Poverty Rate Worse than '65." *Los Angeles Times*, May 11, 1992, sec. A.

———. "The Hard Facts of Life without a Living Wage." *Los Angeles Times*, November 12, 1998, sec. B.

Hunt, Darnell M. *Screening the Los Angeles "Riots."* Cambridge: Cambridge University Press, 1997.

Industry Manufacturers Council. *City of Industry Factbook*. City of Industry, Calif.: Industry Manufacturers Council, 1990.

"The Issue Is the Arena, Period; City Council Shouldn't See Vote as Referendum on Broader Matters." *Los Angeles Times,* January 15, 1997, sec. B.

"Judge Says Test Shows Alatorre Is Using Cocaine." *Los Angeles Times,* September 30, 1998, sec. A.

Kanter, Larry. "L.A. Battlegrounds: Rival Football Teams Head for Showdown." *Los Angeles Business Journal,* September 28–October 4, 1998.

Kaplan, Robert. "Travels into America's Future." *Atlantic Monthly,* August 1998.

Kaufman, Philip A., Carol Reese Dykes, and Carole Caldwell. "Why Going Online for Content Analysis Can Reduce Research Reliability." *Journalism Quarterly* 70 (winter 1993).

Keating, Raymond. "We Wuz Robbed! The Subsidized Stadium Scam." *Policy Review* (March/April 1997).

Keil, Roger. *Los Angeles: Globalization, Urbanization and Social Struggles*. New York: John Wiley, 1998.

"Kings' Sale Cleared by Bankruptcy Judge; Hockey Deal Could Be Final Tuesday." *Los Angeles Times,* October 6, 1995, sec. C.

Koppel, Ted, and Kyle Gibson. *Nightline: History in the Making and the Making of Television*. New York: Times Books, 1996.

Kotkin, Joel. "Los Angeles Riots: Causes, Myths and Solutions." Unpublished manuscript, Progressive Policy Institute, Washington, D.C., 1992.

Krasnowski, Matt. "Developers Step Up Campaign for Arena by Releasing Lease Agreements." Copley News Service, August 27, 1998.

Krikorian, Greg. "Hernandez Is Charged with 1 Drug Felony." *Los Angeles Times,* August 29, 1997, sec. A.

Kyser, Jack. *Manufacturing in Los Angeles* (Los Angeles: Los Angeles County Economic Development Corp., 1999), 2.

LaGanga, Maria L. "At a Career Crossroads? Try the Kitchen." *Los Angeles Times,* March 2, 1997, sec. A.

Larson, Tom, and Miles Finney. *Rebuilding South Central Los Angeles: Myths, Realities and Opportunities* (final report). Los Angeles: California State University, School of Business and Economics, 1996.

Lechner, Ernesto. "Dancing Crowd Celebrates the Talent and Sound of Solis." *Los Angeles Times,* September 15, 1998, sec. F.

Leib, Jeffrey. "Anschutz Group Bidding for Kings, Owners Confirm." *Denver Post,* May 13, 1995, sec. B.

Lichter, Robert S., and Daniel R. Amundson. "Distorted Reality: Hispanic Characters in TV Entertainment." In *Latin Looks: Images of Latinas and Latinos in the U.S. Media,* edited by Clara E. Rodriguez. Boulder, Colo.: Westview, 1997.

Lieberman, Paul. "51% of Riot Arrests Were Latino, Study Says." *Los Angeles Times,* June 18, 1992, sec. B.

Lieberman, Paul, and Richard O'Reilly. "Most Looters Endured Lives of Crime, Poverty." *Los Angeles Times,* May 2, 1993, sec. A.

Light, Ivan, and Elizabeth Roach. "Self-Employment: Mobility Ladder or Economic Lifeboat?" In *Ethnic Los Angeles,* edited by Roger Waldinger and Mehdi Bozorgmehr. New York: Russell Sage Foundation, 1996.

Lockwood, Charles, and Christopher B. Leinberger. "Los Angeles Comes of Age." *Atlantic Monthly,* January 1988.

Lopez, David E., Eric Popkin, and Edward Telles. "Central Americans: At the Bottom, Struggling to Get Ahead." In *Ethnic Los Angeles,* edited by Roger Waldinger and Mehdi Bozorgmehr. New York: Russell Sage Foundation, 1996.

Lopez, Robert J., and Rich Connell. "MTA Probes Charities Promoted by Alatorre." *Los Angeles Times,* July 7, 1997, sec. A.

Los Angeles Area Chamber of Commerce. Southern California Business Directory and Buyers Guide. Los Angeles: Los Angeles Area Chamber of Commerce, 1992.

Los Angeles Unified School District, Information Technology Division, "Ethnic Survey Report: Fall 1998." Publication 131 (Los Angeles, December 1998).

Lummis, Charles Fletcher. *The Landmarks Club Cook Book: A California Collection of the Choicest Recipes from Everywhere . . . Including a Chapter of the Most Famous Old Californian and Mexican Dishes.* Los Angeles: Out West, 1903.

———. *Letters from the Southwest, September 20, 1884 to March 14, 1885.* Edited by James W. Byrkit. Tucson: University of Arizona Press, 1989.

Martinez, Ruben. "Perspective on the Latino Community: 'This Was About Something to Eat.'" *Los Angeles Times,* May 18, 1992. sec. B.

Mayer, Magit. "Politics in the Post-Fordist City." *Socialist Review* 21, no. 1 (1991): 105–24.

McCoy, Thomas S. *Voices of Difference: Studies in Critical Philosophy and Mass Communication.* Cresskill, N.J.: Hampton, 1993.

McDonnell, Patrick. "Riot Aftermath; Scores of Suspects Arrested in Riots Turned over to INS." *Los Angeles Times,* May 6, 1992, sec. B.

McLaren, Peter, and Rodolfo D. Torres. "Racism and Multicultural Education: Rethinking 'Race' and 'Whiteness' in Late Capitalism." In *Critical Multiculturalism: Rethinking Multicultural and Antiracist Education,* edited by Steven May. London: Falmer, 1999.

McPhee, John. *The Control of Nature.* New York: Farrar, Straus & Giroux, 1989.

McWilliams, Carey. *North from Mexico: The Spanish-Speaking People of the United States.* New York: Greenwood, 1948.

Merl, Jean. "Council Endorses Deal to Build Sports Arena." *Los Angeles Times,* January 16, 1997, sec. A.

———. "City Still Viewed as Racially Split." *Los Angeles Times,* April 29, 1997, sec. A.

Meyer, Josh. "County Crackdown on Dirty Restaurants OK'd." *Los Angeles Times,* November 26, 1997, sec. B.

Meyerson, Harold. "Contracting Out of Poverty: Downtown Hotel Pact Sets New Standard for L.A.'s Service Sector." *L.A. Weekly,* January 23–29, 1998.

———. "No Justice, No Growth." *L.A. Weekly,* July 17–23, 1998.

———. "Activists Turned Elected Officials." *L.A. Weekly,* October 2–8, 1998.

———. "Caretakers Take Charge: 75,000 Workers (in 75,000 Work Sites!) Form a Union." *L.A. Weekly,* February 26–March 4, 1999.

Miles, Robert. *Racism.* London: Routledge, 1989.

———. *Racism after Race Relations.* London: Routledge, 1993.

Miller, Gary J. *Cities by Contract: The Politics of Municipal Incorporation.* Cambridge: MIT Press, 1981.

Miron, Louis F. "Corporate Ideology and the Politics of Entrepreneurism in New Orleans." *Antipode* 24 (October 1992).

Morain, Dan, and Victor Valle. "City of Industry: It Has Clout Where It Counts—in the State Capitol." *Los Angeles Times,* April 15, 1984, sec. A.

Moran, Robert. "Mayo Joins Council after Perez Resigns." *Los Angeles Times,* January 20, 1992, sec. J.

Moxley, R. Scott. "No Hits, One Run, 200 Errors: Hermandad Probes' Central Figure Returns from Mexico." *O.C. Weekly,* August 14–20, 1998.

Murray, Bobbi. "Organize! Living Wage Lives in L.A." *Shelterforce Online,* January/February 1998. Available at http://www.nhi.org/online/issues/97/organize.html.

Narayan, Uma. "Eating Cultures: Incorporation, Identity and Indian Food." *Social Identities* 1, no. 1 (1995): 63–86.

National Council of La Raza. "Out of the Picture: Hispanics in the Media." In *Latin Looks: Images of Latinas and Latinos in the U.S. Media,* edited by Clara E. Rodriguez. Boulder, Colo.: Westview, 1997.

Newton, Jim. "Sports Deals Transforming L.A.'s Politics." *Los Angeles Times,* October 26, 1997, sec. A.

———. "Council Size Issue to Be Put to the Voters." *Los Angeles Times,* October 20, 1998, sec. B.

———. "Mayor Won't Block 'Living Wage' at LAX." *Los Angeles Times,* December 2, 1998, sec. A.

"NHL's Board Approves Sale of Kings to Anschutz, Roski." *Los Angeles Times,* September 30, 1995, sec. C.

Noriega, Chon. "Birth of the Southwest: Social Protest, Tourism and D. W. Griffith's *Ramona.*" In *The Birth of Whiteness: Race and the Emergence of U.S. Cinema,* edited by Daniel Bernardi. New Brunswick, N.J.: Rutgers University Press, 1996.

Office of the State Controller. *Annual Report 1989–1990 Financial Transactions Concerning Community Redevelopment Agencies of California.* Los Angeles: California State Division of Local Government Fiscal Affairs, 1991.

Office of the State Controller. "*Annual Report 1991–1992 Financial Transactions Concerning Community Redevelopment Agencies of California.*" Los Angeles: California State Division of Local Government Fiscal Affairs, 1993.

Office of the State Controller. *Annual Report 1994–1995 Financial Transactions Concerning Community Redevelopment Agencies of California.* Los Angeles: California State Division of Local Government Fiscal Affairs, 1996.

Oldenburg, Ray. "Food, Drink, Talk, and the Third Place." *Journal of Gastronomy* 6 (summer 1990): 3–16.

Olivarez, Adriana. "Studying Representations of U.S. Latinos," *Journal of Communication Inquiry* 22 (October 1998).

Orfield, Myron. *Metropolitics: A Regional Agenda for Community Stability.* Rev. ed. Washington, D.C.: Brookings Institution Press, 1998.

———. "Salvaging Suburbia: How to Stop Communities from Growing Farther and Farther Apart." *Los Angeles Times,* November 15, 1998, sec. M.

Orlov, Rick. "City Receives Guarantee from Arena Builders." *Daily News of Los Angeles,* August 22, 1997, Valley edition, sec. N.

———. "Arena Backers OK New Plan to Pay Expenses." *Daily News of Los Angeles,* October 9, 1997, Valley edition, sec. N.

———. "Clippers Will Sail to Staples Center; Murdoch to Buy Part of Downtown Arena." *Daily News of Los Angeles,* April 17, 1998, Valley edition, sec. S.

Ortiz, Vilma. "The Mexican-Origin Population: Permanent Working Class or Emerging Middle Class?" In *Ethnic Los Angeles,* edited by Roger Waldinger and Mehdi Bozorgmehr. New York: Russell Sage Foundation, 1996.

Ouroussoff, Nicolai. "In Search of Material Gain." *Los Angeles Times,* July 31, 1998: sec. F.

"Owners to Cut Ties with Kings." *Los Angeles Times,* September 23, 1995, sec. C.

Padilla, Genaro. "Imprisoned Narrative? Or Lies, Secrets, and Silence in New Mexico Women's Autobiography." In *Criticism in the Borderlands: Studies in Chicano Literature, Culture, and Ideology,* edited by Hector Calderon and José David Saldívar. Durham, N.C.: Duke University Press, 1991.

Paltrow, Scot. "The City of Insiders: How One Man Runs His City." *Los Angeles Herald Examiner,* June 25, 1980, sec. A.

Pastor, Manuel Jr., *Latinos and the Los Angeles Uprising: The Economic Context.* Claremont, Calif.: Tomas Rivera Center, 1993.

———. "Advantaging the Disadvantaged through International Trade." Merril College, University of California, Santa Cruz, 1998. Photocopy.

Perry, Charles. "Fusion Food; Birth of a Nation's Cuisine." *Los Angeles Times,* September 16, 1993, sec. H.

Plaschke, Bill. "Arena Means Downtown Will Party When It's 1999." *Los Angeles Times,* May 24, 1997, sec. C.

Popkin, Eric, Lourdes Arguelles DeSipio, and Harry Pachon. *Constructing the Los Angeles Area Latino Mosaic: A Demographic Portrait of Guatemalans and Salvadorans in Los Angeles.* Claremont, Calif.: Tomas Rivera Policy Institute, 1997.

Preston, Mark. *California Mission Cookery: A Vanished Cuisine—Rediscovered.* Albuquerque, N.M: Border, 1994.

Quiroga, Jorge. "Hispanic Voices: Is the Press Listening?" In *Latin Looks: Images of Latinas and Latinos in the U.S. Media,* edited by Clara E. Rodriguez. Boulder, Colo.: Westview, 1997.

Raabe, Steve. "Industrial Developer Has Big Denver Plans." *Denver Post,* November 28, 1995: sec. D.

Ramos, George. "Latino Middle Class Growing in the Suburbs." *Los Angeles Times,* November 30, 1997, sec. B.

Ramos, George, and Tracy Wilkinson. "Unrest Widens Rifts in Diverse Latino Population." *Los Angeles Times,* May 8, 1992: sec. A.

Rasmussen, Cecilia. "Community Profile: City of Industry." *Los Angeles Times,* November 14, 1995, sec. B.

Reichl, Ruth. "Restaurants in the Eighties; L.A. Discovers the Exotic in Its Own Back Yard." *Los Angeles Times,* December 29, 1989, sec. F.

Rifkin, Jeremy. *The End of Work: The Decline of the Global Labor Force and the Dawn of the Post-Market Era.* New York: Tarcher/Putnam, 1995.

Rios-Bustamante, Antonio. *Mexican Los Angeles: A Narrative and Pictorial History.* Ventura, Calif.: Floricanto, 1992.

Rivera Sedlar, John. *Modern Southwest Cuisine.* New York: Simon & Schuster, 1986.

Robinson, W.W. *Los Angeles from the Days of the Pueblo: A Brief History and Guide to the Plaza Area.* San Francisco: California Historical Society, 1981.

Rodriguez, Gregory. "The Emerging Latino Middle Class." Pepperdine University Institute for Public Policy AT&T paper, October 1996.

———. "The Impending Collision of Eastside and Westside." *Los Angeles Times,* August 3, 1997, sec. M.

Rodriguez, Luis J. *Always Running: La Vida Loca: Gang Days in L.A.* Willimantic, Conn.: Curbstone, 1993.

Rodriguez, Richard. "Mexican Food: Filling Loneliness of American Life." *Los Angeles Times,* July 24, 1994, sec. M.

Rohrlich, Ted. "Wachs Softens Stand against Arena Accord." *Los Angeles Times,* August 29, 1997, sec. A.

———. "Developers Vow to Drop Arena Plan If Initiative Is on Ballot." *Los Angeles Times,* September 18, 1997, sec. B.

———. "Latino Voting in State Surged in 1996 Election." *Los Angeles Times,* December 31, 1997, sec. A.

———. "Living Wage Movement Targets County Government." *Los Angeles Times,* November 4, 1998, sec. A.

———. "L.A. Unions Step Up Demands on Developers." *Los Angeles Times,* December 2, 1998, sec. B.

Romney, Lee. "Hispanic Cheese: Haute Item." *Los Angeles Times,* June 16, 1998, sec. A.

Rosaldo, Renato. *Culture and Truth: The Remaking of Social Analysis.* Boston: Beacon, 1989.

Rosenberg, Howard. "TV's Double-Edged Role in Crisis." *Los Angeles Times,* May 1, 1992, sec. F.

Rosenblatt, Robert A., and Vicki Torres. "Number of Latino Firms Up 76 Percent in 5 Years; California Has Most." *Los Angeles Times,* July 11, 1996, sec. D.

Rosentraub, Mark S. *Major League Losers: The Real Cost of Sports and Who's Paying for It.* New York: Basic Books, 1997.

Rumbaut, Ruben G. "Origins and Destinies: Immigration to the United States since World War II." In *New American Destinies: A Reader in Contemporary Asian and Latino Immigration,* edited by Darrell Y. Hamamoto and Rodolfo D. Torres. London: Routledge, 1997.

Rustin, Michael. "The Politics of Post-Fordism; or, The Trouble with 'New Times.'" *New Left Review,* 175 (May/June 1989).

Said, Edward W. *Culture and Imperialism.* New York: Alfred A. Knopf, 1993.

Saldívar-Hull, Sonia. *Feminism on the Border: Chicana Gender Politics and Literature.* Berkeley, University of California Press, 2000.

Sanchez, George J. *Becoming Mexican-American: Ethnicity, Culture and Identity in Chicano Los Angeles, 1900–1945.* New York: Oxford University Press, 1993.

Sanchez, Jesus. "Inn Trouble: Convention Center Remains Unattractive Site for Hotel Firms Despite Plans for an Arena There." *Los Angeles Times,* May 14, 1997, sec. D.

Sánchez, Rosaura. "Mapping the Spanish Language along a Multiethnic and Multilingual Border." *Aztlan: A Journal of Chicano Studies,* 21, nos. 1–2 (1992–96): 49–104.

Sassen, Saskia. *The Global City: New York, London, Tokyo.* Princeton, N.J.: Princeton University Press, 1991.

———. "New Employment Regimes in Cities: The Impact on Immigrant Workers." *New Community* 22 (October 1996): 579–94.

"Schabarum Fails in Fight for $2 Million Park Funds," *San Gabriel Valley Tribune,* October 8, 1975, sec. B.

Schwada, John. "CRA Girds for Fight to Retrieve Downtown Plan Redevelopment." *Los Angeles Times,* October 19, 1995, sec. B.

Scott, J., and A. S. Paul. "Industrial Development in Southern California, 1970–1987." In *Our Changing Cities,* edited by John Fraser Hart. Baltimore: Johns Hopkins University Press, 1991.

Seager, Susan. "Deal of the Century." *L.A. Weekly,* June 2–8, 1995.

Shah, Hemant, and Michael C. Thorton. "Racial Ideology in U.S. Mainstream News Magazine Coverage of Black Latino Interaction, 1980–1992." *Critical Studies in Mass Communication* 11 (June 1994): 141–61

Shuster, Beth. "Hernandez Question Splits Angry Council." *Los Angeles Times,* October 25, 1997, sec. A.

———. "Tighter Rules Proposed for Living Wage Law." *Los Angeles Times,* August 21, 1998, sec. B.

———. "New Latino Political Picture Offers Opportunity." *Los Angeles Times,* October 5, 1998, sec. A.

———. "Living Wage Law Could Get Boost." *Los Angeles Times,* November 11, 1998, sec. B.

Silvestri, George T. "Occupational Employment to 2005." *Monthly Labor Review* 118 (November 1995): 60–84.

Simers, T. J. "L.A. and Inglewood in Showdown over Arena." *Los Angeles Times,* August 9, 1996, sec. A.

———. "NFL to Be Presented New Coliseum Plan." *Los Angeles Times,* October 13, 1997, sec. A.

Skelton, George. "Now Latinos Are Changing the Face of Both Parties." *Los Angeles Times,* November 23, 1998, sec. A.

Smith, Erna. "Transmitting Race: The Los Angeles Riot in Television News." In *Press Politics, Public Policy,* Research Paper R-11. Cambridge: Harvard University, John F. Kennedy School of Government, 1994.

Small, Steve. "The Contours of Racialization: Structures, Representations, and Resistance in the United States." In *Race, Identity, and Citizenship: A Reader,* edited by Rodolfo D. Torres, Louis F. Miron, and Jonathan Xavier Inda. Malden, Mass.: Blackwell, 1999.

Soboroff, Steven, Marvin D. Selter, and Frank Moran. "Perspective on the Sports Arena: The Initiative Negates Los Angeles' Welcome Sign." *Los Angeles Times,* September 26, 1997, sec. B.

Soja, Edward W. *Thirdspace: Journeys to Los Angeles and Other Real-and-Imagined Places.* Cambridge, Mass.: Blackwell, 1996.

Starr, Kevin. "Field of Dreams." *Los Angeles Times,* April 20, 1997, sec. M.

"Suit against City Officials Alleges Financial Conflict." *Los Angeles Times,* June 8, 1990, sec. B.

Taylor, Clyde. "The Re-birth of the Aesthetic in Cinema." In *The Birth of Whiteness: Race and the Emergence of U.S. Cinema,* edited by Daniel Bernardi. New Brunswick, N.J.: Rutgers University Press, 1996.

"To Save the Plaza: Landmarks Club Will Oppose Any Perversion of It." *Los Angeles Daily Times,* January 29, 1896, Public Service sec.

Torres, Rodolfo D., and Chor Swang Ngin. "Racialized Boundaries, Class Relations, and Cultural Politics: The Asian American and Latino Experience." In *Culture and Difference: Critical Perspectives on the Bicultural Experience in the United States,* edited by Antonia Darder. Westport, Conn.: Bergin & Garvey, 1995.

Torres, Vicki. "Hidden High-Tech Hot Spot." *Los Angeles Times,* December 18, 1996, sec. A.

"The Tradition of the New." *Los Angeles Times,* November 7, 1991, sec. H.

"Un Sencillo Homenaje a la Señorita Fabregas [A Simple Homage to Miss Fabregas]." *La Opinión,* May 13, 1927, Society sec.

"Understanding the Riots, Part I: Path to Fury." Special Section. *Los Angeles Times,* May 11, 1992, sec. T.

"Understanding the Riots—Six Months Later." *Los Angeles Times,* November 16, 1992, sec. JJ.

United Way of Greater Los Angeles. *State of the County Report: Los Angeles, 1998–99* (Los Angeles, March 1999).

United Way of Greater Los Angeles, Research Services. *American Dream Makers: Executive Summary.* Los Angeles, January 2000.

Valle, Victor M. "Return of Life: 5-Mile-Long Habitat Testifies to Nature's Resiliency." *Los Angeles Times,* July 4, 1985, San Gabriel Valley sec.

———. "'Break of Dawn'—Bilingual Experiment." *Los Angeles Times,* July 5, 1987, sec. F.

———. "A Chicano Reporter in 'Hispanic Hollywood': Editorial Agendas and the Culture of Professional Journalism." In *Chicanos and Film: Essays on Chicano Representation and Resistance,* edited by Chon Noriega. Minneapolis: University of Minnesota Press, 1993.

———. *Recipe of Memory: Five Generations of Mexican Cuisine.* New York: New Press, 1995.

———. "A Curse of Tea and Potatoes: A Discourse Analysis of Encarnación Pinedo's *Cocinero Español.*" *Latino Studies Journal* 8 (fall 1997): 1–18.

Valle, Victor M., and Allen Maltun. "Called to Account: Money Laundering at Bank Proved to Be Flaw in Stafford Scheme." *Los Angeles Times,* April 11, 1985, San Gabriel Valley sec.

Valle, Victor M., and Rodolfo D. Torres. "The Economic Landscape of the Greater Eastside: Latino Politics in 'Post-industrial' Los Angeles." *Prism* 1 (fall 1993).

———. "The Idea of Mestizaje and the 'Race' Problematic: Racialized Media Discourse in a Post-Fordist Landscape." In *Culture and Difference: Criticial Perspectives on the Bicultural Experience in the United States,* edited by Antonia Darder. Westport, Conn.: Bergin & Garvey, 1995.

———. "Bank Job: Stafford Called on Roski in Bid to Control Local Lender." *L.A. Weekly,* November 13–19, 1998.

van Dijk, Teun A. *Elite Discourse and Racism.* Newbury Park, Calif.: Sage, 1993.

Waldinger, Roger, and Michael Lichter. "Anglos: Beyond Ethnicity?" In *Ethnic Los Angeles,* edited by Roger Waldinger and Mehdi Bozorgmehr. New York: Russell Sage Foundation, 1996.

Walkup, Carolyn. "Hispanics: Learning the Language of Success." *Nation's Restaurant News,* September 20, 1993.

Wang Yin, Fu-Tung Cheng, and Issac Cronin. "Chinese Cuisine." *California Magazine,* February 1982, 88–98.

Watson, John G. "Busboys' Night Out: Top Latino Restaurant Workers to Be Feted at Ceremony Jan. 17." *Nuestro Tiempo, Los Angeles Times,* November 5, 1992, 2.

Weikel, Dan. "Engineer Hired to Oversee Alameda Work." *Los Angeles Times,* November 20, 1998, sec. B.

West, Cornel. *Race Matters.* New York: Vintage, 1993.

White, George. "Workers Held in Near-Slavery, Officials Say." *Los Angeles Times,* August 3, 1995, sec. A.

Wieviorka, Michel. *The Arena of Racism.* London: Sage, 1995.

Wilgoren, Jodi. "Council Takes Key Step in Building Downtown Arena." *Los Angeles Times,* May 24, 1997, sec. A.

———. "Council Orders Parts of Arena Lease Disclosed." *Los Angeles Times,* July 23, 1997, sec. A.

———. "Arena Builders Ready to Offer Debt Guarantee." *Los Angeles Times,* August 22, 1997, sec. A.

Wilson, William Julius. *The Bridge over the Racial Divide: Rising Inequality and Coalition Politics.* Berkeley: University of California Press, 1999.

Wolff, Geotz. "County Business Patterns, Change in Number of Small Manufacturing Establishments, Los Angeles County (1979–1990)." In U.S. Department of Commerce, *Resources for Employment and Economic Development.* Washington, D.C., May 1994.

———. "Percent Distribution of Race/Latino Groups by Occupation, Los Angeles County, 1990." In U.S. Department of Commerce, *Resources for Employment and Economic Development.* Washington, D.C., September 1994.

Wong, Linda. "The Role of Immigrant Entrepreneurs in Urban Economic Development." *Stanford Law and Policy Review* 7 (summer 1996).

Wood, Ellen Meiksins. *Democracy against Capitalism: Renewing Historical Materialism.* Cambridge: Cambridge University Press, 1995.

———. "Modernity, Postmodernity or Capitalism?" *Monthly Review* 48 (July/August 1996).

Zukin, Sharon. *Landscapes of Power: From Detroit to Disney World.* Berkeley: University of California Press, 1991.

———. *The Culture of Cities.* Cambridge, Mass.: Blackwell, 1995.

# Index

A native of Los Angeles, **Victor M. Valle** worked as a *Los Angeles Times* staff writer for eight years and was awarded a Pulitzer Prize as a member of the reporting team for a series on Southern California's Latino community. He is currently associate professor of ethnic studies at California Polytechnic State University, San Luis Obispo. He is the author of *Recipe of Memory: Five Generations of Mexican Cuisine*, and has written extensively on the politics of culture and food.

Born and raised in East Los Angeles, **Rodolfo D. Torres** teaches urban political economy and social policy at the University of California, Irvine, where he is associate professor of education and a member of the Focused Research Program in Labor Studies. Among his books are *Latino Social Movements* and *Race, Identity, and Citizenship*. He is currently on the editorial boards of *New Political Science*, *Socialist Review*, and *Latino Studies Journal*.

**Saskia Sassen** is professor of sociology at the University of Chicago and Centennial Visiting Professor at the London School of Economics. She is the author of *The Global City*, *Guests and Aliens*, and *Globalization and Its Discontents*, among many other works. Her books have been translated into ten languages.